THE POEMS OF EMILY BRONTË

The Poems of
EMILY BRONTË

EDITED BY
DEREK ROPER
WITH
EDWARD CHITHAM

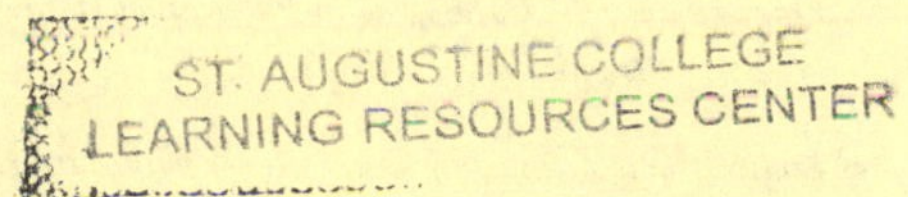

CLARENDON PRESS · OXFORD
1995

Oxford University Press, Walton Street, Oxford OX2 6DP
Oxford New York
Athens Auckland Bangkok Bombay
Calcutta Cape Town Dar es Salaam Delhi
Florence Hong Kong Istanbul Karachi
Kuala Lumpur Madras Madrid Melbourne
Mexico City Nairobi Paris Singapore
Taipei Tokyo Toronto
and associated companies in
Berlin Ibadan

Oxford is a trade mark of Oxford University Press

Published in the United States
by Oxford University Press Inc., New York

British Library Cataloguing in Publication Data
Data available

Library of Congress Cataloging in Publication Data
Brontë Emily, 1818–1848.
[Poems]
The poems of Emily Brontë / edited by Derek Roper with Edward Chitham
I. Roper, Derek. II. Chitham, Edward. III. Title.
PR4172A4. 1994 821.'8—dc20 94-39225
ISBN 0-19-812641-7

1 3 5 7 9 10 8 6 4 2

Typeset by Pure Tech Corporation, Pondicherry, India
Printed in Great Britain
on acid-free paper by
Biddles Ltd,
Guildford and King's Lynn

IN MEMORIAM

L. P. R.

PREFACE

This edition owes a great deal to the work of Dr Edward Chitham, who was originally named as co-editor. His initiative and perseverance led to the decipherment of many of the cancelled readings which are presented for the first time in this volume. His own edition of Emily Brontë's poems, presented at the University of Sheffield as a doctoral thesis, has been freely made available for consultation, and he has responded generously to many requests for advice and information. The editor thanks him warmly for this assistance, while accepting sole responsibility for all shortcomings in the present work. Help and advice have also been given by Dr Christine Alexander, Dr Juliet Barker, Dr Clive Upton, and, with endless patience, by Mrs Margaret Smith.

For permission to transcribe from Emily Brontë's manuscripts and for photographs, thanks are due to the following institutions: the British Library (Additional MS 48483, Ashley MS 175); the Brontë Society (Bonnell MS 127); the New York Public Library, Astor, Lenox and Tilden Foundations (manuscripts in the Henry W. and Albert A. Berg Collection); the Pierpont Morgan Library, New York (MA 2615, 2696 in the Bonnell Collection); the Princeton University Library (manuscripts in the Robert H. Taylor Collection); the Rare Book and Special Collections Library of the University of Illinois at Urbana-Champaign; and the Harry Ransom Humanities Research Center, the University of Texas at Austin. For their friendly help the editor thanks the librarians in all these institutions, and especially the staff of the Brontë Parsonage Museum, Haworth—in past years Dr Juliet Barker and Miss Sally Johnson, and more recently Dr Jane Sellars, Ms Kathryn White, and Ms Ann Dinsdale. Finally, thanks are due to Mr William Self for permission to transcribe from record papers by Emily and Anne Brontë.

D. S. R.

July 1995

CONTENTS

DATED POEMS AND FRAGMENTS

UNDATED POEMS AND FRAGMENTS

ABBREVIATIONS AND SYMBOLS

Except in appendix VI, poem numbers are given in bold type, line numbers in ordinary type, without 'No.' or 'll.'

Persons and Places

A.G.A. — Augusta G. Almeda (the most prominent Gondal character, abbreviated thus in Gondal headings by EB)
BPM — Brontë Parsonage Museum, Haworth
AB — Anne Brontë
BB — Patrick Branwell Brontë
CB — Charlotte Brontë
EB — Emily Jane Brontë

Holographs

A — The 'Honresfeld MS' (from photographs in BPM)
B — Notebook headed 'Gondal Poems', British Library Additional MS 43483
C — Notebook with some leaves removed, British Library Ashley MS 175
D — MSS formerly owned by Mr Henry Houston Bonnell; now in BPM (Bonnell 127), except for three leaves (D1–2, D15) in the Pierpont Morgan Library (Bonnell MA 2615, 2696)
E — MSS in the New York Public Library (Berg Collection)
F — MSS in the Humanities Research Center, University of Texas (from photographs)
T — MSS in Princeton University Library (Robert H. Taylor Collection)

Additional Symbols Used in the Collation

See also the section on pp. 28–9 for an explanation of editorial conventions.

1846 — *Poems by Currer, Ellis, and Acton Bell* (London: Aylott & Jones, 1846)
< > — words or letters cancelled by overwriting, striking through, or erasure
<< >> — cancellation within a longer cancellation
alternative — reading parallel with that of text where neither is cancelled
[ ] — gap in text

———	indecipherable reading; number of indecipherable words uncertain
?	word or attribution that follows is uncertain
unclear	reading of text is uncertain
~ <*word*>	overwriting, priority of reading in text uncertain
or [*word*]	alternative reading of text
ed.	editorial emendation
38+	variant that follows stands after 38 and before any 39 of text

Editions of the Poems Cited in Introduction and Commentary

1846	*Poems by Currer, Ellis, and Acton Bell* (as above)
1850	*Wuthering Heights and Agnes Grey. By Ellis and Acton Bell. . . . with . . . a Selection from their Literary Remains* (London: Smith, Elder & Co., 1850)
1902	*Poems by Charlotte, Emily, and Anne Brontë, Now for the First Time Printed* (New York: Dodd, Mead & Co., 1902)
1910	*The Complete Poems of Emily Brontë*, ed. Clement Shorter (London: Hodder & Stoughton, 1910)
1923	*The Complete Poems of Emily Jane Brontë*, ed. Clement Shorter, arranged and collated, with bibliography and notes, by C.W. Hatfield (London: Hodder & Stoughton [1923])
1934	*The Poems of Emily Jane Brontë and Anne Brontë* (Oxford: Blackwell, 1934; vol. xvii in the Shakespeare Head Brontë), ed. Thomas J. Wise and John Alexander Symington
1938	*Gondal Poems, by Emily Jane Brontë: Now first published from the MS. in the British Museum*, ed. Helen Brown and Joan Mott (Oxford: Blackwell, 1938)
1941	*The Complete Poems of Emily Jane Brontë*, ed. from the manuscripts by C. W. Hatfield (New York: Columbia University Press; London: OUP, 1941)
Gezari	*Emily Jane Brontë: The Complete Poems*, ed. Janet Gezari (Harmondsworth: Penguin Books, 1992)
Lloyd-Evans	*The Poems of Emily Brontë*, ed. Barbara Lloyd-Evans (London: Batsford, 1992)

Other Works Cited

Publication is in London unless otherwise indicated.

BST	*Brontë Society Transactions* (Haworth, 1895–)
Barker	Juliet Barker, *The Brontës* (Weidenfeld & Nicolson, 1994)
CBEW	*An Edition of the Early Writings of Charlotte Brontë*, ed. Christine Alexander (Oxford: Blackwell, 1987–)

Collins	*The Hand of the Arch-Sinner: Two Angrian Chronicles of Branwell Brontë*, ed. Robert Collins (Oxford: Clarendon Press, 1993)
Dingle	Weather records of Abraham Shackleton at Braithwaite, Keighley, near Haworth, reprinted as unpaginated appendix to Herbert Dingle, *The Mind of Emily Brontë* (Martin Brian & O'Keeffe, 1974)
Gérin	Winifred Gérin, *Emily Brontë: A Biography* (Oxford: Clarendon Press, 1971)
GGG	List of Gondal place-names pencilled by AB into a copy (now in BPM) of J. Goldsmith, *A Grammar of General Geography, for the use of Schools and Young Persons* (1823)
GQ	*Gondal's Queen: A Novel in Verse by Emily Jane Brontë*, arranged, with an introduction and notes, by Fannie E. Ratchford (Austin, Tex.: University of Texas Press, 1955)
Grove	Robin Grove, ' "It Would Not Do": Emily Brontë as Poet', in *The Art of Emily Brontë*, ed. Anne Smith (Vision Press, 1976), pp. 33–67
Hardy	Barbara Hardy, 'The Lyricism of Emily Brontë', in *The Art of Emily Brontë*, pp. 94–118
Hewish	John Hewish, *Emily Brontë: A Critical and Biographical Study* (Macmillan, 1969)
Hinkley	Laura L. Hinkley, *The Brontës: Charlotte and Emily* (Hammond, 1947)
Jane Eyre	Charlotte Brontë, *Jane Eyre*, ed. Jane Jack and Margaret Smith (Oxford: Clarendon Press, 1969; corr. repr. 1975)
LL	*The Brontës: Their Lives, Friendships and Correspondence. In Four Volumes*, ed. Thomas J. Wise and Alexander Symington (Oxford: Blackwell, in the Shakespeare Head Brontë, 1933).
Life	Edward Chitham, *A Life of Emily Brontë* (Oxford: Blackwell, 1987)
Miles	Rosalind Miles, 'A Baby God: The Creative Dynamism of Emily Brontë's Poetry', in *The Art of Emily Brontë*, pp. 68–93
OED	*Oxford English Dictionary*
Paden	W. D. Paden, *An Investigation of Gondal* (New York: Bookman Associates, 1958)
Poems of AB	*The Poems of Anne Brontë: A New Text and Commentary*, ed. Edward Chitham (Macmillan, 1979)
Poems of BB	*The Poems of Patrick Branwell Brontë: A New Text and Commentary*, ed. Victor Neufeldt (New York: Garland, 1990)

Roper	Derek Roper, 'The Revision of Emily Brontë's Poems of 1846', *The Library*, 6th ser., 6 (1984), 153–67
Shorter	Clement K. Shorter, *Charlotte Brontë and her Circle* (1896)
Tales of the Genii	[James Ridley] *The Tales of the Genii; or, The Delightful Lessons of Horam, the son of Asmar. Faithfully Translated from the Persian Manuscript . . . by Sir Charles Morell.* 2 vols. (Cooke's British Novelists, n.d., *c.*1805; orig. pub. 1764)
Visick	Mary Visick, *The Genesis of 'Wuthering Heights'* (Hong Kong and London: Hong Kong University Press and Oxford University Press, 1958)
WH	Emily Brontë, *Wuthering Heights*, ed. Hilda Marsden and Ian Jack (Oxford: Clarendon Press, 1976)
Wilks	Brian Wilks, *The Brontës: An Illustrated Biography* (Hamlyn, 1975)

INTRODUCTION

I. THE POETRY

This edition contains all the poetry by Emily Brontë that has survived and been reliably identified. It includes two hundred poems and fragments, of which 168 exist in holograph and one (**124**) as a printed text based on a holograph. Texts of the remaining thirty-one poems are taken from photographs of a notebook known as the Honresfeld MS, or MS A, which may still exist but has been inaccessible to scholars for more than fifty years. One poem of uncertain authorship (**201**) is also included; no manuscript has been found for this poem, printed here from *1850*, in which Charlotte Brontë assigns it to Emily.

At least sixty-seven of the pieces formed part of a continuous imaginative creation based on an invented country called Gondal (discussed more fully in the following section). Anne Brontë also took part in this creation, though she and Emily wrote independently. Gondal originated in childhood 'plays', i.e. games, but the fiction was carried on until Emily ceased to write poetry altogether. As with the parallel game of 'Angria', played by Charlotte and Branwell Brontë, Gondal gave rise to a prose literature in which Emily and Anne chronicled the doings of its characters; but the Gondal prose has been lost. Many of Emily's other poems and fragments describe fictional events and situations, and some of these too may belong to Gondal. The line between fictional and non-fictional poetry cannot be drawn clearly. Nor can the line between 'poems' and 'fragments': some pieces (like **56** and **60**) relate episodes which imply a larger story but may seem complete, as poems, in themselves, and whether they do so depends on a judgement by the reader. But it looks as though about 150 of the 201 are substantially complete.

Luckily, Emily Brontë attached composition dates to nearly all her surviving complete poems and a number of incomplete ones, and repeated these dates when she transcribed or revised them. Her earliest dated poem, 'Will the day be bright or cloudy?', was written on 12 July 1836, not long before her eighteenth birthday.[1] We cannot tell how much poetry she had written before that date. In the Brontë family, verse was as natural a way of writing as prose, and Charlotte's

[1] A few dates are hard to be sure of, and two editors have read the year of **44** as 1832.

first dated poems were written in 1829, when she was thirteen. In 1826 the children had begun the 'Young Men's Play'—the first of their continuous collaborative fictions—and Emily had played a part in this game while it developed through the Glasstown story towards Angria and Gondal.[2] But neither she nor Anne contributed to the *Young Men's Magazine* (1830),[3] in which some of the earliest writings of Charlotte and Branwell are preserved, or left datable manuscripts of that period. We may guess that Emily had had plenty of practice in writing poems before she began to date them, and that some of the undated pieces that have survived were written before the dated ones.

At first she wrote in tiny print on whatever bits of paper came to hand, which was not only economical but in scale with the Glasstown magazines and the rest of the game. These scraps were probably stored in 'the Tin Box' which appears, so labelled, in the sketch Emily drew in 1837 of herself and Anne writing at a table strewn with papers.[4] Accumulations of short poems and passages were fair-copied on to slips of paper, sometimes as many as sixteen to a slip, separated by horizontal lines or rows of crosses; in these storage slips most of the dated poems belong to 1836, 1837, and 1838.

The world of Gondal came into being some time before 24 November 1834. During the whole of her career Emily produced what are clearly Gondal poems in rough alternation with others. By the end of 1838 she had written forty-two dated poems, half of them plainly belonging to Gondal. Her most productive years seem to have been 1838 (twenty-one dated poems) and 1839 (twenty-nine). It was probably late in 1839 or early in 1840 that she started to transcribe selected poems into a note-book (MS C), using an ordinary cursive hand.

From 1840 until 1845 Emily averaged eight or nine dated poems a year, with only two completed and two more begun during her time in Brussels (February–November 1842). In February 1844 she began two more transcription books in tiny printed characters, one headed only by her initials and date, the other also headed 'Gondal Poems'. These are Emily's most important manuscripts, usually known as MSS A and B. By 9 October 1845, when she wrote the piece which became 'The Prisoner', Emily had written 123 dated poems, and probably all or most of the undated poems and fragments had also been written.

[2] Christine Alexander, *The Early Writings of Charlotte Brontë* (Oxford, 1983), esp. pp. 27–8, 62–3.

[3] First called *Branwell's Blackwood's Magazine* and *Blackwood's Young Men's Magazine*.

[4] Record paper of 26 June 1837; see app. V for a list of facsimiles.

Thereafter, though she lived for three more years, she is known to have written only two poems: 'No coward soul is mine' (**125**; 2 January 1846), and a long narrative poem that she never completed (**126–127**). It was apparently in the autumn of 1845 that Charlotte Brontë discovered and read some of Emily's poems, and by doing so caused, at first, great resentment.[5] Perhaps having her poetry brought into the open inhibited Emily from writing more, though the effect need not have been so traumatic as it has appeared to some biographers.[6] The failure of *Poems by Currer, Ellis, and Acton Bell* (1846), which included twenty-one of Emily's best poems, cannot have increased her confidence in her verse. In late 1845 and early 1846 most of her creative energies went into *Wuthering Heights.*

Emily's sixty-seven undoubted Gondal poems are known as such by their inclusion in MS B, or by their Gondal headings or names. Most of them are lyrics to be uttered by a character on some occasion in Gondal history, or in his or her own story. A few are ballads, like **31**, and there are two long narratives (**81** and **126–127**). Apart from the question of reconstructing the Gondal history behind them, which would be interesting and often useful but is not usually essential to their understanding, these poems pose no real problems.

Slightly more difficult are between fifty and sixty poems that plainly deal with fictional situations, but were not included in MS B and have no names or references that link them with Gondal. Examples are **51**, **56**, and **71**. Some of these may simply be Gondal poems that need the lost prose to identify them: Fannie E. Ratchford has fitted **56** and many others into her synthesis.[7] Others may have had their occasions in stories by Emily that had nothing to do with Gondal. It would not be surprising if she invented characters and sequences independent of Gondal, a creation she and Anne nominally shared, though the creators seem largely to have followed separate paths.[8] Then again, such poems need not have formed parts of any continuous fiction. Emily may only have imagined enough of a

[5] See CB's 'Biographical Notice of Ellis and Acton Bell', in *1850*, p. viii; repr. in *WH*, pp. 435–6.

[6] Most recently to Katherine Frank, in the 'Prologue' to her *Emily Brontë: A Chainless Soul* (Harmondsworth, 1992); also to Lloyd-Evans, p. 12. For other possible views, see Visick, pp. 11–12; Roper, pp. 156–8.

[7] *GQ*, pp. 156–7.

[8] Their Gondal poems have almost no characters in common: see app. VI.

situation to establish a scene, a mood, a turn in a relationship, as in Browning's dramatic lyrics.[9]

Confusion most often arises with the third and last class of poems, the eighty or so which at first glance look like personal statements. The confusion has not been caused by the poems, but by the way in which they have been approached. Because in 1844 Emily separated her latest transcripts into Gondal poems and others, many critics have assumed that the 'others' in MS A must spring directly, or more directly, from her own experience. That this was not always so is shown by **83**, spoken in the character of a Stoic philosopher whose 'swift days near their goal', and appropriately titled in *1846* 'The Old Stoic'. In **117** the speaker tells of the death of an intimate and its devastating effect, a record that cannot reasonably be fitted into Emily's life. Likewise, in **68** the speaker works out an attitude to a dead person who cannot be identified with anyone Emily knew: the poem used to be read as an elegy for Branwell, until it was noticed that when it was written he still had nearly nine years to live. Four consecutive poems in MS A (**77**, **38**, **74**, **66**) tell the story of a love once joyful but now lost. It is almost impossible that a lover figured in Emily's life, though candidates have been found. The assumption that MS A was meant for 'personal' poems is best discarded.

None of this is to deny that Emily made use of her own experience in these poems in various degrees, or that she could use them to express her own attitudes: the 'old Stoic' was a figure she could identify with. In some pieces, too, like **125** ('No coward soul is mine'), it is hard not to feel that she is speaking with her own voice. But factual truth was not an important aim for Emily Brontë as a poet, as it was for Wordsworth and Tennyson. Even in apparently autobiographical poems like **39** and **40**, expressing her homesickness while at Law Hill, she transforms the very landscape around Haworth for which she longs into something more like Scotland or Gondal. (In revising them for *1850*, Charlotte replaced Emily's highlands, glens, and deer by lowland, crags, and sheep.)

The best approach to these poems is an open-minded one that allows each to define its nature in its own way. The distinction between Gondal and non-Gondal poems should not be drawn too

[9] In the late 18th and early 19th centuries the 'fragment' became an established genre, e.g. in Wordsworth's 'The Danish Boy', Byron's *The Giaour*. Some poems offered as fragments were genuinely incomplete, others were self-sufficient: cf. Coleridge's *Christabel* with his *Kubla Khan*. But by Browning's day it was no longer necessary to offer a poem like 'Meeting at Night' or 'The Last Ride Together' with the apologetic subtitle 'A Fragment', though Emily did so with 'The Prisoner' in *1846*.

firmly. It has been argued elsewhere[10] that the 'lost love' sequence in MS A could appropriately be addressed to the Gondal character Fernando De Samara by the sweetheart he left behind at Areon, who also speaks **17**. Whether this was so does not matter so much as the fact that the poems would fit that possibility. There are many poems in MS A that could go unchanged into MS B, and were perhaps included in MS A not because they were 'personal' poems but because Emily saw that they had liberated themselves from the Gondal framework. There are also some, like **98**, in MS B that would look quite at home in MS A; others that would need only to have their Gondal headings removed. Dr Peeck-O'Toole points out that 'lyrical expressiveness is what . . . Gondal and non-Gondal have in common'; and writing of the Gondal poems, she argues that we should focus on this quality 'rather than forever trying to reconstruct the vestiges of the narrative'.[11] A parallel argument holds good for most seemingly non-Gondal poems. Instead of 'forever trying to reconstruct the vestiges' of Emily's life and personality, we should take the situations implied by the poems primarily as enabling data for the lyrics.

These poems may still give us clues to her life and art. It is clear from her transcription book projects and from her habits of dating her poems, adding her name or initials, hoarding scraps of verse, and making minute revisions that during her ten or more years as a poet she set much store by her work, however scornfully she may later have spoken of her 'rhymes'.[12] We need not read **108** and **110** literally for a picture of her life at Haworth, but the account given there of the world of the imagination presents it as a valued escape and a deep pleasure. Yet neither they nor the related **95** and **103** say anything about writing: they speak of 'dream', 'Fancy', 'Visions', the power of creating alternative worlds. This power could be controlled but could threaten to dominate, and there was something ambivalent and untrustworthy about its 'phantom bliss' (**108**. 31). Emily was too much of a moralist not to be disturbed by the suspicion that this kind of poetry was an unworthy self-indulgence, and by the strength of feelings it sometimes involved. Nor could she (as we can) defend a poem like **7** in terms of its symbolic mode, any more than Coleridge could theorize *The Ancient Mariner*. Charlotte had felt the same about

[10] By Roper in 'Emily Brontë's Lover', *BST*, 21/1 (1993), 24–30.

[11] Maureen Peeck-O'Toole, *Aspects of Lyric in the Poetry of Emily Brontë* (Amsterdam, 1988), pp. 24–5.

[12] *LL*, ii. 256.

her Angrian fantasies; in her case mistrust became stronger, leading to her 'formal farewell to Angria'[13] and new directions. Emily left no 'Farewell to Gondal', but turned to *Wuthering Heights*. In her novel, even more strictly than in the poetry, it is a rule that the author's own voice is never heard.

II. GONDAL

The story has often been told of how Branwell Brontë was given a box of wooden soldiers in June 1826, and how from a series of 'plays', i.e. games, with these soldiers the Brontë children went on to create alternative worlds.[1] In June 1826 Charlotte was nearly ten years old, Branwell nine, Emily nearly eight and Anne six. Their first game developed into a series of overlapping inventions, and after some years a division had been made: Emily and Anne concerned themselves with two islands called Gondal and Gaaldine, Charlotte and Branwell with Glasstown and the province of Angria.

The earliest known reference to Gondal occurs in a record paper of 24 November 1834: the first of a series of records which Emily and Anne wrote at approximately four-year intervals, to be preserved like family photographs.[2] In 1834 Emily wrote: 'The Gondals are discovering the interior of Gaaldine.' But the idea of an island kingdom goes back to December 1827, when each child chose an island as part of an imaginative exercise that developed into 'The Islanders' Play'. Emily, then aged nine, chose Arran, and named as its 'chief man' Walter Scott.[3] Little is known of Emily's Arran, but the poetry she wrote nine or ten years later suggests that Scott was the presiding genius when the groundwork of Gondal was being laid.

Some Gondal place-names were pencilled by Anne into 'A Vocabulary of Proper Names' in J. Goldsmith's *Grammar of General Geography* (1823).[4] The two most important items are 'GONDAL, a large island in the North Pacific', and 'GAALDINE, a large island newly discovered in the South Pacific'. Gaaldine was evidently colonized from Gondal in the same way that, in the earlier game,

[13] Fannie E. Ratchford, *The Brontës' Web of Childhood* (New York and Oxford, 1941), pp. 148–9.

[1] See e.g. Alexander, *Early Writings of Charlotte Brontë*, ch. 2.

[2] For longer extracts from the record papers quoted here (sometimes called 'birthday notes' or 'diary papers'), see app. V.

[3] *CBEW*, i. 21–2. In an earlier version of this scene, CB wrote that EB chose 'Bute Isle' as well as Arran, and added 'Mr Lockhart, Johnny Lockhart etc.' to Scott (*CBEW*, i. 6).

[4] For a list of these additions see app. V.

parts of an imaginary Africa were colonized from Glasstown, later Verdopolis. Its tropical climate (101. 11) is contrasted with the more bracing weather of Gondal, and Gaaldine may have stood in relation to Gondal rather as England to Scott's Scotland and Angria to Glasstown, as a wealthier but somewhat despised neighbour.

Gondal continued to be part of Emily's and Anne's lives for another twelve years, and is mentioned together with their real-life doings in each of their record papers. On 26 June 1837 Emily noted: 'I [am writing] Agustus-Almedas life 1st v. 1–4th page from the last . . . the Emperors and Empresses of Gondal and Gaaldine [are] preparing to depart from Gaaldine to Gondal to prepare for the coronation which will be on the 12th of July.'

On 30 July 1841, her twenty-third birthday, Emily wrote: 'The Gondals are at present in a threatening state but there is no open rupture as yet—all the princes and princesses of the Royal royaltys are at the palace of Instruction—I have a good many books on hands but I am sorry to say that as usual I make small progress with any.' Meanwhile Anne, in Scarborough, was 'engaged in writing the fourth volume of Solala Vernon's Life'.

Four years later Emily and Anne, reunited after a long separation, went on a visit to York—a wonderful opportunity for shared fantasy and oral improvisation. Emily was now twenty-seven years old.[5] But as Katherine Frank notes,[6] her record says nothing of the Minster or the city, but gives a long list of the Gondal characters that she and Anne 'were' during their excursion, adding: 'The Gondals Still florish bright as ever I am at present writing a work on the First Wars—Anne has been writing some articles on this and a book by Henry Sophona—We intend sticking firm by the rascals as long as they delight us which I am glad to say they do at present.' While Anne noted:

Emily is engeaged in writing the Emperor Julius's life she has read some of it and I want very much to hear the rest—she is writing some poetry, too. . . . We have not yet finished our Gondal chronicles that we began three years and a half ago. . . . The Unique Society above half a year ago were wrecked on a dezart Island as they were returning from Garldin—they are

[5] Of several parallels with the Brontë games, the most interesting is the 'play' carried on by the Canadian novelist Mazo de la Roche with her cousin and companion, Caroline Clement, which began when de la Roche was an adolescent and was still continuing when she was in her fifties. The two women 'were' characters of the play and became deeply attached to some of them. See Joan Givner, *Mazo de la Roche: The Hidden Life* (Toronto, 1989), esp. pp. 14–15, 54–7, 130.

[6] *Emily Brontë: A Chainless Soul*, p. 207.

still there, but we have not played at them much yet—The Gondals in general are not in first rate playing condition.

These records show how the Gondal saga must have been built up. First came inventive play, with parts spoken and perhaps performed. The story was progressive: some idea was always current of what was going on in Gondal 'at present', and perhaps of what was likely to happen soon ('no open rupture as yet'). Different narratives might be carried on at the same time. But invention or opportunity sometimes failed, leaving castaways stranded and perhaps a gap in the story. Later came the chronicling of these events in prose 'lives' and 'books' and in verse, with further invention and elaboration. Eventually writing would become virtually independent of the shared play.

When Emily and Anne were both at home, they could act out Gondal together. Their writing, however, would normally have been done separately. The fact that the dramatis personae of Anne's Gondal poems are quite different from Emily's suggests that by 1836 (when the first dated poems appear) each of the girls was recording the doings of her own favourite characters, probably with exchanges of information. Circumstances encouraged the development of two parallel Gondals, for the sisters were often apart. In 1835 Emily spent three months at school at Roe Head; when she returned, Anne took her place at the school for a longer period. In 1838 Emily was teaching at Law Hill; in 1839 Anne spent some months as a governess at Blake Hall; then came a long separation (probably from May 1840 to June 1845) when Anne was employed at Thorp Green.[7] During those five years Anne wrote only three Gondal poems,[8] two of them during or just after a Christmas visit to Haworth. It was Emily who kept Gondal going, for in the same period she wrote at least two dozen Gondal pieces. As the record papers show, the two enjoyed playing the game when reunited (Emily perhaps more than Anne), and both wrote Gondal poems during 1846. But however close their collaboration in the early years and occasionally later, we can regard Emily's Gondal poetry as a virtually independent creation.

A few of Emily's poems were given 'Gondal dates', which range from 1825 to 1830.[9] But their background is usually more like that

[7] See *Poems of AB*, pp. 10–13 and (for variations in the quantity of AB's Gondal output, judged from the extant poems), p. 208.

[8] These are 15, 29, and 35 in *Poems of AB*.

[9] These dates may derive from earlier games which had to accommodate CB's great hero, the Duke of Wellington.

of a romantically perceived Scotland of the fifteenth and sixteenth centuries: noble persons and families contend for honour, power, or love in a series of intrigues about the throne, conspiracies, revenges, assassinations, sieges, and battles. Scottish names like Douglas, Gleneden, and Lesley recur,[10] and the scenery is mostly mountains, lakes, heather, and snow. Emily's liking for such materials probably goes back to December 1827, when she named Scott as her 'chief man'. In the same month Scott had published the first series of his *Tales of a Grandfather*, and a copy was given to the Brontë children by their aunt as a New Year present in 1828.[11] The book claims to give 'a general view of Scottish History, with a selection of its more picturesque and prominent points', from the time of Macbeth to the accession to the English throne of James VI; in effect, a series of exciting and usually violent stories. A sixth of the book is taken up by Mary Queen of Scots, who is perhaps the main prototype of 'Gondal's queen', the fascinating, passionate, and ambivalent A.G.A. Gondal owes much to Scott's poetry, his novels, and the ballads he collected and imitated. It may also owe something to the work of a minor poet, David Moir, whose contributions to *Blackwood's Magazine* included many ballads and lyrics on Scottish themes.[12] But the other major influence on Gondal was Byron.[13] Emily may have come to him later than to Scott: it is hard not to feel that when she wrote **56**, in July 1839, she had just read and intensely experienced *The Giaour*. In Gondal poetry Byron's moods, themes, and characters, and sometimes his phrases, can be recognized.

Nearly all the Gondal and Angrian manuscripts are written in tiny print-style characters difficult for the unskilled to read. After the plan of keeping to scale with the toy soldiers had lost its point, this script still had the advantage of being almost impenetrable to the casual glances of outsiders. It is unlikely that Mr Brontë or Aunt Branwell would have approved of Charlotte's romantic treatment of promiscuity and adultery in high life in her Angrian novelettes of the later 1830s. Gondal is a more moral world, where sin is usually

[10] Paden suggests (p. 69 n. 63) that 'Gondal's royal race' were Stuarts. Two 'Stewarts' appear in a list of characters by EB (see app. VI); and the royalist 'Claudia' in 51 may be an exile from the England of the Interregnum.

[11] Inscribed copy in BPM, and see Gérin, *Charlotte Brontë: The Evolution of Genius* (Oxford, 1967), p. 28.

[12] See Juliet Barker, *The Brontës* (1994), pp. 274, 889 n. 3.

[13] See Helen Brown, 'The Influence of Byron on Emily Brontë', *Modern Language Review*, 34 (1939), 374–81, where some of the parallels noted in the commentary were first pointed out.

followed by remorse and punishment, but the career of A.G.A. is not exemplary. To each writer in a different degree these fictions had the fascination of a secret conspiracy against the adults, and in this context the phrases used for Angria by Charlotte and Branwell—the 'world below', 'the infernal world'[14]—suggest a realm of pleasure, energy, and transvalued wickedness, like Blake's in *The Marriage of Heaven and Hell.*

We cannot assume that Gondal history was clear and consistent. (A wish to make it more so may have been behind the project of writing 'Gondal chronicles', begun about Christmas 1841 but perhaps never completed.) But certain characters, relationships, and events were well established in Emily's mind, in sequences to which she could return at any time. Thus the death of Alexander, Lord of Elbë, as witnessed by his lover A.G.A., was the subject of a poem in 1837 and another in 1844 (**4**, **114**). In 1838 Emily wrote a ballad describing the pursuit of Douglas, apparently for a crime which she did not begin to put into verse until 1841, completing the poem three years later (**31**, **81**). It follows that the composition dates that Emily attached to her poems are no guide to Gondal chronology.

Many of Emily's Gondal poems imply enough of the fictional situation to be self-explanatory. Others, like **63**, would be clearer if we knew the stories behind them. But some may never have been written down; the prose that was written has been lost; and most of the surviving poems are lyrical or meditative, with only a few narratives. Some poems may have been conceived as 'fragments'; and in some cases we do not know whether they belong to Gondal or not. About forty Gondal characters are known to us only as names in lists or record papers. To reconstruct Gondal history from such evidence is like reconstructing extinct fauna from a few scattered bones. Some ambitious attempts have been made,[15] but they differ widely, and none is altogether convincing. However, the sequence of poems in MS B, where Emily at first arranged them in related groups, is more

[14] *LL*, i. 297; Ratchford, *The Brontës' Web of Childhood*, p. 159.

[15] Notably by Laura L. Hinkley, Fannie E. Ratchford, and (with more rigour) W. D. Paden. Ratchford's synthesis depends on her belief that three Gondal heroines, A.G.A., Rosina Alcona, and Geraldine S., are one and the same person: this belief rests on a long chain of reasoning with some very weak links (*GQ*, pp. 26–7). Tom Winnifrith pertinently asks what our chances of accurately reconstructing the story of *WH* would have been, if all that had survived were a few dialogues between characters identified, for the most part, by first names or initials (*The Brontës* (1977), pp. 36–7). Some solutions offered by these scholars to particular problems are discussed in the commentary, and summaries of their reconstructions are given in app. VII.

suggestive than is usually realized. At the end of this section is placed a summary of what seems fairly solidly established.

The Gondal stories sound melodramatic, but so would a summary of *Wuthering Heights*. The degree of success of each poem depends on the qualities Emily could bring to such tales. Her dated Gondal poems show development not only in technique but in imaginative power: **116** shows a better grasp of what love and fidelity mean than **14**, just as **126** shows a better grasp of what war means than **20**. Even when the nominal subject of a Gondal poem was beyond Emily's imagining, it could supply metaphors for real and intense feelings. An obvious example is the dungeon theme, which provides the subject or setting for fourteen pieces and references in twelve more.[16] Emily probably knew Byron's *The Prisoner of Chillon*, but the power of her own prison poems is of a different kind. The earliest, **7**, has been condemned for its crudeness,[17] and like the rest it would be unconvincing as a sketch of prison life. But it expresses feelings of confinement, despair, and rage with great force, hammered across by the repetitive rhythm and syntax, which dissolve into heartfelt relief with the looser pattern of lines 21–4. These were feelings Emily knew from her time at Roe Head school, if not from Cowan Bridge; probably too from her position as a woman in a male-orientated society.[18] Later, still other feelings could be carried by the dungeon theme. In one of Emily's best-known poems (**123**, **124**), physical imprisonment in Gondal becomes a metaphor for the confinement of soul in body.

Gondal Characters and Stories

A.G.A. (Augusta G. Almeda),[19] the most prominent figure and the speaker of fourteen or more poems, was born in Gondal and loved

[16] The theme had acquired increased significance in the late 18th century as a metaphor for all kinds of restriction and oppression, and is ubiquitous in Gothic literature. The Brontës began to use it early: the extremely deep dungeon of the 'Palace School', invented when EB was nine (*CBEW*, i. 22–4), was re-created in Angria: see CB's 'A Leaf from an Unopened Volume' (1834), *CBEW*, ii/I. 374. In Gondal, dungeons lay beneath the North and South Colleges of the 'Palaces of Instruction', where the young nobility were educated, frequently imprisoned, and wrote poems on their prison walls.

[17] Referring to **7**. 55–8, Derek Stanford calls it 'the poetry of tantrums' (*Emily Brontë*, by Stanford and Muriel Spark (1953), p. 140). Both tantrums and poems can express acute frustration which defeats rational expression: some poems by Sylvia Plath are cases in point.

[18] See, among many, Sandra Gilbert and Susan Gubar, *The Madwoman in the Attic* (New Haven, Conn., and London, 1979), esp. ch. 8; Lyn Pykett, *Emily Brontë* (1989), esp. chs. 3–4.

[19] 'Augusta' may have been suggested by the name of Byron's half-sister; and the name had been proposed for Princess (later Queen) Victoria (in whom the young EB took a close

its mountains, bluebells, heather, and snow, calling herself 'a mountaineer' (18). As a reigning queen we find her sleeping in the heather, drinking from a spring, stabbing her attacker with her own knife (81).[20] It is not clear whether she was originally of 'royal race', and in the course of a stormy life she was imprisoned at least once (18, 114). A passionate beauty with 'dark resplendant hair', she was unscrupulous in love, like Charlotte's Angrian hero Zamorna. After stealing the lover, named Amedeus, of her childhood friend Angelica and involving him in dishonour, she abandoned him and sent him and Angelica into exile (81). Her love for Alexander, Lord of Elbë, ended with his violent death by Lake Elnor, perhaps after a battle (114, 4, 8). As for Alfred ?Sidonia of Aspin Castle, she 'wronged both him and heaven'; after a joyous affair, she left him in remorse, after which he 'failed' and died (76, 130, 104, 25, 48). Fernando De Samara she loved, then imprisoned, then drove to exile and suicide (32, 72, 37; ?6, 17, 63). Finally, when her 'passionate youth was nearly past', she was murdered by the outlaw Douglas, at the instigation of Angelica, while alone on Elmor Hill. She defended herself bravely and Douglas fled wounded, though he managed to escape pursuit (81, 31). The faithful Lord Eldred remained to sum up a life that had inspired both hatred and devotion (81, 107).

Julius Brenzaida, sometimes called Julius Angora (perhaps from his estate),[21] was given a princely education in Gondal, but imprisoned for a spell as a punishment for his involvement with the ambitious Rosina Alcona (112). Another of his loves was Geraldine S., whom he left grieving over her child by Julius in Zadora (34, 35, 87). As King of Almedore in Gaaldine, Julius swore an oath of union (which he had no intention of keeping) with his kinsman Gerald Exina (23). In alliance with Rosina, whom he perhaps married, Julius made war against Gerald for the throne of Gondal; at this time or later Arthur Exina, of the royal house, was imprisoned (190). In his hour of triumph Julius was assassinated in his palace, where Rosina lay ill

interest). The wicked, beautiful and passionate Augusta di Segovia is prominent in BB's Angrian 'Life of Alexander Perey' (1834: see Collins. 'Almeda' probably comes from Almeida in Portugal, dramatically lost and recaptured during Wellington's Peninsular campaigns. In CB's Angria one of the grandchildren of 'Wellington' is Arthur Julius, Lord Almeida (*CBEW*, i. 184 n.). *GQ* would read 'G' as 'Geraldine'.

[20] In her physical hardiness, dark beauty, courage, and treachery she may owe something to Gibbon's account of Zenobia, Queen of Palmyra (*Decline and Fall*, ch. 11), the model for one of CB's early heroines: see Alexander, *Early Writings of Charlotte Brontë*, pp. 23–4.

[21] In 88 Rosina refers to Julius by his name of Brenzaida and his title of Almedore (27, 60). She later describes him as buried 'on Angora's shore' (116. 6).

(**20**, **46**, **88**). Fifteen years later Rosina commemorated their love in one of Emily's best-known poems (**116**).

The Gleneden group and its doings are less clear. This family played a part in restoring peace and order to Gondal after a period of tyranny, but in the fighting a brother (Arthur or Desmond) was killed (**45**, ?**53**) or perhaps only imprisoned (**26**). A woman of the family, E. R. Gleneden, was loved by M. Douglas (**113**). A male E. Gleneden (probably Edmund) persuaded a Mary R. to elope with him (**97**), and we later find R. Gleneden, Edmund, Mary, and Flora sailing to 'Zedoras strand and Ula's Eden sky' in Gaaldine, where a loved one is already waiting for them (**80**). They kept their ties with Gondal, and like M.G. (?Mary Gleneden) preferred its 'mists and moorlands drear' to the sunnier southern climate (**101**). This group called itself the Unique Society, and Anne's last record paper (quoted above) notes their having been shipwrecked on a desert island while returning from Gaaldine.

The wars of the Royalists and Republicans may have been a late development in Gondal history; clear references appear only in the record papers of 1845 and two poems written in or after October 1844 (**109**, **126**). Possibly King Julius's wars were the 'First Wars' chronicled by EB in 1845, and so called because these later conflicts constituted the second. (CB's 'A Leaf from an Unopened Volume', written in 1834 and set in a future of *c.*1858, predicts a successful revolution in Angria leading to the massacre of the royal family.)[22]

III. THE MANUSCRIPTS

After Emily Brontë's death her surviving poetry manuscripts passed to Charlotte Brontë, and after 1855 to Charlotte's widower, Arthur Bell Nicholls. In 1895 Nicholls sold all but one of them to Clement Shorter, who was acting on behalf of Thomas Wise, by whom they were dispersed. Since then all the known manuscripts, with the exception of MS A, have passed into the care of libraries and museums, usually by the generosity of collectors. The smaller manuscripts have been identified and described, and wrong attributions to Emily corrected, largely through the work of C. W. Hatfield.[1]

[22] *CBEW*, ii/I. 346, 359.

[1] Much of the information given below about the history of the manuscripts is drawn from Hatfield's introduction to *1941*. All EB's holographs except those in the Taylor Collection are listed poem by poem in Barbara Rosenbaum and Pamela White, *Index of English Literary Manuscripts*, iv/I (1982), 84–105.

The manuscripts consist of three small notebooks and forty-six scraps of paper or card. The designations A, B, and C were given to the notebooks by Hatfield, who numbered each poem or fragment within them according to sequence (A1, etc.). The collections of single leaves he designated D, E, and F, and within each collection he gave a number to every leaf. The present edition retains Hatfield's system, and adds the designation T for the leaves whose location was unknown to him but are now in the Robert H. Taylor Collection in the University Library at Princeton.

MS A (the Honresfeld Manuscript)

MS A is the transcript book that Emily began in February 1844 for poems not then considered as belonging to Gondal: a notebook of faintly lined pages about 7″ x 4¼″. Wise had the fifteen leaves of text bound in morocco, trimming them slightly in the process, and by 5 February 1897 he had sold the volume to the collector William Law, of Honresfeld, Littleborough, near Rochdale. By 1926 it had passed to Mr A. J. (later Sir Alfred) Law, who permitted three complete typescripts and some photographs to be made by the antiquarian Davidson Cook.[2] In 1934 Sir Alfred allowed the notebook to be reproduced in facsimile in the volume of the Shakespeare Head edition containing Emily's poems. It does not appear to have been seen since, and its location is unknown. Hatfield claims in *1941* only to have seen transcripts and photographs, and no later scholar has been been able to obtain information from Sir Alfred's successors. Fortunately an excellent set of photographs, made either in 1926 or in 1934, can be consulted at the Parsonage Museum. These show pencillings and fine details which cannot be seen in the Shakespeare Head facsimile.

The first page of this notebook is headed 'E J B. Transcribed Febuary 1844.'[3] The first poem, **39**, then follows after two short horizontal lines, which are used throughout to separate the poems. The book contains thirty-one complete poems,[4] neatly if not very legibly copied in small printed characters. In every case but two Emily gave the composition date, placing it at the head of the text on the right; she did not initial the poems, as she did most of the pieces in B. Most of them show only small revisions, though the last stanza of **115** has been heavily revised after the following poem was

[2] Information about the early history of A is taken from Cook's introduction to one of his transcripts, at BPM.

[3] For a list of facsimile reproductions of this page, see commentary to **39**.

[4] For a list of these poems in the order in which they appear in A, see app. II.

entered. Into some poems Charlotte has pencilled alterations and suggestions, including titles, apparently in preparation for *1850*.

Into the first part of the book Emily copied poems that she had waiting to be transcribed; these she arranged approximately by theme.[5] That she paid attention to their sequence is shown by the figure '2' written in ink over **84** and '1' over the next poem, **79**, to show they should be taken in reverse order. Six of the first seven poems express a love for moorland scenery and flowers, or, more generally, for Earth. Then, after two poems drawing on Stoic ideas and a relatable poem in dispraise of earthly life, come four apparently dealing with a lover who is lost, or dies (see above, p. 4). Two transitional poems are followed by four concerning death. Then, after the intermediate **99**, comes **103**, the first of seven poems of self-communion and the imagination. The three remaining poems are of different kinds, but the idea of death is important in each.

In this latter part of A the sequence was partly determined by what was available. With **103** Emily had reached a poem written in the same month that she had begun the book. She then went back to pick up **95**, written ten months before. The last eight poems were all written from March 1844 onwards. Most of these appear in order of composition, but the fact that **118** precedes **117**, though written a few days later, shows that Emily was not simply entering poems as soon as she wrote them. The only one to be substantially revised in A is **115**; the rest were probably drafted on sheets now lost, and copied into A some time after the composition date. The last poem entered is **125**, 'No coward soul', dated 2 January 1846.

MS B (the Gondal Notebook)

MS B is the other transcript book Emily began in February 1844: it is a notebook of sixty-eight lined pages 6″ x 4″, in a red paper cover bearing the price '6d'. This is the manuscript Nicholls kept back when the others were sold to Shorter in 1895. After Nicholls' death it was bought at Sotheby's in 1907 by Mrs George Murray Smith, the widow of Charlotte Brontë's publisher, whose son bequeathed it in 1933 to the British Museum (British Library Additional MS 43483).

The first page is headed, with flourishes, 'Emily Jane Brontë. Transcribed Febuary 1844. | Gondal Poems.'[6] Forty-five poems follow.[7]

[5] Lloyd-Evans is a convenient edition for following the grouping of poems in A, B, and C.

[6] For a list of facsimiles of this page see commentary to 4.

[7] For a list of these poems in the order in which they appear in B, see app. II.

All but two are dated (at the head of the text on the right), and at first nearly all bear Emily's initials, usually just 'E.' before the date. But after entering twenty-seven poems she became less consistent about initials, and for the last twelve she added none. All but three of the poems clearly deal with fictional episodes. Most are spoken by a Gondal character, whose name or initials appear in the heading. In this notebook too Charlotte has pencilled some suggested revisions.

As with A, Emily began by copying in poems she already had by her, arranging them in a preferred order. This is confirmed by the figure '2' written over **45** and '1' over **26**, which follows it in B but should seemingly have come first. The arrangement is by groups of characters and their relationships, and apparently in order of events within each group. Thus the first eight poems deal with the loves of Augusta ?Geraldine Almeda (A.G.A.), seen first grieving for the death of Alexander Elbë and then in love with Alfred ?Sidonia, who also dies. After an interposed narrative poem (**31**), two poems follow about the Gleneden family. Then come four about Julius Brenzaida; the chronology of this group is strange, as the first poem (**88**) tells of Julius's death. Next comes one that may look back on an affair between A.G.A. and Fernando De Samara, followed by two that certainly do look back on it. Then, after two more interposed poems, comes the long narrative centred on the death of A.G.A. (**81**). This was not completed until May 1844, and having entered this poem, another of uncertain relevance, and **106** (an elegy for A.G.A.), Emily seems to have used up all the completed poems that could be arranged into such groups.

Six miscellaneous poems follow, one undated, the rest of various dates between 1841 and 1843. The remaining sixteen poems, with two exceptions, were written between May 1844 and May 1848 and entered roughly in order of composition. The exceptions are **90** and **100**, written in 1842 and 1843. Some of the late poems would obviously have found a place in one of the subject groups if they had been written in time.

After the autumn of 1845, when Emily's poems were discovered and the scheme of publication begun, she lost interest in keeping a tidy transcript book for Gondal poems. The last two poems to be entered in B are **126** and **127**. The first, a long, powerful, unfinished narrative set amid a civil war, is dated at the head '14 September 1846'. Composition probably continued after that date, for revision becomes increasingly heavy and the last hundred lines, which seem to have been composed directly into B, are often illegible. The second, dated 'may 13th 1848', is a new attempt at the same poem, abandoned after twenty-five lines.

MS C (the Ashley Manuscript)

MS C is what remains of an earlier transcript book for both Gondal and non-Gondal poems. It is a notebook that now contains twelve leaves of lined paper 6½″ x 4¾″, with text in a cursive hand. The book passed from Nicholls through Shorter to Wise, and thence to the British Museum as part of the Ashley Library (Ashley MS 175). Its leaves have been rebound and slightly trimmed, and mounted on stubs which mask a few letters of text.

This notebook contains thirteen complete poems (eight of which are not found in other manuscripts) and three incomplete ones.[8] The use of a cursive hand of normal size made it necessary for Emily to tuck up the ends of many lines of verse.[9] The first two poems are signed and dated at the foot; the third and twelfth are unsigned and undated. The others bear no signatures but have their composition dates at the head of the text, on the right. All but one undatable poem (**132**) were written between 19 August 1837 and 15 October 1839. They were probably copied out in late 1839 or early 1840: had the collection been made later, some poems of 1840 would most likely have been included. But we do not have the whole collection. One or more leaves have been removed from the front of the notebook, which now begins in the middle of **8** with a cancelled version of the last five lines. Also, at least two leaves have been removed from the body of the book: one which bore the last stanza of **38** and must have carried other text as well, and another which bore the middle section of **45**, amounting to some thirty lines.

The explanation is that after February 1844 Emily transferred some poems from C to her new fair-copy books A and B, revising as she did so. Superseded texts in C were crossed out and any leaves completely filled by such texts were removed, as happened to one or more leaves from the beginning of the book. But the leaf containing the cancelled ending of **8** also contained **18**, which had not been superseded; so that leaf was allowed to remain, becoming the first in the book. For the same reason an incomplete text of **38**, the beginning and ending of **45**, and a complete but superseded text of **48** were cancelled but left in place.

[8] For a list of these poems in the order in which they appear in C, see app. II.

[9] MS C is reproduced in facsimile in *Wuthering Heights,* ed. Clement K. Shorter (1911), pp. 419–42. For photographs of some pages see Thomas J. Wise, *A Brontë Library* (1929), pp. 36–7; Lloyd-Evans, p. 63.

The first seven poems in C are all Gondal poems. In arranging these Emily may have attempted the kind of grouping she used later in B. Like B, C begins with A.G.A. grieving for Elbë, and then comes another A.G.A. poem; then two about Julius Brenzaida. The four poems known to have been copied from C into B (8, 25, 48, 45) reappear there in the same order, though with other poems interspersed. It may be that the poem which once preceded 8 at the beginning of C was 4, which precedes it in B and would already have been written when C was started. But in 1839 or 1840 Emily seems to have felt no need to segregate her poems by category. Of the nine poems which follow the first seven, one (45) is clearly a Gondal piece. Six are fictional but may have nothing to do with Gondal; for example, in 51 the only country mentioned is England, and the speaker, 'Claudia', appears in no other poem. The remaining two poems are hard to classify, and one of these (38) was transcribed not into B but into A.

MSS D, E, F, T (Single-Leaf Manuscripts)

The forty-six slips now designated MSS D, E, F, and T were among the manuscripts sold by Nicholls to Shorter in 1895. Before being resold by Wise, these were arbitrarily divided into two batches, which were further divided when they came to be sold yet again. One of Wise's two batches, containing sixteen leaves now designated the D MSS, passed to an unidentified American owner and was used in the preparation of *1902*. Subsequently it was bought by the collector H. H. Bonnell, of Philadelphia, who on his death in 1926 bequeathed all but three of these leaves to the Brontë Parsonage Museum (Bonnell 127). The other three (D1–2, D15) passed by way of Mrs Bonnell to the Pierpont Morgan Library (Bonnell MA 2615, 2696).

The second batch, containing the thirty leaves now designated E, F, and T, was bought by H. Buxton Forman, who sold them in 1920. Twenty-two were bought by Harry T. Smith of New York, and of these twenty were eventually resold to another American collector, W. T. H. Howe. These (the E MSS) are now in the Berg Collection of the New York Public Library. The other two leaves from Smith's collection (the F MSS) were bought by the University of Texas, and are now in the Humanities Research Center at Austin. The remaining eight holographs (the T MSS) passed through various hands[10]

[10] Two were bought by Jerome Kern, others by J. Herbert Foster: see Mildred Christian, 'A Census of Brontë Manuscripts in the United States', *The Trollopian*, 2–3 (1947–8), pt. 2, pp. 245–6. Taylor had acquired Kern's manuscripts by 1977 (see *Princeton Library Chronicle*, 38 (1977), 217), and bought the others in 1981.

before coming to rest in the Taylor Collection at Princeton University Library.

'Sheets', though in one sense correct, would be a misleading word for these tiny irregular slips, the smallest of which (T8) measures about 2″ x 1″, the longest (D16) about 6½″ x 3″. Many seem to be parts of leaves of one or more notebooks about 7″ x 4½″, but it has seldom been possible to reconstruct an entire leaf.[11] Some leaves fit the texts as closely as if the edges had been torn to fit what was written; in other cases, like **191**, the text has been cramped to fit the paper. Some are written on odd corners of waste paper, one (**102**) on a piece of mourning stationery, two (**63**, **192**) on scraps of card or cardboard. A few slips carry tiny sketches or fantastic doodles.

These manuscripts contain a number of complete poems not found in other holographs; some shorter pieces which may or may not be seen as complete; ten drafts, complete or partial, of poems for which later holographs exist; and all the smaller fragments.[12] Some pieces, like **166**, consist only of two or three lines that Emily must have liked and perhaps hoped to work into a later poem. The arbitrary way in which these single-leaf manuscripts were divided and dispersed means that their distribution among collections and their arrangement within collections has little significance. Some leaves contain a number of poems and fragments, neatly written and dated; D10 has sixteen. These may be the remains of an early attempt by Emily to collect and fair-copy her verse. As almost all the dated pieces collected in this way are from 1836–9, it may be that the attempt took place in 1839 and was partly superseded by C. But the co-presence on any such storage slip of several short poems and fragments seems to mean only that Emily had these pieces ready for storage at about the same time. To link them in sequences or amalgamate them into poems, as most editors have done in some cases from *1902* onwards, is misleading: on the slips these pieces are regularly separated by lines or rows of crosses, as poems are in the notebooks.

Transcripts by A. B. Nicholls

Before selling Emily's manuscripts to Shorter, Nicholls had copied out most of the poems from MSS A and B that had not already appeared in *1846* or *1850*. It is not known when these transcripts

[11] E8, a scrap in the Berg Collection bearing two fragments, once formed a single leaf with F2 at Texas, bearing a third.

[12] For lists of poems and fragments in their order in the single-leaf manuscripts, see app. II.

were made. The plan may have been suggested by Charlotte, with the idea of producing legible copy from which further instalments of Emily's poetry might be printed. It is possible that some of the copying was done in CB's lifetime, and that she suggested some of the titles that Nicholls added in his transcripts; but she does not seem to have annotated the holographs after *1850* was published. Pencilled markings by Nicholls in B indicate which poems had already been published, and the initials 'A.B.N.' at the head of other B poems were probably added to show which he had transcribed.

Nicholls made two sets of copies of the same poems: the eight that remained unpublished in A, and twenty-six of the thirty in B.[13] One set, copied into a notebook, was sold with other effects in 1914 and is now in the Bonnell Collection at the Pierpont Morgan Library. The other set was probably sold in 1895 to Shorter, who published **26** in *Charlotte Brontë and her Circle* (1896) and **72** in *The Woman at Home* (August 1897). Five years later this set of copies had found its way to the USA and was used in the preparation of *1902*; they are now in the Huntington Library.[14] Nicholls's transcripts have not been collated for the present volume, but the titles he added have been included in the commentary.

Characteristics of the Holographs

Except for MS C, in an ordinary cursive hand, nearly all Emily Brontë's holographs are in the printed characters already described. These are not only very small but often badly formed. The best the editor of *1902* could make of 'Remains its memory dear' (**130**. 31) was 'Beneath its mighty glare'.[15] The *n*, *r*, and *u* are almost interchangeable, and some letters, especially the *e*, are often so small as virtually to disappear. The *t* is not always crossed and the *m* often has a spiky crown, so that in several places one can only tell from the sense of the passage whether Emily wrote 'thy' or 'my'; and the sense is not always decisive, as in **7**. 26.

Revisions are frequent: Emily seldom copied a poem without changing it, and could disfigure the first poem in a new transcript book by alterations, as with **4**. We have few examples of her apparently composing straight on to paper, but this may be because

[13] The poems in each set are listed by Rosenbaum and White, *English Literary Manuscripts*, iv/I. 82.

[14] It would have been easier for Nicholls to make one set of transcripts and recopy them, but variants in his readings suggest that for each set he consulted the holographs, at least for difficult words: thus in **86**. 1 Pierpont Morgan has 'hideous', Huntington 'piteous'.

[15] *1902*, p. 180; the source of the reading is a draft of **130** on D8.

superseded drafts were discarded, as with pages of C. Each complete poem has probably passed through several stages of improvement, of which we see only the latest. Except where a change occurred to her in mid-line, her usual method of revising was by overwriting; then, if another change was to be made, the overwritten words would be crossed out and new ones written above the line. Such third thoughts are particularly hard to read because of the tiny irregular spaces into which they have been crammed.

In the absence of any manuscript of *Wuthering Heights*, these revisions in the holographs give us our only chance of watching Emily's mind at work. Some are fairly trivial, like the substitution of *yet* for *but*, or the use of a homonym to avoid repetition; but even small changes can be illuminating. In 15, 'Sleep brings no joy to me', '<r>joy' in line 1 suggests that Emily began to write 'rest', but decided to keep 'rest' for stanza 2. In 15. 10, '<d>soundest' suggests that she began to write 'deepest', then realized that 'deepen' was coming two lines later. This shows the poem in an unexpectedly fluid state at a time when it was already being copied on to a storage slip. The cancelled draft of 8 reveals a version of Elbë's absence in which he literally takes a sea voyage, whereas in the final text the sea is a metaphor for his death. In 82, 'And like myself lone wholey lone', the changes in pronouns play out the whole question of the relation of speaker to bird, one fundamental to the interpretation of the poem. The present edition is the first to attempt to record as many revisions as possible.

Emily was highly sensitive to the sound of words, less so to their appearance, as is shown by the fact that she sometimes writes a perfectly metrical line but forgets at first to go back to the left to start it (see collation at 1. 10–11, 26. 11–12). Normally she leaves a space between stanzas, sets all lines over on the left without indentations, and begins each new line with a capital (though if the first word is revised, she often forgets to use one for the new word). Nearly all her poems were originally untitled, apart from Gondal headings that show who is speaking and sometimes to whom.

Emily's spelling is unorthodox, and in a few cases bizarre; for a discussion and a list of the more confusing forms, see appendix I. In the single-leaf manuscripts and in C she uses very little punctuation. In A and B it is fuller in some poems than in others, and often unconventional. A favourite mark is a horizontal dab of the pen that ranges in length between a short hyphen and a long dash, and in position from mid-height to slightly below the line. Occasionally she uses a question mark with a comma at the bottom instead of a full stop: logically this should indicate a question in mid-sentence, but this is not always the case. Her use of capitals is more orthodox, and her unconventional uses are sometimes deliberate: in several places she changes initial lower-case to a capital to mark emphasis or status (e.g. in **26**, **37**). The small print-style script often makes it difficult to be sure whether a large or small letter is intended, especially with *f*, *k*, *s*, and *w*. Sometimes a large one may have been used because it was easier to form without making a blot; this looks likely to have happened in some cases with *S* and with the square-topped *F*. But unmistakable capitals occur in unexpected places, as in 'heart and Eyelids' (**43**. 20), 'Bless thee Bright Sea' (**7**. 25), 'The night was Dark' (**43**. 1), 'O Hinder me by no delay' (**142**. 1).

IV. THE EARLY EDITIONS

1846

Twenty-one poems[1] by Emily Brontë were included in *Poems by Currer, Ellis, and Acton Bell* (1846). The story of this project was first told by Charlotte[2] and has often been embroidered by others. The known facts are that on 29 or 30 January 1846 Aylott & Jones agreed to publish a volume of poems at the authors' expense; the copy was parcelled up on 6 February and posted the next day; proofs were being read during March; and the volume appeared about the end of May.[3] We have no direct testimony about the method used for preparing the copy. By far the most likely method is that each of the sisters chose her own contributions and wrote out each poem separately, using for the printer's benefit the clear cursive hand they used for writing letters. The poems were then put into sequence for printing, with a piece first by one, then another sister in rotation, with slight variations. In due course each author corrected her own proofs.[4]

That Emily overcame her initial reluctance and played her part in the project is shown by the final layer of revisions in her hand in MSS A and B, from which her contributions were drawn. These show her supplying titles for **99**, **103**, **108**, and other poems (not all of which were finally included in *1846*), and removing the Gondal

[1] For a list of these poems see app. III.

[2] In a letter of Sept. 1848 to W. S. Williams, *LL*, ii. 256; in *1850*, pp. viii–x.

[3] Letters in *LL*, ii. 81–5, 93–4.

[4] Roper, pp. 159–61; see this article for a more detailed account of *1846*.

name 'Julian' from **123**. 65. She made many more revisions, either in the printer's copy or in proof. The most striking and successful of these was the creation of **124** ('The Prisoner') by removing these lines from their Gondal setting in **123**. Smaller verbal changes first appearing in *1846* affect sixty-nine lines of her poems.[5] Gondal headings and place-names are removed, though not 'Iernë' in **111**. The printed volume also normalizes spelling, punctuation, and capitals, indents lines to show stanza patterns, and occasionally alters the spacing between stanzas. Such changes to accidentals are much more likely to have been made by the printer than the poet.

The selection that Emily made for *1846* includes some of her best poems, fifteen of them from A (almost half the A poems) and six from B. In view of her initial resentment when Charlotte 'intruded upon her mind and feelings'[6] by reading her work, it is surprising that she chose to publish some of the most apparently self-revealing poems: **93**, **95**, **103**, **108**, **110**, and **118**.[7] Fourteen of the chosen poems date from 1844 and 1845, but **125**, 'No coward soul is mine', which bears the date 2 January 1846, was excluded. Perhaps in February Emily was still working on it; or perhaps she recognized that its scorn for 'the thousand creeds That move men's hearts' might be offensive, though Charlotte published the poem in *1850*.

In Emily's signed and dated copy of *1846* she is said to have entered the composition dates of her own poems.[8] Possibly the printed volume satisfied in part the need which led her to make successive transcript books, and if it occurred to her to make revisions in those poems, she may have done so in that volume. The whereabouts of that copy is unknown.[9] Only two copies of the original issue were sold;[10] but in October or November 1848, when

[5] Ibid. 162–6.

[6] 'My sister Emily was not a person . . . on the recesses of whose mind and feelings, even those nearest and dearest to her could, with impunity, intrude unlicensed' (CB, in *1850*, p. viii).

[7] A point first made by Visick, who adds that the poems chosen 'are, quite simply, the best poems' (p. 11).

[8] A. Mary F. Robinson, *Emily Brontë* (1883), pp. 128, 141.

[9] It was apparently this copy which passed to the Brontës' servant Martha Brown, who sold it to William Law of Honresfeld. On 16 Nov. 1895 Law wrote to Nicholls mentioning this purchase of 'her copy of the "Poems", with notes written in it in her handwriting and autograph' (transcript at BPM). This copy does not seem to have been heard of since. It cannot be the copy of the 1848 reissue now at the University of Illinois (see below, n. 11): it is conceivable, though very unlikely, that EB annotated an early copy of that reissue before she died, but the annotations to the Illinois copy give the date of **115** as 'Feb. 1845', whereas Robinson reports the month given in EB's copy as October.

[10] CB to Thomas De Quincey, 16 June 1847: *LL*, ii. 136.

the Brontës had become known through their novels, the sheets were rebound and reissued by Smith, Elder with more success. On the title-page of this reissue the publishers' names were changed, but the date '1846' was retained. The signature 'Emily J. Brontë' in the copy owned by the University of Illinois is probably spurious.[11]

1850

In 1850, after the death of both her sisters, Charlotte Brontë prepared for Smith, Elder a one-volume reprint of *Wuthering Heights* and *Agnes Grey*.[12] To this she added selections from her sisters' unpublished poetry, with notes and a biographical introduction. She included sixteen poems[13] undoubtedly by Emily, eight from A and eight from B. To these she added **201** ('Often rebuked'), for which no manuscript has been found.

The texts from A and B incorporate all Emily's revisions in those manuscripts, plus some that Charlotte can be seen to have pencilled into A, plus others that appear for the first time in *1850*. It is hard to imagine how this last group could include late revisions by Emily: they must have been made by Charlotte herself, and they are extensive. She made **112** into a different poem by dropping the last thirty-two lines and adding six new ones; fitted the first twelve lines of **123** with a new eight-line ending; dropped sixteen lines from **42**; added five lines to **85**, and four to **120**. She also made small verbal alterations in every poem, affecting eighty-five other lines.

However misconceived this editorial work, the extent to which it was used as a means of interpreting or re-creating Emily has perhaps been exaggerated.[14] Some changes were made to disencumber **39** and **40**, read by Charlotte as autobiographical, from fictional touches. The reconstructions of **112** and **123** were carried through to make Gondal poems accessible. Most others seem to be attempts at local improvement, such as Charlotte must have felt Emily would have made had

[11] Library of the University of Illinois at Urbana (X821.B78.1848); described by Rosenbaum and White (*English Literary Manuscripts*, iv/I. 83) as a copy of *1846*. The date 'May 7th 1846' written under the signature must be spurious, and casts doubt on the other annotations. The composition dates added in pencil are in at least two different hands, neither of them Emily's.

[12] *Wuthering Heights and Agnes Grey. By Ellis and Acton Bell. A New Edition revised, with a Biographical Notice of the Authors, a Selection from their Literary Remains, and a Preface, By Currer Bell.*

[13] For a list of these poems in the order in which they appear, see app. III.

[14] See Romer Wilson, *All Alone: The Life and Private History of Emily Jane Brontë* (1928), pp. 245–6; Emily Tresselt Schmidt, 'From Highland to Lowland: Charlotte Brontë's Editorial Changes in Emily's Poems', *BST*, 15/78 (1968), 221–6.

she seen *1850* through the press, and had made during the preparation of *1846*.[15] We do not need to pronounce on their merits, since the only poem for which *1850* has any authority—is, indeed, the sole authority—is **201**. Hatfield suspected that Charlotte wrote this poem herself,[16] and as the selection shows her passing off twenty-three lines of her own as Emily's we cannot say she was incapable of it. It was by this poem, if she wrote it, and in the biographical preface and notes that Charlotte tried to make Emily more intelligible and acceptable to readers without departing from the essential truth.

For notes on some editions after *1850*, see appendix IV.

V. THIS EDITION

Canon

There is no problem with the authenticity of MSS A and B; nor with MS C, though unsigned and in a cursive hand, because poems were transcribed from it into A and B. But the sales by Wise confused the state of the single-leaf manuscripts, especially as Wise sometimes passed off Branwell's poems as the work of Emily (which commanded a higher price), and was not above forging signatures. All four Brontës wrote most of their poetry in the tiny printed characters already described, but small differences enable their work in this script to be told apart. The canon of Emily's poems (apart from the uncertain **201**) was established by Hatfield, who after long experience was able to verify his hypotheses by predicting the characteristics that a collector would find in a given manuscript.[1] Repeated readings have brought increased respect for Hatfield's judgement, and the canon is essentially that which he established in *1941*.[2] But the reappearance

[15] The change of 'frozen snow' to 'winter snow' in line 12 of the reconstructed **123** seems pointless, until it is noticed that the phrase 'frozen snow' appears in line 16 of **89**, on the same page of the selection. Many of EB's revisions were made to avoid such repetitions.

[16] *1941*, p. 255; for discussion see commentary to **201**.

[1] See *1941*, p. 7.

[2] I concur with Hatfield in rejecting the Angrian poem 'To the horse black Eagle', printed as EB's in *1910* and attributed at different times to CB and BB. (For a text of this poem from the Berg MSS, see *The Poems of Charlotte Brontë*, ed. Victor A. Neufeldt (New York, 1985), pp. 374–5.) It is not quite true that 'there is no evidence that Emily was ever involved with Angria' (ibid., p. 375); her record paper of June 1837 shows that she then knew the whereabouts of its two main characters, Zamorna and Northangerland. But we have no other poems by EB that identify themselves as Angrian, and the only grounds for assigning 'To the horse black Eagle' to EB is that Dr Tom Winnifrith believed it to be in her handwriting (*Brontë Facts and Brontë Problems* (with Edward Chitham, 1983), p. 17).

of the holograph of 'I've been wandering in the greenwoods' (Hatfield's J297), which Hatfield knew only from *1910* and assumed to be one of Emily's poems from the T group, has shown it to be the work of Charlotte.[3] And the rediscovery of the T MSS has made it possible to redistribute some texts within the canon. It is now clear that **3**, **195**, **196**, and **197**, which Hatfield printed as one poem (J270), are four separate fragments on one leaf, separated by rules, and that Emily's composition date applies only to **3**.

Sequence

In A and B Emily began by arranging her poems in related groups, and if she could have sustained this method there would have been a strong case for following her sequence for these poems. But in the latter part of A and B and in all other manuscripts the sequence is largely arbitrary. The obvious alternative, the one adopted here, is to place as many poems as possible in chronological order. For this method to have value, it was necessary to make a clear distinction between dated and undated poems, since where Emily has not attached a composition date it is not possible to date the piece with any confidence.[4] The dated poems and fragments are given first; in the few cases where the reading of a date is uncertain, this is signalled in the collation. After the dated pieces come the undated poems and fragments, manuscript by manuscript. Within each manuscript the leaves and poems follow each other in the numerical sequences assigned by Hatfield, though he did not always follow them in *1941*.

Text

Except in the case of **201**, the base text used for every poem and fragment is a holograph. For the missing MS A and the two leaves of F I have relied upon photographs; in other cases upon the manuscripts themselves, sometimes under high magnification. In the thirteen cases where more than one holograph has survived, the text used is that which the evidence of cancellations and revisions shows to be the latest. For **201** the text is taken from *1850*.

On these grounds Gezari includes it as a poem of uncertain authorship. The writing is, in fact, distinctly different from anything we have from EB or from BB, and bears a close resemblance to MSS by CB. I am grateful to have confirmation on this point from Dr Christine Alexander and Mrs Margaret Smith.

[3] The holograph is now in the library of Roger W. Barrett, of Chicago (see *Poems of Charlotte Brontë*, ed. Neufeldt, pp. xv, 21).

[4] The attempt to fit undated poems into a chronological sequence, sometimes on no better evidence than proximity in a single-leaf manuscript, is the least successful aspect of *1941*.

The only other texts of authority are the printed texts of the twenty-one poems that appear in *1846*. The substantive variants in those texts, affecting seventy-nine lines (besides the recasting of 123), I believe to be Emily's final revisions. The decision had to be made whether to regard them as the last stage of authorial improvement, or as alterations made to fit the texts for a special purpose, like an acting version of an Elizabethan play. In the latter case, manuscript and printed texts would each be allowed to keep their own integrity. Either view could be justified; but the revisions of *1846* correspond so closely, both in their kinds and in their general pattern, with revisions previously made in the manuscripts, that the first view seems to have more truth in it.[5] The verbal readings of *1846* have accordingly been adopted here, with two exceptions. First, Gondal names have been preserved in 113, 114 and 116. The removal of these names, which might have puzzled the Brontës' first readers, from *1846* is the only kind of revision clearly done for a special purpose, and their retention preserves links with other Gondal poems. Gondal headings have likewise been retained, together with the 'Gondal date' in 114. Secondly, 'The Prisoner' is given in both its printed form (124) and its manuscript form as part of a longer poem (123).

A few obvious slips of the pen have been corrected: these include failure to close quotation marks, the accidental deletion of too many words when revising, and the omission of 'not' in 5. 28. Such corrections are noted in the collation. Where Emily seems deliberately to have cancelled all readings, and where words are indecipherable, a gap has been left in the text. Uncertainty of reading is noted when this is acute.

Treatment of Accidentals

No policy is easy, because of the unclear nature of many letters and punctuation marks in the holographs. 'To give Emily Brontë's poems exactly as she wrote them'[6] can be achieved only by photographic facsimiles, which are much too laborious for ordinary reading. This aim is, however, more nearly achieved in the present edition than in any previous one. To follow the holographs as closely as their nature and ordinary typography permit seemed preferable both to complete normalization, which would be necessary in another kind of edition, and to a policy of compromise, which calls for so many arbitrary

[5] For evidence and argument see Roper, pp. 162–6.

[6] The professed aim of Philip Henderson in *The Complete Poems of Emily Brontë* (1951), p. ix. His edition normalizes spelling, punctuation, and capitals.

decisions that consistency becomes impossible. A normalized or semi-normalized text would also have made it very difficult to show revisions clearly in the collation, a major purpose of this edition. It is realized that Emily's punctuation and spelling will irritate some readers, but others may be glad to read what are virtually her only surviving manuscripts in something like their original form. The texts now presented follow what can be seen rather than what expectations would suggest, but where letters are completely equivocal due weight has been given to probability. The only other departures from the details of the base text are:

1. Where Emily has added her name or initials, these have been transferred to the commentary.
2. Composition dates have uniformly been placed where Emily usually placed them, at the head of the poem on the right, and set in italic.
3. Gondal headings have likewise been placed at the head of the poem on the left, except where they form part of a centred title.
4. In a few cases where the absence of punctuation, in mid-line, could cause confusion, a short space has been silently inserted into the text.
5. The indeterminate horizontal punctuation-mark described above (p. 21) has been standardized to a dash.
6. The question-mark with a comma at the bottom (see pp. 21–2) has likewise been normalized.

Collation

All holographs and *1846* have been collated. The base text for each poem is identified at the beginning of its collation by manuscript and poem (for MSS A, B, and C) or manuscript collection and leaf (for MSS D, E, F, and T). Substantive departures from the base text, usually where an *1846* reading has been adopted, are recorded; likewise substantive variants in other holographs. The line and stanza arrangements of *1846* are also shown, but not its punctuation or spelling. The editions of 1850, 1902, and 1910 have been consulted for possible readings of words now indecipherable: though each ultimately depends on existing holographs, those holographs may have been copied when they were in a better state than they are today. All legible cancelled readings have been recorded, except for a very few completely insignificant slips that Emily corrected.

All readings in the collation for a given poem are from the base text, unless another source is indicated. Thus '20 <g>God' shows that in the base text Emily changed the lower-case 'g' to a capital; '2 blowing] <raging>' shows that in the base text she first wrote 'raging', then replaced it by 'blowing'; '9 lonely] noble *D*' shows that where the base text (identified in the headnote as from B) reads 'lonely', the D text reads 'noble'; '79 moan] ~ <groan>' means that in the base text one of these words is written over the other, and though 'moan' seems the more likely final reading, it is impossible to be certain; '24 eyes] *ed.*; eye' means that the base text (of 5) reads 'eye', a slip corrected editorially to 'eyes'. After the headnote, the base text is specified only where a reading is adopted from *1846* ('11 Weary to watch] *1846*; I'm sick to see *A*'), or in a case of three readings complicated by a cancellation or emendation (thus, where the base text is from B, '9 small] <thick> *B*; young *C*'). Substantive agreement with the base text is assumed, except where agreement follows a cancellation. Thus where a base text from B is collated with C, '7 wan] <fair> wan *C*' shows that where B has 'wan', C first had 'fair', then 'wan'.

Other symbols used in the collation are explained above, pp. xiii–xiv. The form '4 wert] *or* went' indicates that the appearance of the manuscript makes the two readings equally plausible and that 'went' cannot be excluded on grounds of meaning, though 'wert' has been preferred.

Commentary

The commentary regularly records authorial signatures, the date of first publication, and the location of photographic facsimiles. Also included are Charlotte Brontë's revisions and suggestions, both in the manuscripts and in *1850*. Where interpretation is difficult, I have tried to indicate a range of views. Some sources and parallels are noted; and the explanatory notes include some attempts made by Ratchford and other scholars to elucidate Gondal relationships.

DATED POEMS AND FRAGMENTS

I

July 12 1836

Will the day be bright or cloudy?
Sweetly has its dawn begun
But the heaven may shake with thunder
Ere the setting of the sun

Lady whach Appollos journy
Thus thy first borns course shall be—
If his beams through summer vapours
Warm the earth all placidly
Her days shall pass like a pleasant dream in sweet tranquility

If it darken if a shadow
Quenche his rays and summon rain
Flowers may open buds may blossom
Bud and flower alike are vain
Her days shall pass like a mournful story in care and tears and pain

If the wind be fresh and free
The wide skies clear and cloudless blue
The woods and feilds and golden flowers
Sparkling in sunshine and in dew
Her days shall pass in Glorys light the worlds drear desert through

2

December 13 1836

High waveing heather 'neath stormy blasts bending
Midnight and moon light and bright shineing stars

1. *Text from D10*
10 shadow <quenc>
2. *Text from D11*

Darkness and glory rejoiceingly blending
Earth riseing to heaven and heaven descending
Mans spirit away from its drear dongoen sending
Bursting the fetters and breaking the bars

All down the mountain sides wild forests lending
One mighty voice to the life giveing wind
Rivers their banks in the jubilee rending
Fast through the vallys a reckless course wending
Wider and deeper their waters extending
Leaving a desolate desert behind

Shineing and lowering and swelling and dieing
Changeing for ever from midnight to noon
Roaring like thunder like soft music sighing
Shadows on shadows advanceing and flying
Lightening bright flashes the deep gloom defying
Comeing as swiftly and fadeing as soon

3

Febuary 1837

Red breast early in the morning
Dark and cold and cloudy grey
Wildly tender is thy music
Chaseing merry thoughts away

4

A.G.A. *March 6th 1837*

There shines the moon, at noon of night.
Vision of Glory—Dream of light!
Holy as heaven—undimmed and pure,
Looking down on the lonely moor—
And lonlier still beneath her ray
That drear moor stretches far away

3. *Text from T3*
4. *Text from B1*
   2 <g>Glory—<d>Dream

Till it seems strange that aught can lie
Beyond its zone of silver sky—

Bright moon—dear moon! when years have past
My weary feet return at last—
And still upon Lake Elnor's breast
Thy solemn rays serenely rest
And still the firn-leaves sighing wave
Like mourners over Elbë's grave
And Earth's the same but Oh to see
How wildly Time has altered me!
Am I the being who long ago
Sat whaching by that water side
The light of life expiring slow
From his fair cheek and brow of pride?
Not oft these mountains feel the shine
Of such a day—as fading then,
Cast from its fount of gold devine
A last smile on the heathery plain
And kissed the far-off peaks of snow
That gleaming on the horizon shone
As if in summers warmest glow
Stern winter claimed a loftier throne—
And there he lay among the bloom
His red blood dyed a deeper hue
Shuddering to feel the ghastly gloom
That coming Death around him threw—
Sickening to think one hour would sever
The sweet, sweet world and him forever
To think that twilight gathering dim
Would never pass away to him—
No—never more! That aweful thought
A thousand dreary feelings brought
And memory all her powers combined
And rushed upon his fainting mind.

Wide, swelling woodlands seemed to rise
Beneath soft, sunny, southern skies—
Old Elbë Hall his noble home
Towerd mid its trees, whose foliage green
Rustled with the kind airs that come

17 who] <that> 23 gold] <lig> 30 d<i>yed

From summer Heavens when most serene—
And bursting through the leafy shade
A gush of golden sunshine played;
Bathing the walls in amber light
And sparkling in the water clear
That stretched below—reflected bright
The whole, wide world of cloudless air—
And still before his spirit's eye
Such wellknown scenes would rise and fly
Till, maddening with dispair and pain
He turned his dying face to me
And wildly cried, "Oh once again
"Might I my native country see!
"But once again—one single day!
"And must it—can it *never* be?
"To die—and die so far away
"When life has hardly smiled for me—
"Augusta—you will soon return
"Back to that land in health and bloom
"And then the heath alone will mourn
"Above my unremembered tomb
"For you'll forget the lonely grave
"And mouldering corpse by Elnor's wave"—

5

June 10th 1837

The night of storms has past
The sunshine bright and clear
Gives glory to the verdant waste
And warms the breezy air

And I would leave my bed
Its cheering smile to see
To chase the visions from my head
Whose forms have troubled me

62 smiled] <bloomed>   64 bloom] <joy>   66 Above <——> <on> my <*?*tearless> unremembered tomb   66+ <And years will steal away the *?*trace | Of my *?*last—— < <love> > and——kiss>

5. *Text from D2*

In all the hours of gloom
My soul was wrapt away
I dreamt I stood by a marble tomb
Where royal corpses lay

It was just the time of eve
When parted ghosts might come
Above their prisoned dust to greive
And wail their woeful doom

And truely at my side
I saw a shadowy thing
Most dim and yet its presence there
Curdled my blood with ghastly fear
And ghastlier wondering

My breath I could not draw
The air seemed ranny
But still my eyes with maddening gaze
Were fixed upon its fearful face
And its were fixed on me

I fell down on the stone
But could not turn away
My words died in a voiceless moan
When I began to pray

And still it bent above
Its features full in veiw
It seemed close by and yet more far
Than this world from the farthest star
That tracks the boundless blue

Indeed 'twas not the space
Of earth or time between
But the sea of deaths eternity
The gulph o'er which mortality
Has never never been

O bring not back again
The horror of that hour
When its lips opened and a sound
Awoke the stillness reigning round

24 eyes] *ed.*; eye 28 could not] *ed.*; could 41 again <t>

Faint as a dream but the earth shrank
And heavens lights shivered neath its power

"Woe for the day Regina's pride
Reginas hope is in the grave
And who shall rule my land beside
And who shall save

"Woe for the day with gorey tears
My countrys sons this day shall rue
Woe for the day a thousand years
Can not repair what one shall do

"Woe for the day" mixt with the wind
That sad lament was ringing
It almost broke my heart to hear
Such dreary dreary singing

6

July 1837

I saw thee child one summers day
Suddenly leave thy cheerful play
And in the green grass lowly lying
I listened to thy mournful sighing

I knew the wish that waked that wail
I knew the source whence sprung those tears
You longed for fate to raise the veil
That darkend over comeing years

The anxious prayer was heard and power
Was given me in that silent hour
To open to an infants eye
The portals of futurity

But child of dust the fragrant flowers
The bright blue sky and velvet sod
Were strange conductors to the bowers
Thy daring footsteps must have trod

46 <g>shivered 52 countr<ie>ys 54 Can] <Shall>

6. *Text from D2*
Date Ju<ne>ly

I whached my Time and summer pass'd
And Autumn waneing fleeted by
And dollful winter nights at last
In cloudy mourning clothed the sky

And now I'm come this evening fell
Not stormily but stilly drear
A sound sweeps o'er thee like a knell
To banish joy and welcome care

A fluttering blast that shakes the leaves
And wistles round the gloomy wall
And lingering long lamenting greives
Fernando 'tis the spectre call

He hears me   what a sudden start
Sent the blood icy to that heart
He wakens and how ghastly white
That face looks in the dim lamplight

Those tiny hands in vain essay
To thrust the shadowy feind away
There is a horror on his brow
An anguish in his bosom now
A fearful anguish in his eyes
Fixed strainedly on the vacant air
Heavely bursts in long drawn sighs
His panting breath enchained by fear

Poor child if Spirits such as I
Could weep o'er human misery
A tear might flow aye many a tear
To see the road that lies before
To see the sunshine disapear
And hear the stormy waters roar
Breaking upon a desolate shore
Cut off from hope in early day
From power and glory cut away
But it is doomed and mornings light
Must image forth the scowl of night
And childhoods flower must waste its bloom
Beneath the shadow of the tomb

17 pass'd] <past>   19 dollful] <dreary>   28 Fernando] <——o'er>
30 that] <this>   45 sunshine] <storm>

7

August 7 1837

O God of heaven! the dream of horror
The frightful dream is over now
The sickened heart The blasting sorrow
The ghastly night the ghastlier morrow
The aching sense of utter woe

The burning tears that would keep welling
The groans that mocked at every tear
That burst from out their dreary dwelling
As if each gasp were life expelling
But life was nourished by dispair

The tossing and the anguished pineing
The grinding teeth and stareing eye
The agony of still repineing
When not a spark of hope was shineing
From gloomy fate's relentless sky

The impatient rage the useless shrinking
From thoughts that yet could not be borne
The soul that was forever thinking
Till nature maddened tortured sinking
At last refused to mourn—

—Its over now—and I am free
And the oacen wind is carressing me
The wild wind from that wavey main
I never thought to see again

Bless thee Bright Sea—and glorious dome
And my own world my spirits home
Bless thee Bless all—I can not speak
My voice is chocked but not with greif
And salt drops from my haggard cheek
Descend like rain upon the heath

How long they've wet a dongoen floor—
Falling on flag-stones damp and grey
I used to weep even in my sleep
The night was dreadful like the day

7. *Text from D4*
12 star<i>eing   26 my . . . my] *unclear; see commentary*   31 <O> How

I used to weep when winters-snow
Whirled through the grateing stormily
But then it was a calmer woe
For every thing was drear as me

The bitterest time the worst of all
Was that in which the summer sheen
Cast a green luster on the wall
That told of feilds of lovelier green

Often I've sat down on the ground
Gazing up to that flush scearce seen
Till heedless of the darkness round
My soul has sought a land serene

It sought the arch of heaven devine
The pure blue heaven with clouds of gold
It sought my Fathers home and mine
As I remembered it of old

O even now too horribly
Come back the feelings that would swell
When with my face hid on my knee
I strove the bursting groans to quell

I flung myself upon the stone
I howled and tore my tangled hair
And then when the first gush had flown
Lay in unspeakable dispair

Sometimes a curse some times a prayer
Would quiver on my parched tongue
But both without a murmer there
Died in the breast from whence they sprung

And so the day would fade on high
And darkness quench that lonely beam
And slumber mold my misery
Into some strange and specteral dream
Whose phantom horrors made me know
The worst extent of human woe—

But this is past and why return
O'er such a past to brood and mourn?

49 my] *or* thy 68 worst] <last>

Shake off the fetters Break the chain
And live and love and smile again.

The waste of youth the waste of years
Departed in that dongoens thrawl
The gnawing greif the hopeless tears
Forget them—O forget them all—

8

A.G.A. to A.E. *August 19th 1837*

Lord of Elbë, on Elbë hill
The mist is thick and the wind is chill
And the heart of thy freind from the dawn of day
Has sighed for sorrow that thou wert away—

Lord of Elbë, how pleasant to me
The sound of thy blithesome step would be
Rustleing the heath that, only now
Waves as the night-gusts over it blow

Bright are the fires in thy lonely home
I see them far off, and as deepens the gloom
Gleaming like stars through the high forest-boughs
Gladder they glow in the parks repose—

O Alexander! when I return,
Warm as those hearths my heart would burn,
Light as thine own, my foot would fall
If I might hear thy voice in the hall

But thou art now on a desolate sea—
Parted from Gondal and parted from me—
All my repining is hopless and vain,
Death never yeilds back his victims again—

8. *Text from B2, collated with C1 (16–20 only) and cancelled draft in D6*
No title B; Song *D*
A.G.A. to A.E.] A G A *D*
3 dawn] dawning *D* 4 wert] *or* went *B*, *D* 8 Waves] Moans *D* 9 lonely] noble *D* 11 Gleaming] Shineing *D* 14 my] *?*thy *D* 15 foot] step *D* 17 a] <the> a *C*; the *D* 18 Thinking of Gondal, and greiving for me *C* (*B's readings added above*), *D* 19 Longing to be in sweet Elbë again *C* (*B's readings added below*), *D* 20 Thinking and greiving and longing in vain *C*, *D*; Death never gives back his victim again *added below in C*

9

August 1837

Alone I sat the summer day
Had died in smiling light away
I saw it die I watched it fade
From misty hill and breezless glade

And thoughts upon my soul were rushing
And my heart bowed beneath their power
And tears within my eyes were gushing
Because I could not speak the feeling
The solemn joy around me stealing
In that devine untroubled hour

I asked my self O why has heaven
Denied the precious gift to me
The glorious gift to many given
To speak their thoughts in poetry

Dreams have encircled me I said
From careless childhoods sunny time
Visions by ardent Fancy fed
Since life was in its morning prime

But now when I had hoped to sing
My fingers strike a tuneless string
And still the burden of the strain
Is strive no more 'tis all in vain

10

August 1837

The battle had passed from the height
And still did evening fall
While heaven with its hosts of Light
Gloriously canopied all

9. *Text from D6*
5 upon] <within> <g>rushing 7 <r>gushing 15 Dreams] *ed.*; Dream 19 The vows to sing *alternative, in margin* 20 strike] <?struck> a] my *alternative, in margin*
10. *Text from D12*

The dead around were sleeping
On heath and granite grey
And the dieing their last whachs were keeping
In the closeing of the day

11

October 14 1837

A sudden chasm of ghastly light
Yawned in the city's reeling wall
And a long thundering through the night
Proclaimed our triumph—Tyndarum's fall

The shreiking wind sank mute and mild
The smothering snow-clouds rolled away
And cold—How cold! wan moonlight smiled
Where those black ruins smoldering lay

'Twas over—all the Battles madness
The bursting fires the cannon's' roar
The yells the groans the frenzied gladness
The death the danger warmed no more

In plundered churches piled with dead
The weary charger neighed for food
The wornout soldier laid his head
Neath roofless chambers splashed with blood

I could not sleep through that wild seigh
My heart had fiercly burned and bounded
The outward tumult seemed to asswage
The inward tempest it surrounded

But calm a seared soul cannot bear
And silence whets the fang of pain
I felt the full flood of dispair
Returning to my breast again

11. *Text from T2*
Date <15th>14
8 smoldering] <?smoking> 16 Neath] *ed.*; Nneath 21 seared] *unclear*

My couch lay in a ruined Hall
Whose windows looked on the minster-yard
Where chill chill whitness covered all
Both stone and urn and withered sward

The shattered glass let in the air
And with it came a wandering moan
A sound unutterably drear
That made me shrink to be alone

One black yew tree grew just below
I thought its boughs so sad might wail
Their ghostly fingers flecked with snow
Rattled against an old vault's rail

I listened—no 'twas life that still
lingered in some deserted heart
O God what caused that shuddering thrill?
That anguished agonizing start?

An undefined an awful dream
A breath of what had been before
A memory whose blighting beam
Was flitting o'er me ever more

A frightful feeling frenzy born—
I hurried down the dark oak stair
I reached the door whose hinges torn
Flung streaks of moonshine here and there

I pondered not I drew the bar
An icey glory leapt on high
From that wide heaven were every star
glowed like a dying memory

And there the great cathedral rose
Discrowned but most majestic so
It looked down in serene repose
On its own realm of buried woe

48+ <What they reveald I dared not ponder | I sprang out with a careless bound | And *?*stood the <<dark>> great cathedral under | Whose dark [ ] downward frowned> 50 leapt on high] <blessed> my <gaze> mine eye *alternative* 52 glowed like a] <*?*Lent——>

12

October 1837

lines

Far away is the land of rest
Thousand miles are strecched between
Many a mountains stormy crest
Many a desert void of green

Wasted worn is the traveller
Dark his heart and dim his eye
Without hope or comforter
faultering faint and ready to die

Often he looks to the ruthless sky
Often he looks o'er his dreary road
Often he wishes down to lie
And render up lifes tiresome load

But yet faint not mournful man
Leagues on leagues are left behind
Since your sunless course began
Then go on to toil resigned

If you still dispair control
Hush its wispers in your breast
You shall reach the final goal
You shall win the land of rest

13

Oct 1837

The Old church tower and Garden wall
Are black with Autumn rain
And dreary winds forboding call
The darkness down again

I whached how evening took the place
Of glad and glorious day

12. *Text from C15*
2 between *ed.*; betwe (*leaf masked by stub*) 18 breast *ed.*; breas (*leaf masked*)
13. *Text from T3*

I whached a deeper gloom efface
The evenings lingering ray

And as I gazed on the cheerless sky
Sad thoughts rose in my mind

14

November 1837

Now trust a breast that trusts in you
And firmly say the word adeiu
Be sure wereever I may roam
My heart is with your heart at home

Unless there be no truth on earth
And vows ment true are nothing worth
And mortal man have no controul
Over his own unhappy soul

Unless I change in every thought
And memory will restore me nought
And all I have of virture die
Beneath far Gondals Forign sky

The mountain peasant loves the heath
Better than richest plains beneath
He would not give one moorland wild
For all the feilds that ever smild

And whiter brows than yours may be
And rosier cheeks my eyes may see
And lightning looks from orbs devine
About my path may burn and shine

But that pure light changless and strong
Cherished and whached and nursed so long
That love that first its glory gave
Shall be my pole star to the grave

14. *Text from D11*
Date November] <?June>
1 breast] <heart> 15 one] *ed.*; on 23 love] <?star>

15

A G A *November 1837*

Sleep brings no joy to me
Remembrance never dies
My soul is given to misery
And lives in sighs

Sleep brings no rest to me
The shadows of the dead
My wakeing eyes may never see
Surround my bed

Sleep brings no hope to me
In soundest sleep they come
And with their doleful Imagry
Deepen the gloom

Sleep brings no strength to me
No power renewed or brave
I only sail a wilder sea
A darker wave

Sleep brings no freind to me
To sooth and aid to bear
They all gaze oh how scornfuly
And I despair

Sleep brings no wish to knit
My harrased heart beneath
My only wish is to forget
In the sleep of death

16

November 1837

The night is darkening round me
The wild winds coldly blow
But a tyrant spell has bound me
And I cannot cannot go

15. *Text from D11*
A G A] *written twice*
1 <r> joy 10 <d> soundest
16. *Text from D6*

The giant trees are bending
Their bare boughs weighed with snow
And the storm is fast descending
And yet I cannot go

Clouds beyond Clouds above me
Wastes beyond Wastes below
But nothing drear can move me
I will not cannot go

17

December 14 1837

O mother I am not regreting
To leave this wretched world below
If there be nothing but forgeting
In that dark land to which I go

Yet though 'tis wretched now to languish
Deceived and tired and hopless here
No heart can quite repress the anguish
Of leaveing things that once were dear

Twice twelve short years and all is over
And day and night to rise no more
And never more to be a rover
Along the feilds the woods the shore

And never more at early dawning
To whach the stars of midnight wane
To breath the breath of summer morning
And see its sunshine ne'er again

I hear the Abbey bells are ringing
Methinks their chime sound faint and drear
Or else the wind is adverse winging
And wafts its music from my ear

The wind the winter night is speaking
Of thoughts and things that should not stay
Mother come near my heart is breaking
I can not bear to go away

17. *Text from D9*
3 be] <is>   17 Abbey] <minster>   21 The] <That>

And I *must* go whence no returning
To sooth your greif or calm your care
Nay do not weep that bitter mourning
Torturs my soul with wild dispair

No tell me that when I am lieing
In the old church beneath the stone
Youll dry your tears and check your sighing
And soon forget the spirit gone

Youve asked me long to tell what sorrow
Has blanched my cheek and quenched my eye
And we shall sever ere to morrow
So I'll confess before I die

Ten years ago in last September
Fernando left his home and you
And still I think you must remember
The anguish of that last adieu

And well you know how wildly pineing
I longed to see his face again
Through all the Autumns drear declining
Its stormy nights and days of rain

Down on the skirts of Areons Forest
There lies a lone and lovely glade
And there the hearts together nourished
Their first their fatal parting made

The afternoon in softened glory
Bathed each green swell and waveing tree
beyond the broard park spread before me
Streched faraway the boundless sea

And there I stood when he had left me
With ashy cheek but tearless eye
Whaching the ship whose sail bereft me
Of life and hope and peace and joy

It past that night I sought a pillow
Of sleepless woe and greiving lone
My soul still hovered o'er the billow
And mourned a love forever flown

48 first] <last>   51 beyond] <And o'er>   54 but] <and>

Yet smiling bright in recollection
One blissful hour returns to me
One letter told of firm affection
Of safe deliveranc from the sea

But not another fearing hopeing
Spring winter harvest glided o'er
And time at length brought power for copeing
With thoughts I could not once endure

And I would seek in summers evening
The place that saw our last farewell
And there a chain of visions weaveing
I'de linger till the cerfew bell

18

December 1837

To a Wreath of snow
by A G Almeda—

O transient voyager of heaven!
O Silent sign of winter skies!
What adverse wind thy sail has driven
To dungeons where a prisoner lies?

Methinks the hands that shut the sun
So sternly from this mourning brow
Might still their rebel task have done,
And checked a thing so frail as thou

They would have done it had they known
The talisman that dwelt in thee,
For all the suns that ever shone
Have never been so kind to me!

For many a week, and many a day,
My heart was weighed with sinking gloom
When morning rose, in mourning grey
And faintly lit my prison room,

But angel-like, when I awoke,
Thy silvery form so soft and fair

18. *Text from C2, collated with E13 (22–8 and fragments only)*
5 Methinks] *ed.*; "Methinks   7 rebel] <tyrant>   14 sinking] *unclear*

Shining through darkness, sweetly spoke
Of cloudy Skies and mountains bare

The dearest to a mountaineer,
Who, all life long has loved the snow
That crowned her native summits drear,
Better, than greenest plains below

And voicless, souless, messenger
Thy presence waked a thrilling tone
That comforts me while thou art here
And will sustain when thou art gone

19

December 1837

Lines

I die but when the grave shall press
The heart so long endeared to thee
When earthly cares no more distress
And earthly joys are nought to me

Weep not, but think that I have past
Before thee o'er a sea of gloom
Have anchored safe and rest at last
Where tears and mourning cannot come

'Tis I should weep to leave thee here
On that dark Oecan sailing drear
With storms around and fears before
And no kind light to point the shore

But long or short though life may be
'Tis nothing to eternity
We part below to meet on high
Where blissful ages never die

26 waked] <——> touched *E*

19. *Text from C8*

9 here] *ed.*; h (*leaf masked by stub*) 11 around] <behind> before] *ed.*; be (*leaf masked*) 12 shore] *ed.*; shor (*leaf masked*)

20

December 1837

song by Julius Angora

Awake! awake! how loud the stormy morning
Calls up to life the nations resting round;
Arise, Arise, is it the voice of mourning
That breaks our slumber with so wild a sound?

The voice of mourning? listen to its pealing
That shout of triumph drowns the sigh of woe
Each tortured heart forgets its wonted feeling,
Each faded cheek resumes its longlost glow—

Our souls are full of gladness, God has given
Our arms to victory, our foes to death;
The crimson ensign waves its sheet in heaven
The sea-green Standard lies in dust beneath

Patriots, no stain is on your country's glory
Soldiers, preserve that glory bright and free
Let Almedore in peace, and battle gorey,
Be still a nobler name for victory!

21

? 1837

Fall leaves fall die flowers away
Lengthen night and shorten day
Every leaf speaks bliss to me
Fluttering from the autumn tree
I shall smile when wreaths of snow
Blossom where the rose should grow
I shall sing when nights decay
Ushers in a drearier day

20. *Text from C3, collated with cancelled text in D6*
Date D only
song . . . Angora] Song *D* (J A *below date*).
5 pealing] <?clamour> pealing *D* 11 ensign] <?banner>
21. *Text from E12*
Date <1837> *in r.h. margin*

22

Febuary H G 1838

Weaned from life and torn away
In the morning of thy day
Bound in everlasting gloom
Buried in a hopless tomb

Yet upon thy bended knee
Thank the power banished thee
Chain and bar and dongoen wall
Saved thee from a deadlier thrall

Thank the power that made thee part
E're that parting broke thy heart
Wildly rushed the mountain spring
From its source of firn and ling
How invincible its roar
Had its waters won the shore

23

march 1838

The wide cathedral Isles are lone
The vast crowds vanished every one
There can be nought beneath that dome
But the Cold tenants of the tomb

O look again for still on high
The lamps are burning gloriously
And look again for still beneath
A thousand thousand live and breathe

All mute as death regard the shrine
That gleams in lustre so devine
Were Gondals monarchs bending low
After the hush of silent prayer
Take in heavens sight their awful vow

22. *Text from E13*
14 won<n>
23. *Text from D5*

And never dying Union swear
King Julius lifts his impious eye
From the dark marble to the sky
Blasts with that Oath his perjurd soul
And changless is his cheek the while
Though burning thoughts that spurn control
Kindle a short and bitter smile
As face to face the Kinsmen stand
His false hand clasped in Geralds hand

24

A G A *May 9 1838*

Why do I hate that lone green dell?
Buried in moors and mountains wild
That is a spot I had loved too well
Had I but seen it when a child

There are bones whitening there in the summers heat
But it is not for that and none can tell
None but one can the secret repeat
Why I hate that lone green dell

Noble foe I pardon thee
All thy cold and scornful pride
For thou wast a priceless freind to me
When my sad heart had none beside

And leaning on thy generous arm
A breath of old times over me came
The earth shone round with a longlost charm
Alas I forgot I was not the same

Before a day—an hour passed by
My spirit knew itself once more
I saw the gilded vapours fly
And leave me as I was before

24. *Text from D9*
2 moors] <mount> 9 <would> pardon

25

A.G.A. to A.S. *may 20th 1838*

O wander not so far away!
O love, forgive this selfish tear.
It may be sad for thee to stay
But how can I live lonely here?

The still may morn is warm and bright
young flowers look fresh and grass is green
And in the haze of glorious light
Our long low hills are scearcely seen—

The woods—even now their small leaves hide
The blackbird and the stockdove well
And high in heaven so blue and wide
A thousand strains of music swell—

He looks on all with eyes that speak
So deep, so drear a woe to me!
There is a faint red on his cheek
Not like the bloom I used to see—

Can Death—yes, Death, he is thine own!
The grave must close those limbs around
And hush, for ever hush the tone
I loved above all earthly sound.

Well, pass away with the other flowers
Too dark for them, too dark for thee
Are the hours to come, the joyless hours
That Time is treasuring up for me—

If thou hast sinned in this world of care
T'was but the dust of thy drear abode—
Thy soul was pure when it entered here
And pure it will go again to God!

25. *Text from B6, collated with cancelled C5*
A.G.A. to A.S.] Lines by A G A to A S *C*
6 young flowers look] Sweet flowers are *C* 9 The] Our *C* small] <thick> *B*; young *C* 10 stockdove] throstle *C* 18 must] shall *C*

26

May 21st 1838

Gleneden's Dream

Tell me, whacher, is it winter?
Say how long my sleep has been?
Have the woods, I left so lovely,
Lost their robes of tender green?

Is the morning slow in coming?
Is the night time loath to go?
Tell me, are the dreary mountains
Drearier still with drifted snow?

"Captive, since thou sawest the forest
"All its leaves have died away
"And another March has woven
"Garlands for another May—

"Ice has barred the Artic water,
"Soft southwinds have set it free
"And once more to deep green vally
"Golden flowers might welcome thee"—

Watcher, in this lonely prison,
Shut from joy and kindly air
Heaven, descending in a vision
Taught my soul to do and bear—

It was night, a night of winter;
I lay on the dungeon floor,
And all other sounds were silent—
All, except the river's roar—

Over Death, and Desolation,
Fireless hearths, and lifeless homes
Over orphans heart-sick sorrows;
Patriot fathers bloody tombs;

Over friends that my arms never
Might embrace, in love, again—
Memory pondered untill maddness
Struck its poignard in my brain—

26. *Text from B11*
11 woven <g> 13 water<s> 17 W<ha>atcher

Deepest slumber followed raving,
Yet, methought, I brooded still—
Still I saw my country bleeding,
Dying for a Tyrant's will—

Not because *my* bliss was blasted
Burned within, the avenging flame—
Not because my sceattered Kindred
Died in woe, or lived in shame.

God doth know, I would have given
Every bosem dear to me
Could that sacrifice have purchased
Tortured Gondals Liberty!

But, that at Ambition's bidding
All her cherished hopes should wane;
That her noblest sons should muster,
Strive, and fight and fall in vain—

Hut and castle, hall and cottage,
Roofless, crumbling to the ground—
Mighty Heaven, a glad Avenger
Thy eternal Justice found!

Yes, the arm that once would shudder
Even to peirce a wounded deer,
I beheld it, unrelenting,
Choke in blood its soverign's prayer—

Glorious Dream! I saw the city
Blazing in imperial shine;
And, among adoring thousands,
Stood a man of form devine—

None need point the princely victim
Now he smiles with royal pride!
Now his glance is bright as lightening!
Now—The Knife is in his side!

Ha, I saw how Death could darken—
Darken that triumphant eye!
His red heart's blood drenched my dagger;
My ear drank his dying sigh!

51 <a>Avenger   57 <d>Dream

Shadows come! What means this midnight?
O my God, I know it all!
—Know the fever-dream is over;
Unavenged, the Avengers fall!

27

May 1838

Song to A A

This shall be thy lullaby
Rocking on the stormy sea
Though it roar in thunder wild
Sleep stilly sleep my dark haird child

When our shuddering boat was crossing
Elderns lake so rudely tossing
Then twas first my nursling smiled
Sleep softly sleep my fair-browed child

Waves above thy cradle break
Foamy tears are on thy cheek
Yet the Oacens self grows mild
When it bears my slumbering child

28

May 1838

Darkness was over Gondall every face
Seemed clouded with a drear and ominous gloom
In Hut or hall smiled out no resting place
There was no resting place but one—the tomb

All our hearts were the mansions of distress
And noone laughed and none seemd Free from care
Our children felt their fathers wretchedness
Our homes our all were shadowed with dispair

It was not fear that made the land so sad

27. *Text from C6, collated with cancelled draft in D6*
Song to A A] Song *D* (Blanche *after date*)
4 my dark] thou bright *D* 5 shuddering] shivering *D* 8 my] thou *D*
12 When it bears] <*?*rolling round> When it clasps *D*
28. *Text from T3*

29

June 1838

None of my kindred now can tell
The featurs once beloved so well
These dark brown locks that used to deck
A snowy brow in ringlets small
Now wildly shade my sunburnt neck
And streaming down my sholders fall

The pure bright red of noble birth
Has deepened to a gipsy glow
And care as quenched the smile of mirth
And formed my heart to welcome woe

Yet you must know in infancy
Full many an eye whached over me
Sweet voices to my slumber sung
My downy couch with silk was hung

And music soothed me when I cried
And when I laughed they all replied
And "rosy Blanche" how oft was heard
In hall and bower that wellknown word

Through gathering Summers still carest
In Kingly courts a favorite guest
A Monarchs hand would pour for me
The richest gifts of royalty

But clouds will come too soon they came
For not through age and not through crime
Is Blanche a now forgotten name
True heart and brows unmarked by time
These tresured blessings still are mine

30

June 1838

'Twas one of those dark cloudy days
That sometimes come in summers blaze

29. *Text from T7*
18 word] *ed.*; words   20 favorite] <welcome>   26 brows] *ed.*; brown

30. *Text from D10*
1 'Twas] *ed.*; 'T twas

When heaven drops not when earth is still
And deeper green is on the hill

31

July 11th 1838

Douglases Ride—

Well narrower draw the circle round
And hush that organ's solemn sound,
And quench the lamp and stir the fire
To rouse its flickering radiance higher;
Loop up the window's velvet veil
That we may hear the night-wind wail
For wild those gusts and well their chimes
Blend with a song of troubled times—

Song

What Rider up Gobelrins glen
Has spurred his straining steed,
And fast and far from living men
Has pressed with maddening speed?

I saw his hoof-prints mark the roak
When swift he left the plain
I heard deep down, the echoing shock
Reecho back again.

From cliff to cliff, through roak and heath
That coal-black courser bounds;
Nor heeds the river pent beneath,
Nor marks how fierce it sounds.

With streaming hair and forehead bare
And mantle waveing wide
His master rides; the eagles there
Soar up on every side:

31. *Text from B9*
Title <G> Douglases
9 <r>Rider   12 pressed] <prest>

The goats fly by with timid cry
Their realm so rashly won:
They pause—he still ascends on high
They gaze, but he is gone.

O gallant horse hold on thy course!
The road is tracked behind—
Spur, rider, spur, or vain thy force
Death comes on every wind.

Roard thunder loud from that pitchy cloud?
Drowns it the torrents flow?
Or woke the breeze in the swaying trees
That frown so dark below?

He breathes at last, when the valley is past;
He rests on the grey roak's brow—
What ails thee steed? At thy master's need,
Wilt thou prove faithless now?

No, hardly checked, with ears erect,
The charger champed his rein,
Ere his quivering limbs, all foam-beflecked,
Were off like light again—

Hark through the pass, with threatening crash
Comes on the increasing roar!
But what shall brave the deep, deep wave?
The deadly path before?

Their feet are dyed in a darker tide
Who dare those dangers drear—
Their breasts have burst through the battle's worst
And why should they tremble here?

Strong hearts they bear and arms as good
To conquer or to fall
They dash into the boiling flood,
They gain the roak's steep wall—

"Now my bold men this one pass more
"This narrow chasm of stone
"And Douglas—for our soveriegn's gore
"Shall yeild us back his own"—

33 from] <in>   34 Drowns] *unclear*   49 d<i>yed

I hear their ever nearing tread
Sound through the granite glen—
There is a tall pine overhead
Laid by the mountain-men

That dizzy bridge which no horse could track
Has checked the outlaw's way;
There like a wildbeast he turns back:
And grimly stands at bay—

Why smiles he so when far below
He sees the toiling chase?
The ponderous Tree sways heavily
And totters from its place—

They raise their eyes for the sunny skies
Are lost in sudden shade,
But Douglas neither shrinks nor flies—
He need not fly the dead—

32

A. G. A. *August 30th 1838*

For him who struck thy foreign string
I ween this heart hath ceased to care
Then why dost thou such feelings bring
To my sad spirit, Old guitar?

It is as if the warm sunlight
In some deep glen should lingering stay
When cloudes of tempest and of night
Had wrapt the parent Orb away—

It is as if the glassy brook
Should image still its willows fair
Though years ago, the woodman's stroke
Laid low in dust their gleaming hair:

64 Laid by] <——over> 69 when] <as> below] *ed.*; beblow 70 He] <The>

32. *Text from B16*
2 hath] <has> 8 wrapt] <wrapped>

Even so, guitar, thy majic tone
Hath moved the tear and woke the sigh
Hath bid the ancient torrent flow
Although its very source is dry!

33

September 23 1838

The evening sun was sinking down
On low green hills and clustered trees
It was a scene as fair and lone
As ever felt the soothing breeze

That bends the grass when day is gone
And gives the wave a brighter blue
And makes the soft white clouds sail on
Like spirits of etherial dew

Which all the morn had hovered o'er
The azure flowers where they were nursed
And now return to heaven once more
Where their bright glories shone at first

34

October 17th 1838

Song by Julius Brenzaida.
to G.S.

Geraldine, the moon is shining
With so soft, so bright a ray,
Seems it not that eve, declining
Ushered in a fairer day?

While the wind is whispering only,
Far—accross the water borne
Let us, in this silence lonely
Sit beneath the ancient thorn—

14 Hath] <Has> woke] <waked> 15 Hath] <Has>

33. *Text from E12*

34. *Text from B13*
4 <He> Ushered

Wild the road, and rough and dreary;
Barren all the moorland round;
Rude the couch that rests us weary;
Mossy stone and heathy ground—

But when winter storms were meeting
In the moonless midnight dome
Did we heed the tempest's beating
Howling round our spirits' home?

No, that tree, with branches riven
Whitening in the whirl of snow,
As it tossed against the heaven,
Sheltered happy hearts below—

And at Autumn's mild returning
Shall our feet forget the way?
And in Cynthia's silver morning,
Geraldine, wilt thou delay?

35

October 17th 1838

Song by J. Brenzaida to G.S.

I knew not 't was so dire a crime
To say the word, Adieu—
But, this shall be the only time
My slighted heart shall sue.

The wild moorside, the winter morn,
The gnarled and ancient tree—
If in your breast they waken scorn
Shall wake the same in me.

I can forget black eyes and brows
And lips of rosey charm
If you forget the sacred vows
Those faithless lips could form—

If hard commands can tame your love,
Or prison walls can hold

35. *Text from B14*
6 <k>gnarled 7 your] <thy>

I would not wish to greive above
A thing so false and cold—

And there are bosoms bound to mine
With links both tried and strong;
And there are eyes, whose lightening shine
Has warmed and blessed me long:

Those eyes shall make my only day,
Shall set my spirit free
And chase the foolish thoughts away
That mourn your memory!

36

A G A *October 1838*

Where were ye all? and where wert thou
I saw an eye that shone like thine
But dark curls waved around his Brow
And his stern glance was strange to mine

And yet a dreamlike comfort came
Into my heart and anxious eye
And trembling yet to hear his name
I bent to listen whachfuly

This voice though never heard before
Still spoke to me of years gone by
It seemed a vision to restore
That brought the hot tears to my eye

37

November 1st 1838

F. De Samara to A.G.A.

Light up thy halls! 'Tis closing day;
I'm drear and lone and far away—
Cold blows on my breast, the northwind's bitter sigh
And Oh, my couch is bleak beneath the rainy sky!

36. *Text from D11*
9 This] *or* <I> his
37. *Text from B18*

Light up thy halls—and think not of me;
That face is absent now, thou has hated so to see—
Bright be thine eyes, undimmed their dazzlling shine,
For never, never more shall they encounter mine!

The desert moor is dark; there is tempest in the air;
I have breathed my only wish in one last, one burning prayer—
A prayer that would come forth although it lingered long;
That set on fire my heart, but froze upon my tongue—

And now, it shall be done before the morning rise;
I will not whach the sun ascend in yonder skies.
One task alone remains—thy pictured face to view
And then I go to prove if God, at least, be true!

Do I not see thee now? Thy black resplendant hair;
Thy glory-beaming brow, and smile how heavenly fair!
Thine eyes are turned away—those eyes I would not see;
Their dark, their deadly ray would more than madden me

There, go, Deceiver, go! My hand is streaming wet;
My heart's blood flows to buy the blessing—To forget!
Oh could that lost heart give back, back again to thine
One tenth part of the pain that clouds my dark decline!

Oh could I see thy lids weighed down in cheerless woe;
Too full to hide their tears, too stern to overflow;
Oh could I know thy soul with equal greif was torn—
This fate might be endured—this anguish might be borne!

How gloomy grows the Night! 'Tis Gondal's wind that blows
I shall not tread again the deep glens where it rose—
I feel it on my face—where, wild Blast, dost thou roam?
What do we, wanderer, here? So far away from home?

I do not need thy breath to cool my death-cold brow
But go to that far land where She is shining now;
Tell Her my latest wish, tell Her my dreary doom
Say, that *my* pangs are past, but *Hers* are yet to come—

Vain words—vain, frenzied thoughts! No ear can hear me call—
Lost in the vacant air my frantic curses fall—

15 alone] <on>   26 too] *ed.*; to   34 <s>She   35 <h>Her . . . <h>Her

And could she see me now, perchance her lip would smile
Would smile in carless pride and utter scorn the while!

And yet, for all Her hate, each parting glance would tell
A stronger passion breathed, burned in this last farewell—
Unconquered in my soul the Tyrant rules me still—
Life bows to my control, but, *Love* I cannot kill!

38

November 5th 1838

O Dream, where art thou now?
Long years have past away
Since last, from off thine angel brow
I saw the light decay—

Alas, alas for me
Thou wert so bright and fair,
I could not think thy memory
Would yeild me nought but care!

The sun-beam and the storm,
The summer-eve devine,
The silent night of solemn calm,
The full moons cloudless shine

Were once entwined with thee
But now, with weary pain—
Lost vision! 'tis enough for me—
Thou canst not shine again—

39

November 11th 1838

Loud without the wind was roaring
  Through the waned autumnal sky,

41 <h>Her   42 breathed] <*?*lived>

38. *Text from A12, collated with C10 (1–12 only)*
3 thine] thy *C*   13 W<h>ere
39. *Text from A1, collated with draft of 1–10 in E12*
Date Nov—1838 *E*
2–4 *not indented in E*

Drenching wet, the cold rain pouring
  Spoke of stormy winters nigh.

  All Too like that dreary eve
  Sighed within repining greif—
  Sighed at first—but sighed not long
  Sweet—How softly sweet it came!
  Wild words of an ancient song—
  Undefined, without a name—

"It was spring, for the skylark was singing."
Those words they awakened a spell—
They unlocked a deep fountain whose springing
Nor Absence nor Distance can quell.

In the gloom of a cloudy November
They uttered the music of May—
They kindled the perishing ember
Into fervour that could not decay

Awaken on all my dear moorlands
The wind in its glory and pride!
O call me from valleys and highlands
To walk by the hill-rivers side!

It is swelled with the first snowy weather;
The roaks they are icy and hoar
And darker waves round the long heather
And the firn-leaves are sunny no more

There are no yellow-stars on the mountain
The blue-bells have long died away
From the brink of the moss-bedded fountain,
From the side of the wintery brae—

But lovlier than corn-fields all waving
In emerald and scarlet and gold
Are the slopes where the north-wind is raving
And the glens where I wandered of old—

"It was morning, the bright sun was beaming—"
How sweetly that brought back to me
The time when nor labour nor dreaming
Broke the sleep of the happy and free

5 Too] to *E*   6 within] without *E*

But blithely we rose as the dusk heaven
Was melting to amber and blue
And swift were the wings to our feet given
While we traversed the meadows of dew.

For the moors, for the moors where the short grass
Like velvet beneath us should lie!
For the moors, for the moors where each high pass
Rose sunny against the clear sky!

For the moors, where the linnet was trilling
Its song on the old granite stone—
Where the lark—the wild sky-lark was filling
Every breast with delight like its own.

What language can utter the feeling
That rose when, in exile afar,
On the brow of a lonely hill kneeling
I saw the brown heath growing there:

It was scattered and stunted, and told me
That soon even that would be gone
It wispered; "The grim walls enfold me
"I have bloomed in my last summer's sun—"

But not the loved music whose waking
Makes the soul of the swiss die away
Has a spell—more adored and heart-breaking
Than in its half-blighted bells lay—

The spirit that bent 'neath its power
How it longed, how it burned to be free!
If I could have wept in that hour
Those tears had been heaven to me—

Well, well the sad minutes are moving
Though loaded with trouble and pain—
And sometime the loved and the loving
Shall meet on the mountains again—

57 <t>"The

40

December 4th 1838

A little while, a little while
The noisy crowd are barred away;
And I can sing and I can smile—
A little while I've holyday!

Where wilt thou go my harassed heart?
Full many a land invites thee now;
And places near, and far apart
Have rest for thee, my weary brow—

There is a spot mid barren hills
Where winter howls and driving rain
But if the dreary tempest chills
There is a light that warms again

The house is old, the trees are bare
And moonless bends the misty dome
But what on earth is half so dear—
So longed for as the hearth of home?

The mute bird sitting on the stone,
The dank moss dripping from the wall,
The garden-walk with weeds o'e'r-grown
I love them—how I love them all!

Shall I go there? or shall I seek
Another clime, another sky—
Where tongues familiar music speak
In accents dear to memory?

Yes, as I mused, the naked room,
The flickering firelight died away
And from the midst of cheerless gloom
I passed to bright, unclouded day—

A little and a lone green lane
That opened on a common wide
A distant, dreamy, dim blue chain
Of mountains circling every side—

40. *Text from A2*
18 moss] *ed.*; mossy

A heaven so clear, an earth so calm,
So sweet, so soft, so hushed an air
And, deepening still the dreamlike charm,
Wild moor sheep feeding every where—

That was the scene—I knew it well
I knew the pathways far and near
That winding o'er each billowy swell
Marked out the tracks of wandering deer

Could I have lingered but an hour
It well had paid a week of toil
But truth has banished fancy's power
I hear my dungeon bars recoil—

Even as I stood with raptured eye
Absorbed in bliss so deep and dear
My hour of rest had fleeted by
And given me back to weary care—

41

December 7th 1838

How still, how happy! those are words
That once would scearce agree together
I loved the plashing of the surge—
The changing heaven the breezy weather

More than smooth seas and cloudless skies
And solemn, soothing, softened airs
That in the forest woke no sighs
And from the green spray shook no tears

How still, how happy! now I feel
Where silence dwells is sweeter far
Than laughing mirths most joyous swell
However pure its raptures are

Come sit down on this sunny stone
'Tis wintery light o'er flowerless moors—

43 fanc<ie>y's

41. *Text from A3*
5 smooth<e>

But sit—for we are all alone
And clear expand heaven's breathless shores

I could think in the withered grass
Spring's budding wreaths we might discern
The violet's eye might shyly flash
And young leaves shoot among the firn

It is but thought—full many a night
The snow shall clothe those hills afar
And Storms shall add a drearier blight
And winds shall wage a wilder war

Before the lark may herald in
Fresh foliage twined with blossems fair
And summer days again begin
Their glory-haloed crown to wear

Yet my heart loves December's smile
As much as July's golden beam
Then let us sit and whach the while
The blue ice curdling on the stream—

42

December 18th 1838

The bluebell is the sweetest flower
That waves in summer air
Its blossems have the mightest power
To soothe my spirit's care

There is a spell in purple heath
Too wildly, sadly dear
The violet has a fragrant breath
But fragrence will not cheer

The trees are bare, the sun is cold
And seldom, seldom seen—
The heavens have lost their zone of gold
The earth its robe of green

22 clothe<s> 30 golden] <?sunny>

42. *Text from A4*
6 d<r>ear

And ice upon the glancing stream
Has cast its sombre shade
And distant hills and valleys seem
In frozen mist arrayed—

The blue bell cannot charm me now
The heath has lost its bloom
The violets in the glen below
They yeild no sweet perfume

But though I mourn the heather-bell
'Tis better far, away
I know how fast my tears would swell
To see it smile to day

And that wood flower that hides so shy
Beneath the mossy stone
Its balmy scent and dewy eye
Tis not for them I moan

It is the slight and stately stem
The blossem's silvery blue
The buds hid like a sapphire gem
In sheathes of emerald hue

'Tis these that breathe upon my heart
A calm and softening spell
That if it makes the tear-drop start
Has power to soothe as well

For these I weep, so long devided
Through winter's dreary day
In longing weep—but most when guided
On withered banks to stray

If chilly then the light should fall
Adown the dreary sky
And gild the dank and darkened wall
With transient brilliency

How do I yearn, how do I pine
For the time of flowers to come
And turn me from that fading shine
To mourn the fields of home—

25 wood] ~ <wild> 26 the] <its> 32 In] <?With> 39 longing] <?silence> <sadness> 45 yearn] ~ <weep>

43

Janury 12th 1839

The night was Dark yet winter breathed
With softened sighs on Gondals shore
And though its wind repining greived
It chained the snow swollen streams no more

How deep into the wilderness
My horse had strayed, I cannot say
But neither menace nor caress
Would urge him farther on the way

So loosening from his neck the rein
I set my worn companion free
And billowy hill and Boundless plain
Full soon devided him from me

The sullen clouds lay all unbroken
And blackening round the horizon drear
But still they gave no certain token
of heavy rain or tempests near

I paused confounded and distressed
Down in the heath my limbs I threw
Yet wilder as I longed for rest
More wakeful heart and Eyelids grew

It was about the middle night
And under such a starless dome
When gliding from the mountains height
I saw a shadowy spirit come

Her wavey hair on her sholders bare
It shone like soft clouds round the moon
Her noisless feet like melting sleet
Gleamed white a moment then were gone

What seek you now on this bleak moors brow
Where wanders that form from heaven decending
It was thus I said as her graceful head
The spirit above my couch was bending

43. *Text from D7*
1 yet] <but> 17 distres<t>sed 25 her] <the>

This is my home where whirlwinds blow
Where snowdrifts round my path are swelling
T'is many a year tis long ago
Since I beheld another dwelling

When thick and fast the smothering blast
Ore welmed the hunter on the plain
If my cheek grew pale in its loudest gale
May I never tread the hills again

The shepherd had died on the mountainside
But my ready aid was near him then
I led him back ore the hidden track
And gave him to his native glen

When tempests roar on the lonly shore
I light my beacon with sea-weeds dry
And it flings its fire through the Darkness dire
And gladdens the sailors hopless eye

And the scatered sheep I love to keep
Their timid forms to guard from harm
I have a spell and they know it well
And I save them with a powerful charm

thy own good steed on his freindless bed
A few hours since you left to die
But I knelt by his side and the saddle untied
And life returned to his glazing eye

And Deem thou not that quite forgot
My mercy will forsake me now
I bring thee care but not Dispair
Abasement but not over throw

To a silent home thy foot may come
And years may follow of toilsome pain
But yet I swear by that Burning Tear
The loved shall meet on its hearth again

39 its] <the> 52 a powerful charm] <my single arm> 53 thy] <Your> 62 of] <in>

44

A G A *March 27 ?1839*

What winter floods what showers of Spring
Have drenched the grass by night and day
And yet beneath that spectre ring
Unmoved and undiscovered lay

A mute remembrancer of crime—
long lost concealed forgot for years
It comes at last to cancel time
And waken unavailing tears

45

By R. Gleneden— *April 17th 1839*

From our evening fireside now,
Merry laugh and cheerful tone,
Smiling eye and cloudless brow,
Mirth and music all are flown:

Yet the grass before the door
Grows as green in April rain;
And as blithely as of yore
Larks have poured their day-long strain.

Is it fear, or is it sorrow
Checks the stagnant stream of joy?
Do we tremble that tomorrow
May our present peace destroy?

For past misery are we weeping?
What is past can hurt no more;
And the gracious Heavens are keeping
Aid for that which lies before—

One is absent, and for one
Cheerless, chill is our hearthstone—

44. *Text from E5*
Date 1839 *or* 1832; *see commentary*
1 showers] <storms> 6 <Forg> long
45. *Text from B10, collated with C13 (1–3, 34–44 only)*
By R. Gleneden—] Lines by R G *C*
13 weeping?] <greiving>

One is absent, and for him
Cheeks are pale and eyes are dim—

Arthur, brother, Gondal's shore
Rested from the battle's roar—
Arthur, brother, we returned
Back to Desmond lost and mourned:

Thou didst purchase by thy fall
Home for us and peace for all;
Yet, how darkly dawned that day—
Dreadful was the price to pay!

Just as once, through sun and mist
I have climbed the mountain's breast
Still my gun with certain aim
Brought to earth the fluttering game;

But the very dogs repined,
Though I called with wistle shrill
Listlessly they lagged behind,
Looking backward oer the hill—

Sorrow was not vocal there;
Mute their pain and my dispair
But the joy of life was flown
He was gone, and we were lone—

So it is by morn and eve—
So it is in field and hall—
For the absent one we greive,
One being absent, saddens All—

46

April 20th 1839

Song

King Julius left the south country
His banners all bravly flying

35 Listlessly they] Tay and Carlo *C* 38 pain] woe *C* d<e>ispair 40 gone] <dea> gone *C* 44 being] <been> *B*; been *C* <a>All

46. *Text from C4*
2 brav<e>ly

His followers went out with Jubilee
But they shall return with sighing

Loud arose the triumphal hymn
The drums were loudly rolling
Yet you might have heard in distance dim
How a passing-bell was tolling

The sword so bright from battles soon
With unseen rust is fretting
The evening comes before the noon
The scearce risen sun is setting

While princes hang upon his breath
And nations round are fearing
Close by his side a daggered Death
With sheathless point stands sneering

That death he took a certain aim
For Death is stoney-hearted
And in the zenith of his fame
Both power and life departed

47

April 28th 1839

lines

The soft unclouded blue of air
The earth as golden-green and fair
And bright as Edens used to be
That air and earth have rested me

Laid on the grass I lapsed away
Sank back again to Childhoods day
All harsh thoughts perished memory mild
Subdued both greif and passion wild

but did the sunshine even now
That bathed his stern and swarthy brow
Oh did it wake I long to know
One wisper one sweet dream in him

47. *Text from C16*
4 rested] *unclear*

One lingering joy that years ago
Had faded—lost in distance dim
That iron man was born like me
And he was once an ardent boy
he must have felt in infancy
The glory of a summer sky

Though storms untold his mind have tossed
He cannot utterly have lost
remembrance of his early home
So lost that not a gleam may come

No vision of his mother's face
When she so fondly would set free
Her darling child from her embrace
To roam till eve at liberty

Nor of his haunts nor of the flowers
His tiney hand would grateful bear
Returning from the darkening bowers
To weave into her glossy hair

I saw the light breeze kiss his cheek
His fingers mid the roses twined
I whached to mark one transient streak
Of pensive softness shade his mind

The open window showed around
A glowing park and glorious sky
And thick woods swelling with the sound
Of Natures mingled harmony

Silent he sat. That stormy breast
At length I said has deigned to rest
At length above that spirit flows
The waveless ocean of repose

Let me draw near 'twill soothe to view
His dark eyes dimed with holy dew
Remorse even now may wake within
And half-unchain his soul from sin

21 remembrance] <So lost that> 24 fondly] <sweetly> 39 That] *ed.*; 'That 44 dimed] *unclear*

Prehaps this is the destined hour
When Hell shall lose its fatal power
And heaven itself shall bend above
To hail the soul redeemed by love

Unmarked I gazed   my idle thought
Passed with the ray whose shine it caught
One glance revealed how little care
He felt for all the beauty there

Oh crime can make the heart grow old
Sooner than years of wearing woe
Can turn the warmest bosom cold
As winter wind or polar snow

48

A. G. A. *May 9th 1839*

To the bluebell—

Sacred whacher, wave thy bells!
Fair hill flower and woodland child!
Dear to me in deep green dells—
Dearest on the mountains wild—

Blue bell, even as all devine
I have seen my darling shine—
Bluebell, even as wan and frail
I have seen my darling fail—
Thou hast found a voice for me—
And soothing words are breathed by thee—

Thus they murmer, "Summers Sun
"Warms me till my life is done—
"Would I rather choose to die
"Under winters ruthless sky?

"Glad I bloom—and calm I fade
"Weeping twilight dews my bed

48. *Text from B7, collated with C7*
Title To a Blue bell | by A G A *C*
7 wan] <fair> wan *C*   9 Lift thy head and speak to me *C*   10 And soothing words] Soothing thoughts *C*   11 murmer] wisper *C*   12 lights me till my life is done *alternative above* Lights <my> course commenced and done *C*   13 I] <a> *C*   14 ruthless] <cruel> stormy *C*   16 Dews of heaven are round me shed *C*

"Mourner, mourner dry thy tears.
"Sorrow comes with lenghened years!"

49

May 17 1839

I am the only being whose doom
No tongue would ask no eye would mourn
I've never caused a thought of gloom
A smile of joy since I was born

In secret pleasure—secret tears
This changful life has slipped away
As freindless after 18 years
As lone as on my natal day

There have been times I cannot hide
There have been hours when this was drear
When my sad soul forgot its pride
And longed for one to love me here

But those were in the early glow
of feelings not subdued by care
And they have died so long ago
I hardly now beleive they were

First melted off the hope of youth
Then Fanceys rainbow fast withdrew
And then experience told me truth
in mortal bosoms never grew

T'was greif enough to think mankind
All [ ] searvile insincere
But worse to trust to my own mind
And find the same corruption there

49. *Text from T1*
1 being] <one> 2 eye] <heart> 6 has] <as> 14 not subdued] <unsubdued> 16 now] <can> 21 think mankind] <know my kind> 22 All <hollow lying> searvile (<Deceitful> *in l.h. margin)* 23 trust] <turn>

50

25th of May 1839

May Flowers are opening
And leaves unfolding free
There are bees in every blossom
And birds on every tree

The sun is gladly shineing
The stream sings merrily
And I only am pining
And all is dark to me

O—Cold cold is my heart
It will not cannot rise
It feels no sympathy
With those refulgent skys

Dead dead is my joy
I long to be at rest
I wish the damp earth covered
This desolate breast

If I were quite alone
It might not be so drear
When all hope was gone
At least I could not fear

But the glad eyes around me
must weep as mine have done
And I must see the same gloom
Eclipse their morning sun

If heaven would rain on me
That future storm of care
So their fond hearts were free
I'd be content to bear

Alas as lightening withers
The young and aged tree
Both they and I shall fall beneath
The fate we cannot flee

50. *Text from E1*
7 pin<e>ing   19 When] <If>   27 fond] <young>

51

May 28th 1839

Lines by Claudia

I did not sleep 'twas noon of day
I saw the burning sunshine fall
The long grass bending where I lay
The blue sky brooding over all

I heard the mellow hum of bees
And singing birds and sighing trees
And far away in woody dell
the Music of the sabbath bell

I did not dream remembrance still
Clasped round my heart its fetters chill
But I am sure the soul is free
To leave its clay a little while
Or how in exile misery
Could I have seen my country smile

In English feilds my limbs were laid
With English turf beneath my head
My spirit wandered o'er that shore
Where nought but it may wander more

Yet if the soul can thus return
I need not and I willnot mourn
And vainly did ye drive me far
With leagues of oecan streched between
My mortal flesh you might debar
But not the eternal fire within

My Monarch died to rule forever
A heart that can forget him never
And dear to me aye doubly dear
Though shut within the silent tomb
His name shall be for whom I bear
This longsustained and hopless doom

And brighter in the hour of woe
Than in the blaze of Victorys pride

51. *Text from C14*
28 Though] *ed.*; Thought

That glory shedding star shall glow
For which we fought and bled and died

52

June 8th 1839

I know not how it falls on me
This summer evening hushed and lone
Yet the faint wind comes soothingly
With something of an olden tone

Forgive me if I've shunned so long
Your gentle greeting earth and air
But sorrow withers even the strong
And who can fight against dispair

53

June 14th 1839

Written on returning to the P. of I.
on the 10th of January 1827—

The buissy day has hurried by
And hearts greet kindred hearts once more
And swift the evening hours should fly
But—what turns every gleaming eye
So often to the door?

And then so quick away—and why
Does sudden silence chill the room?
And laughter sink into a sigh—
And merry words to whispers die—
And gladness change to gloom?

52. *Text from E14*

53. *Text from B19 collated with E14 (where a cancelled draft of 1–5 is followed by an uncancelled draft of 1–6)*

Title B only

1 buissy day has hurried] <toils> hours of day have glided *E14a*; buisy day has glided *E14b* 3 And voices murmer cheerily *E14a* 5 door] unopened door *E14ab* 7 Does] <Doth>

O we are listening for a sound
We know, shall ne'er be heard again
Sweet voices in the halls resound;
Fair forms, fond faces gather round
But all in vain—in vain!

Their feet shall never waken more
The echoes in these galleries wide,
Nor dare the snow on the mountain's brow,
Nor skim the river's frozen flow,
Nor wander down its side—

They who have been our Life—our soul—
Through summer-youth, from childhood's spring—
Who bound us in one vigorous whole
To stand 'gainst Tyrrany's control
For ever triumphing—

Who bore the brunt of battle's fray
The first to fight, the last to fall
Whose mighty minds—with kindred ray
Still led the van in Glory's way—
The idol cheifs of all—

They, they are gone! not for a while
As golden suns at night decline
And even in death our greif beguile
Fortelling, with a rose-red smile
How bright the morn will shine—

No these dark towers are lone and lorn;
This very crowd is vacancy;
And we must whach and wait and mourn
And half look out for their return;
And think their forms we see—

And fancy music in our ear
Such as their lips could only pour
And think we feel their presence near
And start to find they are not here
And never shall be more!

12 ne'er] <not>   16 *Their*] *in sloping letters*

54

June 18th 1839

Month after month year after year
My harp has poured a dreary strain—
Atlength a livelier note shall cheer
And pleasure tune its chords again

What though the stars and fair moonlight
Are quenchd in morning dull and grey
They were but tokens of the *night*
And *this* my soul is day

55

July 12th 1839

A Farewell to Alexandria—

I've seen this dell in July's shine
As lovely as an angels dream;
Above, heavens depth of blue devine;
Around, the evening's golden beam—

I've seen the purple heather-bell
Look out by many a storm-worn stone
And Oh, I've known such music swell,
Such wild notes wake these passes lone—

So soft, yet so intensley felt—
So low, yet so distinctly heard
My breath would pause, my eyes would melt
And my tears dew the green heath-sward—

I'd linger here a summer day
Nor care how fast the hours flew by
Nor mark the suns departing ray
Smile sadly glorious from the sky—

54. *Text from T8*
Date 1839 *or* 1837; *see commentary*
1 Month . . . month] <Day . . . day> 5 moon<s>light
55. *Text from B22*
8 Such] *ed.*; Suth

Then, then I might have laid thee down
And deemed thy sleep would gentle be
I might have left thee, darling one
And thought thy God was guarding thee!

But now, there is no wandering glow
No gleam to say that God is nigh:
And coldly spreads thy couch of snow
And harshly sounds thy lullaby.

Forests of heather dark and long
Wave their brown branching arms above
And they must soothe thee with their song
And they must sheild my child of love!

Alas the flakes are heavily falling
They cover fast each guardian crest:
And chilly white their shroud is palling
Thy frozen limbs and freezing breast—

Wakes up the storm more madly wild
The mountain drifts are tossed on high—
Farewell unblessed, unfriended child,
I cannot bear to whach thee die!

56

July 12th 1839

And now the housedog streched once more
His limbs upon the glowing floor
The children half resumed their play
Though from the warm hearth scared away
The goodwife left her spinning wheel
And spread with smiles the evening meal
The Shepherd placed a seat and pressed
To their poor fare his unknown guest
And he unclasped his mantle now
And raised the covering from his brow

20 <g>God 24 thy] *or* my

56. *Text from D1*
9 <H> And

Said, voyagers by land and sea
Were seldom feasted daintily
and checked his host by adding stern
He'd no refinement to unlearn
A silence settled on the room
The cheerful welcome sank to gloom
But not those words though cold and high
So froze their hospitable joy
No—there was something in his face
Some namless thing they could not trace
And something in his voices tone
Which turned their blood as chill as stone
The ringlets of his long black hair
Fell o'er a cheek most ghastly fair
Youthful he seemed—but worn as they
Who spend too soon their youthful day
When his glance drooped 'twas hard to quell
Unbidden feelings sudden swell
And pity scearce her tears could hide
So sweet that brow with all its pride
But when upraised his eye would dart
An icey shudder through the heart
Compassion changed to horror then
And fear to meet that gaze again
It was not hatreds tiger-glare
Nor the wild anguish of dispair
It was not sullen misery
Which mocks at friendships symathy
No—lightening all unearthly shone
Deep in that dark eye's circling zone
Such withering lightening as we deem
None but a spirit's look may beam
And glad they were when he turned away
and wrapt him in his mantle grey
leant down his head upon his arm
And veiled from view their basilisk charm

13–14 *in margin* 13 stern] *ed.*; ste (*edge of leaf*) 37 sullen] <——less>
41 Such] <As> *or* <A> 42 spirit's] <spectre's> 43 And] <Full> <Right>
45 <And> leant <with> down

57

July 19 1839

Come hither child—who gifted thee
With power to touch that string so well?
How daredst thou rouse up thoughts in me
Thoughts that I would—but can not quell

Nay chide not lady   long ago
I heard those notes in Ula's hall
And had I known they'd waken woe
I'd weep their music to recall

But thus it was   one festal night
When I was hardly six years old
I stole away from crowds and light
And sought a chamber dark and cold

I had no one to love me there
I knew no comrade and no freind
And so I went to sorrow where
heaven only heaven saw me bend

Loud blew the wind 'twas sad to stay
From all that splendor barred away
I imaged in the lonely room
A thousand Forms of fearful gloom

And with my wet eyes raised on high
I prayed to God that I might die
Suddenly in that silence drear
A sound of music reached my ear

And then a vioce I hear it yet
So full of soul so deeply sweet
I thought that Gabriel's self had come
To take me to my fathers home

57. *Text from D3*
3 rouse up] <waken>   5 long] <years>   6 hall<s>   9 festal] <windy>   10+ <From>   16 <No careless eyes might see me bend>   17 sad] <drear>   18 splendor] <pleas>   21 on high] <in prayer>   22 <g>God   23 that] <the>   24 A sound of] <then dreadful>   24+ <O then my heart froze *?* icyer still>   25 vioce] *unclear*   28 fathers] <heavenly> *in cancelled draft of 28 placed above 25*

Three times it rose that seraph strain
then died nor heard I such again
But still the words and still the tone
dwell round my heart when all alone

58

July 26th 1839

Shed no tears o'er that tomb
For there are Angels weeping
Mourn not him whose doom
Heaven itself is mourning

Look how in sable gloom
The clouds are earthward sweeping
And earth recives them home
Even darker clouds returning

Is it when good men die
That sorrow wakes above?
Greive saints when other spirits fly
To swell thier choir of love?

Ah no with louder sound
The golden harp-strings quiver
When good men gain thc happy ground
Where they must dwell forever

But he who slumbers there
His bark will strive no more
Accross the waters of dispair
To reach that glorious shore

The time of grace is past
And mercy scorned and tried
Forsakes to utter wrath at last
The soul so steeled by pride

29 rose] <spoke> 30 then] <And> nor heard I such] *unclear* 32 dwell round my heart] <?Dwell in my thought>

58. *Text from C11*
Date 1839 *or* 1837
4–5 *no stanza-break* 6 s<p>weeping 18 will] <shall>

That wrath will never spare
Will never pity know
Will mock its victims maddened prayer
Will triumph in his woe

Shut from his Maker's smile
The accursed man shall be
For mercy reigns a little while
But Hate eternaly—

59

July 27th 1839

Mild the mist upon the hill
Telling not of storms to morow
No the day has wept its fill
Spent its store of silent sorrow

O I'm gone back to the days of youth
I am a child once more
And neath my fathers sheltering roof
And near the old hall door

I whach this cloudy evening fall
After a day of rain
Blue mists sweet mists of summer pall
The horizons mountain chain

The damp stands on the long green grass
As thick as mornings tears
And dreamy scents of fragrance pass
That breathe of other years

31 For mercy] Compassion *as alternative above* 32 But Hate] Revenge *as alternative above*

59. *Text from T4*
4 silent] <childish> 4/5 *horizontal line* 6 once more] <again> 13 damp stands] <dew is> 16 <t> years

60

August 12th 1839

How long will you remain the midnight hour
Has tolled its last note from the minster tower
Come come the fire is dead the lamp burns low
Your eyelids droop a weight is on your brow
Your cold hands hardly hold the usless pen
Come morn will give recovered strength again
No let me linger leave me let me be
A little longer in this reverie
I'm happy now and would you tear away
My blissful dream that never comes with day
a vision dear though false for well my mind
Knows what a bitter waking waits behind
Can there be pleasure in this shadowy room
With windows yawning on intenser gloom
And such a dreary wind so bleakly sweeping
Round walls were only you are vigil keeping
Besides your face has not a sign of joy
And more than tearful sorrow fills your eye
Look on those woods look on that [ ] lorn
And think how changed they'll be tomorrow morn
The dome of heaven expanding bright and blue
The leaves the green grass sprinkled thick with dew
And sweet mists rising on the rivers breast
And wildbirds bursting from their songless nest
And your own childrens merry voices chaseing
The fancies greif not pleasure has been tracing
Aye speak of these—but can you tell me why
Day breathes such beauty over earth and sky
And waking sounds revive restore again
Dull hearts that all night long have throbbed in pain
Is it not that the sunshine and the wind
lure from itsself the mourners woe worn mind

60. *Text from D14* (*for 10, 19, 22, 23, see commentary*)
1 the midnight hour] <'tis midnight now> 7 <No leave me let me linger yet 'tis long> 10 blissful dream] <——ghost> 11 mind] <brain> 13 in this] <where a> 15 so bleakly] <in gusts *?*is> 19 that <shadowy> *?*heaven lorn 22 leaves] *ed.*; leave 23 sweet] *ed.*; sweets on] <from> 24 songless] <long> 26 fancies] <phantoms> 27 can you] <canst thou> 28 Day] <May> beauty over] <beauties o'er the> 30 Dull] <The>

And all the joyous music breathing by
And all the splendour of that cloudless sky
Regive him shadowy gleams of infancy
And draw his tired gaze from futurity

61

August 13th 1839

"The starry night shall tidings bring
Go out upon the breezy moor
Whach for a bird with sable wing
And beak and talons dropping gore

Look not around look not beneath
But mutely trace its airy way
Mark were it lights upon the heath
Then wanderer kneel thee down and pray

What Futur may await thee there
I will not and I dare not tell
But heaven is moved by fervant prayer
And God is mercy—fare thee well"

62

August 30th 1839

Fair sinks the summer evening now
In softened glory round my home;
The sky upon its holy brow
Wears not a cloud that speaks of gloom—

The old tower, shrined in golden light,
Looks down on the decending sun—

34 that] <the>

61. *Text from T6, collated with eight cancelled lines of E12*
Date Nov 1838 *E*
No quotation marks in E
1 tidings] comfort *E* 5–12 It will perch on a heathy swell | Against the light of the coming moon | Then poor wretch thy misery tell | Thou shalt have the wishedfor boon *E* 9 Futur] <?truths>
62. *Text from A5*

So gently evening blends with night
You scearce can say that day is done—

And this is just the joyous hour
When we were wont to burst away,
To 'scape from labours tyrant power
And cheerfuly go out to play—

Then why is all so sad and lone?
No merry foot-step on the stair—
No laugh—no heart-awaking tone
But voiceless silence everywhere—

I've wandered round our garden-ground
And still it seemed at every turn
That I should greet approaching feet
And words upon the breezes borne

In vain—they will not come today
And morning's beam will rise as drear
Then tell me—are they gone for aye
Our sun blinks through the mists of care?

Ah no, reproving Hope doth say
Departed joys 'tis fond to mourn
When every storm that hides their ray
Prepares a more devine return

63

September 6th 1839

Alcona in its changing mood
My soul will sometimes overfly
The long long years of solitude
That 'twixt our time of meeting lie

Hope and dispair in turns arise
This doubting dreading heart to move
And now mid smiles and bitter sighs
Tell how I fear tell how I love

7 gently] <?softly> 26 joys] <?suns>

63. *Text from D16* (*for undeciphered words see commentary*)

And now I think "In Areon Hall"
(Alas that such a dream should come
When well I know what ere befall
Sweet Areon is no more my home)

Yet let me say "In Areon Hall"—
The first faint red of morning shines
And one right gladly to its call
The restless breath of greif resigns

Her faded eye her pallid face
Would win the soft awaking wind
All earth is breathing of the peace
She long has sought but can not find

How sweet it is to whach the mist
From that bright silent lake ascend
And high o'er wood and mountain crest
With heaven's grey clouds as greyly blend

How sweet it is to mark those clouds
Break brightly in the rising day
To see the sober veil that shrouds
This summer morning melt away

O sweet to some but not to her
[ ] once at natures shrine
She now kneels down a worshipper
A mad adorer love to thine

The time is come when hope that long
Revived and sunk at length is o'er
When faith in him however strong
Dare prompt her to beleive no more

The tears which day by day o'erflowd
Their heart deep source begin to freeze
And as she gazes on the road
That glances through those [ ] trees

No throbbing flutter checks her breath
To mark a horse man hastening by
Her haggard brow is calm as death
And cold like death her dreary eye

9 think] <say> 18 win] *or* woo 22 that] <*?*the> <its> 40 those <— —> <*?*gloomy> trees

64

Sept 30th 1839

The organ swells the trumpets sound
The lamps in triumph glow
And none of all those thousands round
regards who sleeps below

Those haughty eyes that tears should fill
Glance clearly cloudlessly
Those bounding breasts that greif should thrill
From thought of greif are free

His subjects and his soldiers there
They blessed his rising bloom
But none a single sigh can spare
To breathe above his tomb

Comrades in arms I've looked to mark
One shade of feeling swell
As your feet trod above the dark
Recesses of his cell

65

October 15th 1839

Song

O between distress and pleasure
Fond affection cannot be
Whreched hearts in vain would treasure
Freindship's joys when others flee

Well I know thine eye would never
Smile while mine greived willingly
Yet I know thine eye forever
Could not weep in symphathy

Let us part the time is over
When I thought and felt like thee

64. *Text from F1*
Date 1839 *or* 1837
65. *Text from C9*
4 when] <while>

I will be an Ocean rover
I will sail the desert sea

Isles there are beyond its billow
Lands where woe may wander free
And beloved thy midnight pillow
Will be soft unwatched by me

Not on each returning morrow
When thy heart bounds ardently
Needst thou then dissemble sorrow
Marking my dispondancy

Day by day some dreary token
Will forsake thy memory
Till at last all old links broken
I shall be a dream to thee

66

October 29th 1839

The wind I hear it sighing
With Autum's saddest sound
Withered leaves as thick are lying
As spring-flowers on the ground—

This dark night has won me
To wander far away—
Old feelings gather fast upon me
Like vultures round their prey—

Kind where they once, and cherished
But cold and cheerless now—
I would their lingering shades had perished
When their light left my brow

'Tis like old age pretending
The softness of a child,

16 me] <thee>

66. *Text from A14*
12 my] *or* thy; *see introduction, p. 20*

My altered hardened spirit bending
To meet their fancies wild

Yet could I with past pleasures,
past woe's oblivion buy—
That by the death of my dearest treasures
My deadliest pains might die,

O then another daybreak
Might haply dawn above—
Another summer gild my cheek,
My Soul, another love—

67

October 1839

There was a time when my cheek burned
To give such scornful feinds the lie
Ungoverned nature madly spurned
The law that bade it not defye
O in the days of ardent youth
I would have given my life for truth

For truth for right for liberty
I would have gladly freely died
But now I calmly hear and see
The vain man smile the fool deride
Though not because my heart is tame
Though not for fear though not for shame

My soul still chafes at every tone
Of selfish and self-blinded error
My breast still braves the world alone
Steeled as it ever was to terror
Only I know however I frown
The same world will go rolling on

67. *Text from E7*
Date in margin opposite 12–13
2 feinds] <?sneers> 9 But] <And> 12 Though . . . though] <And . . . and> 17 frown] *unclear*

68

November 14th 1839

Stanzas to——

"Well, some may hate and some may scorn
"And some may quite forget, thy name
"But my sad heart must ever mourn
"Thy ruined hopes, thy blighted fame"—

'T was thus I thought an hour ago
Even weeping o'er that wretche's woe—
One word turned back my gushing tears
And lit my altered eye with sneers—

Then "Bless the friendly dust" I said—
"That hides thy unlamented head
"Vain as thou wert, and weak as vain
"The slave of falsehood, pride and pain—
"My heart has nought akin to thine—
"Thy soul is powerless over mine"

But these were thoughts that vanished too
Unwise, unholy and untrue—
Do I despise the timid deer
Because his limbs are fleet with fear?
Or would I mock the wolf's death-howl
Because his form is guant and foul?
Or hear with joy the leverts cry
Because it cannot bravely die?

No—then above his memory
Let pity's heart as tender be
Say "Earth, lie lightly on that breast,
"And kind Heaven, grant that spirit rest!"

68. *Text from A17, with substantive revisions of 1846*
Title 1846; not in A
No stanza-breaks at 4, 8 in 1846
1–4 *no quotation marks in 1846* 9 Then "Bless] *1846*; "Then bless *A* friendly] <kindly> 13 has] <is> 24 heart] <eye> 26 rest!"] *ed.*; rest!

69

November 23r 1839

The wind was rough which tore
That leaf from its parent tree
The fate was cruel which bore
Its withering corps to me

70

Nov 28th 1839

That wind I used to hear it swelling
With joy devinely deep
you might have seen my hot tears welling
But rapture made me weep

I used to love on winter nights
To lie and dream alone
Of all fond hopes and real delights
My Lonly years had known

And oh above the rest of those
That coming time should bear
like heavens own glorious stars they rose
Still beaming bright and fair

71

Dec 19th 1839

Heavens glory shone where he was laid
In lifes decline
I turned me from that young saints bed
To gaze on thine—

It was a summer day that saw
His spirits flight

69. *Text from E3*
1 rough which] <cruel that>
70. *Text from D13*
7 fond] <the> real] <?vain> 10 bear] <bring>
71. *Text from E10*
Date Dec | <A> 19th 1839

Thine parted in a time of awe
A winter-night

72

F. De Samara. *January 6th 1840*

Written in the Gaaldine prison caves
To A. G. A.

Thy sun is near meridian height
And my sun sinks in endless night;
But if that night bring only sleep
Then I shall rest, while thou wilt weep—

And say not, that my early tomb
Will give me to a darker doom—
Shall those long agonizing years
Be punished by eternal tears?

No, *that* I feel can never be;
A God of *hate* could hardly bear
To whach, through all eternity,
His own creations dread dispair!

The pangs that wring my mortal breast
Must claim from Justice, lasting rest:
Enough, that this departing breath
Will pass in anguish worse than death.

If I have sinned, long, long ago
That sin was purified by woe—
I've suffered on through night and day;
I've trod a dark and frightful way—

Earth's wilderness was round me spread
Heaven's tempests beat my naked head—
I did not kneel—in vain would prayer
Have sought one gleam of mercy there!

How could I ask for pitying love
When that grim concave frowned above

72. *Text from B17*
6 darker] <?drearier> 18 purif<y>ied

Hoarding its lightenings to destroy
My only and my priceless joy?

They struck—and long may Eden shine
Ere I would call its glories mine
All Heaven's undreamt felicity
Could never blot the past from me—

No, years may cloud and death may sever
But what is done, is done for ever—
And thou False freind, and treacherous guide,
Go sate thy cruel heart with pride—

Go, load my memory with shame;
Speak but to curse my hated name;
My tortured limbs in dungeons bind
And spare my life to kill my mind—

Leave me in chains and darkness now
And when my very soul is worn;
When reasons light has left my brow
And madness cannot feel thy scorn;

Then come again,—thou wilt not shrink;
I know thy soul is free from fear
The last full cup of triumph drink;
Before the blank of death be there—

Thy raving, dying victim see;
Lost, cursed, degraded all for thee!
Gaze on the wretch—recall to mind
His golden days left long behind.

Does memory sleep in Lethian rest?
Or wakes its wisper in thy breast?
O memory, wake! let scenes return
That even her haughty heart must mourn!

Reveal, where o'er a lone green wood
The moon of summer pours
Far down from heaven, its silver flood
On deep Elderno's shores—

There, lingering in the wild embrace
Youth's warm affections gave

32 blot] <?hide>   43 When] <Where>

She sits, and fondly seems to trace
His features in the wave—

And while, on that reflected face
Her eyes intently dwell;
"Fernando, Sing to night, she-says,
"The Lays I love so well—"

He smiles and sings though every air
Betrays the faith of yesterday;
His soul is glad to cast for her
Virtue and faith and Heaven away—

Well, thou hast paid me back my love!
But, if there be a God above
Whose arm is strong, whose word is true
This hell shall wring thy spirit too!

73

March 1840

Far, far away is mirth withdrawn;
'Tis three long hours before the morn
And I whach lonely, drearily—
So come thou shade commune with me

Deserted one! thy corpse lies cold
And mingled with a forign mould—
Year after year the grass grows green
Above the dust where thou hast been.

I will not name thy blighted name
Tarnished by unforgotten shame
Though not because my bosom torn
Joins the mad world in all its scorn—

Thy phantom face is dark with woe
Tears have left ghastly traces there,
Those ceasless tears! I wish their flow
Could quench thy wild dispair—

They deluge my heart like the rain
On cursed Gommorrah's howling plain—

73. *Text from A18*

Yet when I hear thy foes deride
I must cling closely to thy side—

Our mutual foes—they will not rest
From trampling on thy buried breast—
Glutting their hatred with the doom
They picture thine—beyond the tomb—

But God is not like human kind
Man cannot read the Almighty mind
Vengeance will never torture thee
Nor hunt thy soul eternaly—

Then do not in this night of greif
This time of overwelming fear
O do not think that God can leave
Forget, forsake, refuse to hear!—

What have I dreamt? He lies asleep
With whom my heart would vainly weep
He rests—and *I* endure the woe
That left his spirit long ago—

74

April 1840

It is too late to call thee now—
I will not nurse that dream again
For every joy that lit my brow
Would bring its after storm of pain—

Besides the mist is half withdrawn,
The barren mountain-side lies bare
And sunshine and awaking morn
Paint no more golden visions there—

yet ever in my grateful breast
Thy darling shade shall cherished be
For God alone doth know how blest
My early years have been in thee!

23 <gr> doom 28 hunt] *or* hurt 33 have I dreamt] <do I dream> lies] <rests at>

74. *Text from A13*
3 lit] <lig>

75

May 4th 1840

Stanzas

I'll not weep that thou art going to leave me
There's nothing lovely here,
And doubly will the dark world greive me
While thy heart suffers there—

I'll not weep—because the summer's glory
Must always end in gloom
And follow out the happiest story,
It closes with a tomb—

And I am weary of the anguish
Increasing winters bear—
Weary to watch the spirit languish
Through years of dead dispair—

So if a tear when thou art dying
Should haply fall from me
It is but that my soul is sighing
To go and rest with thee—

76

May 6th 1840

A.G.A. to A.S. *July 28th 1843*

At such a time, in such a spot
The world seems made of light
Our blissful hearts remember not
How surely follows night—

I cannot, Alfred, dream of ought
That casts a shade of woe;
That heaven is reigning in my thought

75. *Text from A10, with substantive revisions of 1846*
Title 1846; not in A
Alternate lines indented in 1846
8 a] *1846*; <a> the *A* 11 Weary to watch] *1846*; I'm sick to see *A* 14 Should] <Doth>
76. *Text from B3*

Which wood and wave and earth have caught
From skies that overflow—

That heaven which my sweet lover's brow
Has won me to adore.
Which from his blue eyes beaming now
Reflects a still intenser glow
Than nature's heaven can pour—

I know our souls are all devine
I know that when we die
What seems the vilest, even like thine
A part of God himself shall shine
In perfect purity.

But coldly breaks November's day;
Its changes charmless all
Unmarked, unloved, they pass away
We do not wish one hour to stay
Nor sigh at evening's fall

And glorious is the gladsome rise
Of June's rejoicing morn
And who, with unregretful eyes
Can whach the lustre leave its skies
To twilights shade forelorn?

Then art thou not my golden June,
All mist and tempest-free?
As shines earths sun in summer noon
So heaven's sun shines in thee—

Let others seek its beams devine
In cell and cloister drear
But I have found a fairer shrine
A happier worship here—

By dismal rites they win their bliss
By penance, fasts and fears—
I have one rite—a gentle kiss—
One penance—tender tears—

8 Which] <That> 20 coldly] <dreary> 24 Nor] <Or> 27 <in>unregretful 28 Can] <Would> 37 A<nd>

O could it thus forever be
That I might so adore—
I'd ask for all eternity,
To make a paradise for me,
My love—and nothing more!

77

May 18 1840

If greif for greif can touch thee,
If answering woe for woe,
If any ruth can melt thee
Come to me now!

I cannot be more lonley,
More drear I cannot be!
My worn heart throbs so wildly
'Twill break for thee—

And when the world despises—
When Heaven repells my prayer—
Will not mine angel comfort?
Mine idol hear?

Yea by the tears I've poured,
By all my hours of pain
O I shall surely win thee
Beloved, again!

78

May 19th 1840

Tis moon light summer moonlight
All soft and still and fair
The solemn hour of midnight
Breaths sweet thoughts everywhere

77. *Text from A11*
1 touch] <melt> 13 Yea] *or* Yes
78. *Text from E11*
2 soft] <bright> <sweet> still] <still> <soft> 4 Breaths] <Brings> sweet thoughts] <*?*comfort>

But most were trees are sending
Their breezy boughs on high
Or stooping low are lending
A shelter from the sky

And there in those wild bowers
A lovely form is laid
Green grass and dew steeped flowers
Wave gently round her head

79

September 11th 1840

The night wind

In summer's mellow midnight
  A cloudless moon shone through
Our open parlour-window
And rosetrees wet with dew—

I sat in silent musing—
  The soft wind waved my hair
It told me Heaven was glorious
And sleeping Earth was fair—

I needed not its breathing
To bring such thoughts to me
But still it wispered lowly
"How dark the woods will be!—

"The thick leaves in my murmer
"Are rustling like a dream,
"And all their myriad voices
"Instinct with spirit seem"

I said, "go gentle singer,
"Thy wooing voice is kind
"But do not think its music
"Has power to reach my mind—

9 wild] <green>

79. *Text from A7*
9 breathing] <*?*trembling *or* troubling>

"play with the scented flower,
"The young tree's supple bough—
"And leave my human feelings
"In their own course to flow"

The Wanderer would not leave me
Its kiss grew warmer still—
"O come," it sighed so sweetly
"I'll win thee 'gainst thy will—

"Have we not been from childhood friends?
"Have I not loved thee long?
"As long as thou hast loved the night
"Whose silence wakes my song?

"And when thy heart is resting
"Beneath the churcheyard stone
"I shall have time for mourning
"And thou for being alone"—

80

R. Gleneden *September 17th 1840*

Companions all day long we've stood
The wild winds restless blowing
All day we've whached the darkened flood
Around our vessel flowing

Sunshine has never smiled since morn
And clouds have gathered drear
And heavier hearts would feel forlorn
And weaker minds would fear

But look in each young shipmates eyes
Lit by the evening flame
And see how little stormy skys
Our joyous blood can tame

33 resting] <laid at rest> 35 for mourning] <enough to mourn> 36 for being] <to be>

80. *Text from D15*

R. Gleneden] *unclear; in sloping letters*

2 blowing] <raging> 3 darkened] <?tumbling> 8 minds] <heads>

No glance the same expression wears
No lip the same soft smile
Yet kindness warms and courage cheers
Nerves every breast the while

It is the hour of dreaming now
Our red fire brightly gleams
And sweetest in a red fire's glow
The hour of dreaming seems

I may not trace the thoughts of all
But some I read as well
As I can hear the ocaens fall
And sullen surging swell

Edmunds swift soul is gone before
It threads a forest wide
Whose bowers are bending to the shore
And gazing on the tide

And one is there I know the vioce
The thrilling stirring tone
That makes his bounding pulse rejoice
Yet makes not *his* alone

mine own hand longs to clasp her hand
mine eye—to greet her eye
Win white sails win Zedoras strand
And Ula's Eden sky

Mary and flora oft their gaze
Is clouded pensivly
And what that ernest aspect says
Is all revealed to me

Tis but two years or little more
Since first they dared the main
And such a night may well restore
That first time back again

15 kindness] <fondnes> 18 <And> <We all have secret dreams> <The night-fire> 21 may not] <cannot> 23 hear] <?scan> ocaens] <storms> 26 a] <some> 32 Yet makes not *his*] <And not *his* pulse> 33 her] <that> 36 Eden] <tranquil> 38 <Has ?sought the ?sounding sea> 41 or] <and> 42 <Since last in England's isle> (far *uncancelled above* last) 43 And such a night] <Two children> may] <can>

The smotherd sigh the lingering late
The longed for dreaded hour
The parting at the mossgrown gate
The last look on the tower

I know they think of these and then
The evenings gathering gloom
And they alone with foreign men
To guard their cabin room

81

January 1841—
May 1844—

A. G. A. The Death of

Were they Shepherds, who sat all day
On that brown mountain's-side?
But neither staff nor dog had they;
Nor wooly flock to guide—

They were clothed in savage attire;
Their locks were dark and long;
And at each belt a weapon dire
Like bandit-knife was hung—

One was a woman tall and fair;
A princess she might be
From her stately form and her features rare
And her look of majesty—

But oh, she had a sullen frown—
A lip of cruel scorn—
As sweet tears never melted down
Her cheeks since she was born!

'Twas well she had no sceptre to wield,
No subject land to sway;
Fear might have made her vassels yeild
But Love had been faraway—

45 smotherd] *unclear* 51 with] <amid> (<from> *above line*)

81. *Text from B21*

7 each belt a weapon] <their belts the weapons> 8 bandit-knife was] <bandit-knives were>

Yet, Love was even at her feet
In his most burning mood—
That Love, which will the wicked greet
As kindly as the Good—

And he was noble too, who bowed
So humbly by her side—
Entreating, till his eyes o'erflowed,
Her spirit's icy pride—

"Angelica, from my very birth
"I have been nursed in strife,
"And lived upon this weary Earth
"A wanderer, all my life;

"The baited Tiger could not be
"So much athirst for gore,
"For men and Laws have tortured me
"Till I can bear no more—

"The guiltless blood upon my hands
"Will shut me out from Heaven
"And here, and even in foriegn lands
"I can not find a haven—

"And in all space, and in all time,
"And through Eternity,
"To aid a spirit lost in crime,
"I have no hope but thee—

"Yet will I swear, No Saint on high
"A truer faith could prove—
"No angel, from that holy sky,
"Could give thee purer love!

"For thee, through never ending years
"I'd suffer endless pain;
"But—only give me back my tears
"Return my love again!"

Many a time, unheeded, thus
The reckless man would pray;
But something woke an answering flush
On his lady's brow to day,

26 by] <at>

And her eye flashed flame, as she turned to speak,
In concord with her reddening cheek—

"I've known a hundred kinds of Love—
"*All*, made the loved one rue;
"And what is thine, that it should prove,
"Than other love, more true?

"Listen, I've known a burning heart
"To which my own was given
"Nay, not in passion, do not start—
"Our love was love from heaven;
"At least if heavenly love be born
"In the pure light of childhood's morn
"Long ere the poison-tainted air
"From this worlds plague-fen rises there:

"That heart was like a tropic sun
"That kindles all it shines upon;
"And never Majian devotee
"Gave worship half so warm as I
"And never radiant bow could be
"So welcome in a stormy sky
"My soul dwelt with her day and night
"She was my all sufficing light—
"My childhoods mate, my girlhood's guide
"My only blessing, only pride

"But cursed be the very earth
"That gave that fiend her fatal birth!
"With her own hand she bent the bow
"That laid my best affections low;
"Then mocked my greif and scorned my prayers
"And drowned my bloom of youth in tears—
"Warnings, reproaches, both were vain;
"What recked she of another's pain?
"My dearer self she would not spare—
"From Honours voice, she turned his ear:
"First made her love his only stay;
"Then snatched the treacherous prop away!
"Douglas, he pleaded bitterly—

58 redden<ed>ing 63 known] <know> 65 in] <with> 74 I] <me *or* she> 75 radiant] <guiding> <glistering glittering> 77 dwelt] <*?*lived>

"He pleaded, as *you* plead to me,
"For life-long chains or timeless tomb
"Or any, but an Exile's doom:
"We both were scorned—both sternly driven
"To shelter 'neath a foriegn heaven;
"And darkens o'er that dreary time
"A wildering dream of frenzied crime—
"I would not now those days recall;
"The oath within that caverned hall
"And its fulfilment, those you know;
"We both together struck the blow;
"But—you can never know the pain
"That my lost heart did then sustain
"When, severed wide by guiltless gore,
"I felt that *one* could love no more!
"Back maddening Thought!—the grave is deep
"Where my Amedeus lies asleep,
"And I have long forgot to weep—

"Now hear me, in these regions wild
"I saw to day my enemy
"Unarmed, as helpless as a child
"She slumbered on a sunny lea;
"Two Friends, no other guard had she;
"And they were wandering on the braes;
"And chasing, in regardless glee,
"The wild goat o'er his dangerous ways—

"My hand was raised—my knife was bare;
"With stealthy tread I stole along
"But a wild bird sprang from his hidden lair
"And woke her with a sudden song:
"Yet moved she not; she only raised
"Her lids and on the bright sun gazed
"And uttered such a dreary sigh
"I thought, just then she should not die
"Since living was such misery—

"Now Douglas, for our hunted band—
"For future joy and former woe,
"Assist me, with thy heart and hand

97 sternly] <*?* harshly>   121 tread] <*?* step>

"To send to hell my mortal foe—
"Her friends fall first, that she may drain
"A deeper cup of bitterer pain;
"Yonder they stand and whach the waves
"Dash in among the echoing caves—
"Their farewell sight of earth and sea;
"Come, Douglas, rise and go with me—"

. . . .

The Lark sang clearly overhead
And sweetly hummed the Bee
And softly, round their dying bed,
The wind blew from the sea—

Fair Surry would have raised her eyes
To see that water shine;
To see once more, in mountain skies
The summer sun decline:

But ever, on her fading cheek,
The languid lid would close
As weary that such light should break
Its much-desired repose—

And she was waning fast away—
Even Memory's voice grew dim;
Her former life's eventful day
Had dwindled to a dream;

And hardly could her mind recall
One thought of joy or pain;
That cloud was gathering over all
Which never clears again!

In vain—in vain, you need not gaze
Upon those features now!
That sinking head you need not raise,
Nor kiss that pulseless brow—

Let out the greif that chokes your breath;
Lord Lesley, set it free;
The sternest eye, for such a death
Might fill with sympathy.

140 hum<d>med

The tresses o'er her bosom spread
Were by a faint breeze blown;
"Her heart is beating, Lesley said,
"She is not really gone!"

And still that form he fondly pressed,
And still of hope he dreamed
Nor marked, how from his own young breast
Life's crimson current streamed—

At last, the sunshine left the ground,
The laden bee flew home
The deepdown sea, with sadder sound
Impelled its waves to foam;

And the corpse grew heavy on his arm,
The starry heaven grew dim,
The summer night so mild and warm
Felt wintery chill to him.

A troubled shadow, o'er his eye
came down, and rested there;
The moors and sky went swimming by
Confused and strange and drear

He faintly prayed, "Oh, Death, delay
"Thy last fell dart to throw
"Till I can hear my sovereign say,
"The traitors heads are low!—

"God, guard her life, since not to me
"That dearest boon was given;
"God, bless her arm with victory
"Or bless not me with heaven!"

Then came the cry of agony;
The pang of parting pain;
And he had overpassed the sea
That none can pass again—

. . . .

Douglas leaned above the well;
Heather banks around him rose;
Bright and warm the sunshine fell
On that spot of sweet repose—

With the blue heaven bending o'er
And the soft wind singing by
And the clear stream, evermore
Mingling harmony—

On the shady side reclined,
He whached its waters play
And sound and sight had well combined
To banish gloom away—

A voice spoke near—"She'll come, it said,
"And Douglas, thou shallt be
"My Love, although the very dead
"Should rise to rival thee!

"Now only let thine arm be true
"And nerved, like mine, to kill;
"And Gondals' royal race shall rue
"This day on Elmor Hill!"—

They wait not long, the rustling heath
Betrays their royal foe;
With hurried step and panting breath
And cheek almost as white as death,
Augusta sprang below—

Yet marked she not where Douglas lay
She only saw the well;
The tiney fountain, churning spray
Within its mossy cell—

"Oh, I have wrongs to pay, she cried,
"Give life, give vigour now!"
And, stooping by the waters side
She drank its crystal flow.

And brightly, with that draught, came back
The glory of her matchless eye
As, glancing o'er the moorland track,
She shook her head impatiently—

Nor shape, nor shade—the mountain flocks
quietly feed in grassy dells;

237 quietly] all quiet *alternative ?CB*

Nor sound, except the distant roaks
Echoing to their bells—

She turns—she meets the Murderer's gaze:
Her own is scorched with a sudden blaze—
The blood streams down her brow;
The blood streams through her coal-black hair—
She strikes it off with little care;
She scearcely feels it flow,—

For she has marked and known him too
And his own hearts ensanguined dew
Must slake her vengeance now!

False friend! no tongue save thine can tell
The mortal strife that then befell;
But, ere night darkened down
The stream in silence sang once more
And, on its green bank, bathed in gore
Augusta lay alone!

False Love! no earthly eye did see,
Yet Heavens pure eye regarded thee
Where thy own Douglas bled—
How thou didst turn in mockery
From his last hopless agony
And leave the hungry hawk to be
Sole whacher of the dead!

. . . .

Was it a deadly Swoon?
Or was her Spirit really gone?
And the cold corpse, beneath the moon
Laid like another mass of dust and stone?

The moon was full that night—
The sky was almost light like day:
You might have seen the pulse's play
Upon her forehead white;

You might have seen the dear, dear sign of life
In her uncovered eye

240 turns—she meets] <turned—she met> 247 <in>ensanguined 258 thou <g> didst

And her cheek changing in the mortal strife
Betwixt the pain to live and agony, to die—

But nothing mutable was there!
The face, all deadly fair,
Showed a fixed impress of keen suffering past,
And the raised lid did show
No wandering gleam below
But a dark anguish, self-destroyed at last—

Long he gazed and held his breath,
Kneeling on the blood-stained heath;
Long he gazed those lids beneath
Looking into Death!

Not a word from his followers fell,
They stood by mute and pale;
That black treason uttered well
Its own heart-harrowing tale—

But earth was bathed in other gore;
There were crimson drops accross the moor
And Lord Eldred, glancing round
Saw those tokens on the ground;

"Bring him back! he hoarsly said,
"Wounded is the traitor fled,—
"Vengeance may hold but minutes breif
"And you have all your lives for greif"—

He is left alone—he sees the stars
Their quiet course continueing
And, far away, down Elmor scars
He hears the stream its waters fling:
That lulling monotone did sing
Of broken roak and shaggy glen—
Of welcome for the moorcock's wing,
But, not of wail for men!

Nothing in heaven or earth to show
One sign of sympathizing woe—
And nothing but that agony
In her now unconscious eye

272 cheek <g> changing 276 impress<ed> 294 hold] <have>

To weigh upon the labouring breast
And prove she didnot pass at rest—
But he who whached, in thought had gone
Retracing back her lifetime flown;
Like sudden ghosts, to memory came
Full many a face, and many a name,
Full many a heart, that in the tomb
He almost deemed, might have throbbed again
Had they but known her dreary doom,
Had they but seen their idol—there,
A wreck of desolate dispair,
Left to the wild birds of the air
And mountain winds and rain!
For him—no tear his stern eye shed
As he looked down upon the dead—

"Wild morn—he thought—and doubtful noon;
"But, yet it was a glorious sun
"Though comet-like its course was run;
"That sun should never have been given
"To burn and dazzel in the heaven
"Or, night has quenched it far too soon!
"And thou art gone—with all thy pride,
"Thou, so adored, so deifyed!
"Cold as the earth, unweeting now
"Of love, or joy, or mortal woe—

"For what thou wert, I would not greive,
"But much, for what thou wert to be—
"That life, so stormy and so breif,
"That death, has wronged us more than thee!
"Thy passionate youth was nearly past
"The opening sea seemed smooth at last
"Yet vainly flowed the calmer wave
"Since fate had not decreed to save—
"And vain too must the sorrow be
"Of those who live to mourn for thee;
"But Gondal's foes shall not complain
"That thy dear blood was poured in vain!"

337 past] <passed> 339 Yet] <But> the] <that>

82

Feb 27 1841

And like myself lone wholey lone
It sees the days long sunshine glow
And like myself it makes its moan
In unexhausted woe

give me the hills our equal prayer
Earths breezy hills and heavens blue sea
I ask for nothing further here
But my own heart and liberty

Ah could my hand unlock its chain
How gladly would I whach it soar
And ne'er regret and ne'er complain
To see its shining eyes no more

But let me think that if to day
it pines in cold captivity
To morrow both shall soar away
Eternaly entirely Free—

83

March 1st 1841

The Old Stoic

Riches I hold in light esteem
And Love I laugh to scorn
And Lust of Fame was but a dream
That vanished with the morn—

And if I pray—the only prayer
That moves my lips for me
Is—"Leave the heart that now I bear
"And give me liberty"—

82. *Text from E9*
5 me] <her> <us>   hills] <sky>   7 I] <I> <We>   8 my] <our>   heart] *ed.*; hearts   9 its] <thy>   10 whach it] <see thee>   12 shin<y>ing *or* shin<g>ing   14 it] <We>

83. *Text from A8, with substantive revisions of 1846*
Title 1846; not in A
Alternate lines indented in 1846
6 <W> That

Yes, as my swift days near their goal
'Tis all that I implore—
In Life and death, a chainless soul
With courage to endure!—

84

May 16th 1841

Shall Earth no more inspire thee,
Thou lonely dreamer now?
Since passion may not fire thee
Shall Nature cease to bow?

Thy mind is ever moving
In regions dark to thee;
Recall its usless roving—
Come back and dwell with me—

I know my mountain breezes
Enchant and soothe thee still—
I know my sunshine pleases
Despite thy wayward will—

When day with evening blending
Sinks from the summer sky,
I've seen thy spirit bending
In fond idolatry—

I've whached thee every hour—
I know my mighty sway—
I know my magic power
To drive thy greifs away—

Few hearts to mortals given
On earth so wildly pine
Yet none would ask a Heaven
More like the Earth than thine—

Then let my winds caress thee—
Thy comrade let me be—

11 In] *1846*; Through *A*

84. *Text from A6*
19 ma<j>gic   23 a<n> Heaven   24 <e>Earth

Since nought beside can bless thee—
Return and dwell with me—

85

July 6th 1841

Aye there it is! It wakes to night
Sweet thoughts that will not die
And feeling's fires flash all as bright
As in the years gone by!—

And I can tell by thine altered cheek
And by thy kindled gaze
And by the words thou scearce dost speak,
How wildly fancy plays—

Yes I could swear that glorious wind
Has swept the world aside
Has dashed its memory from thy mind
Like foam-bells from the tide—

And thou art now a spirit pouring
Thy presence into all—
The essence of the Tempest's roaring
And of the Tempest's fall—

A universal influence
From Thine own influence free—
A principle of life intense
Lost to mortality—

Thus truely when that breast is cold
Thy prisoned soul shall rise
The Dungeon mingle with the mould—
The captive with the skies—

85. *Text from A9*
12 Like] <As> 19 intense] *ed.*; intend<s>

86

July 17th 1841

I see around me tombstones grey
Stretching their shadows far away—
Beneath the turf my footsteps tread
Lie low and lone the silent dead—
Beneath the turf, beneath the mould—
Forever dark, forever cold—
And my eyes cannot hold the tears
That memory hoards from vanished years
For Time and Death and Mortal pain
Give wounds that will not heal again—
Let me remember half the woe
I've seen and heard and felt below
And Heaven itself, so pure and blest
Could never give my spirit rest—
Sweet land of light! thy children fair
Know nought akin to our dispair,—
Nor have they felt, nor can they tell
What tenants haunt each mortal cell
What gloomy guests we hold within—
Torments and madness, tears and sin!
Well—may they live in extacy
Their long eternity of joy;
At least we would not bring them down
With us to weep, with us to groan,
No—Earth would wish no other sphere
To taste her cup of sufferings drear;
She turns from Heaven a cursless eye
And only mourns that *we* must die!
Ah mother, what shall comfort thee
In all this boundless misery?
To cheer our eager eyes a while
We see thee smile, How fondly smile!
But who reads not through that tender glow
Thy deep, unutterable woe?
Indeed no dazzeling land above

86. *Text from A19*
1 tombstones] <pillars> 2 stre<c>tching 10 will] <can> 25 <e>Earth

Can cheat thee of thy childrens love—
We all in life's departing shine
Our last dear longings blend with thine;
And struggle still, and strive to trace
With clouded gaze thy darling face
We would not leave our native home
For *any* world beyond the Tomb
No—rather on thy kindly breast
Let us be laid in lasting rest
Or waken but to share with thee
A mutual immortality—

87

August 17th 1841

Geraldine

'Twas night, her comrades gathered all
Within their city's rocky wall;
When flowers were closed and day was o'er
Their joyous hearts awoke the more

But lonely, in her distant cave
She heard the river's restless wave
Chafeing its banks with dreamy flow;
Music for mirth, and wail for woe—

Palmtrees and cedars towering high
Deepened the gloom of evening's sky
And thick did raven ringlets veil
Her forehead, drooped like lily pale

yet I could hear my lady sing;
I knew she did not mourn,
For never yet from sorrow's spring
Such witching notes were born

Thus poured she in that cavern wild
The voice of feelings warm

87. *Text from B15*

As, bending o'er her beauteous child
She clasped its sleeping form—

"Why sank so soon the summer sun
"From our Zedora's skies?
"I was not tired, my darling one,
"Of gazing in thine eyes—

"Methought the heaven whence thou hast come
"Was lingering there awhile
"And Earth seemed such an alien home
"They did not dare to smile.

"Methought each moment, something strange
"Within their circles shone
"And yet, through every majic change
"They were Brenzaida's own.

"Methought—What thought I not, sweet love?
"My whole heart centered there;
"I breathed not but to send above
"One gush of ardent prayer.

"Bless it, my gracious God! I cried,
"Preserve thy mortal shrine
"For thine own sake, be thou its guide
"And keep it still devine!

"Say, sin shall never blanche that cheek
"Nor suffering charge that brow
"Speak, in thy mercy maker, speak
"And seal it safe from woe!

"Why did I doubt? In God's control
"Our mutual fates remain
"And pure as now, my angel's soul
"*Must* go to heaven again!"

The revellers in the city slept,
my lady, in her woodland bed;
I, whaching o'er her slumber wept
As one who mourns one dead!

42 charge] *or* change 52 one dead] *or* the dead

88

September 1st 1841

Rosina

Weeks of wild delirium past—
Weeks of fevered pain,
Rest from suffering comes at last—
Reason dawns again—

It was a pleasant April day
Declining to the afternoon—
Sunshine upon her pillow lay
As warm as middle June.

It told her how unconsciously
Early Spring had hurried by
"Ah Time has not delayed for me!"
She murmered with a sigh—

"Angora's hills have heard their tread
"The crimson flag is planted there—
"Elderno's waves are rolling red,
"While *I* lie fettered here!

"—Nay, rather, Gondals shaken throne
"Is now secure and free;
"And my King Julius reigns alone,
"Debtless, alas, to me!"

Loud was the sudden gush of woe
From those who whached around;
Rosina turned and sought to know
Why burst that boding sound—

"What then, my dreams are false," she said
"Come maidens, answer me—
"Has Almedore in battle fled?
"Have slaves subdued the free?

"I know it all, he could not bear
"To leave me dying far away—
"He fondly, madly lingered here
"And we have lost the day!

88. *Text from B12*

"But check those coward sobs, and bring
"My robes and smoothe my Tangled hair;
"A noble victory you shall sing
"For every hours dispair!

"When will he come? 'T will soon be night—
"He'll come when evening falls—
"Oh I shall weary for the light
"To leave my lonely halls!"

She turned her pallid face aside
As she would seek repose;
But dark Ambitions thwarted pride
Forbade her lids to close—

And still on all who waited by
Oppressive mystry hung;
And swollen with greif, was every eye
And chained was every tongue—

They wispered nought, but, "Lady, sleep,
"Dear Lady, slumber now!
"Had we not bitter cause to weep
"While you were laid so low?

"And Hope can hardly deck the cheek
"With sudden signs of cheer
"When it has worn through many a week
"The stamp of anguish drear."

Fierce grew Rosina's gloomy gaze
She cried, "Dissemblers, own
"Exina's arms in victory blaze
"Brenzaida's crest is down"

"Well, since it must be told, Lady,
"Brenzaida's crest *is* down
"Brenzaida's sun is set, Lady,
"His empire overthrown!

"He died beneath this palace dome—
"True hearts on every side—
"Among his guards, within his home
"Our glorious monarch died

46 m<i>ystry   57 Fierce] *ed.*; "Fierce

"I saw him fall—I saw the gore
"From his heart's fountain swell
"And, mingling on the marble floor
"His murderers life-blood fell—

"And now, mid northern mountains lone
"His desert grave is made;
"And, Lady, of your love, alone
"Remains a mental shade!"

89

A S to G S *December 19th 1841*

I do not weep, I would not weep;
Our Mother needs no tears:
Dry thine eyes too, 'tis vain to keep
This causless greif for years

What though her brow be changed and cold,
Her sweet eyes closed for ever?
What though the stone—the darksome mould
Our mortal bodies sever?

What though her hand smoothe ne'er again
Those silken locks of thine—
Nor through long hours of future pain
Her kind face o'er thee shine?

Remember still she is not dead
She sees us Gerald now
Laid where her angel spirit fled
Mid heath and frozen snow

And from that world of heavenly light
Will she not always bend,
To guide us in our lifetimes night
And guard us to the end?

Thou knowst she will and well mayst mourn
That we are left below

89. *Text from B28*
5 brow] *or* brows 14 Gerald] Sister *alternative ?by CB*

But not that she can ne'er return
To share our earthly woe—

90

H.A. and A.S. *May 17th 1842*

In the same place, when Nature wore
The same celestial glow;
I'm sure I've seen these forms before
But many Springs ago;

And only *he* had locks of light
And *she* had raven hair;
While now, his curls are dark as night
And hers, as morning, fair.

Besides, I've dreamt of tears whose Traces
Will never more depart
Of agony that fast effaces
The verdure of the heart—

I dreamt, one sunny day like this
In this peerless month of May
I saw her give the unanswered Kiss
As his spirit passed away:

Those young eyes that so sweetly shine
Then looked their last adieu
And pale Death changed that cheek devine
To his unchanging hue

And earth was cast above the breast
That beats so warm and free
Where her soft ringlets lightly rest
And move responsively

Then She, upon the covered grave—
The grass-grown grave did lie—

90. *Text from B37*
11 agony that] <that wild greif wh> 19 And <death> pale Death <blanched>
25 upon] <above>

A tomb not girt by Gondal's wave
Nor arched by Gondal's sky—

The sod was sparkling bright with dew
But brighter still with tears
That welled from mortal greif, I knew
Which never heals with years—

And if he came not for her woe
He would not now return;
He would not leave his sleep below
When she had ceased to mourn—

O Innocence, that cannot live
With heart-wrung anguish long
Dear childhood's Innocence, forgive,
For I have done thee wrong!

The bright rosebuds, those hawthorns shroud
Within their perfumed bower
Have never closed beneath a cloud
Nor bent before a shower—

Had darkness once obscured their sun
Or kind dew turned to rain
No storm-cleared sky that ever shone
Could win such bliss again—

91

July 28th 1842

Had there been falshood in my breast
No thorns had mared my road
This Spirit had not lost its rest
These tears had never flowed

32 Which] <That>   41 The] <Those>

91. *Text from D8*
Date 1842 *or* 1843

92

August 20th 1842
Febuary 6th 1843

Written in Aspin Castle—

How do I love on summer nights
To sit within this Norman door
Whose sombre portal hides the lights
Thickening above me evermore!

How do I love to hear the flow
Of Aspins water murmering low
And hours long listen to the breeze
That sighs in Rockden's waving trees

To night, there is no wind to wake
One ripple on the lonely lake—
To night the clouds subdued and grey
Starlight and moonlight shut away

'Tis calm and still and almost drear
So utter is its solitude;
But still I love to linger here
And form my mood to nature's mood—

There's a wild walk beneath the roaks
Following the bend of Aspins side
'Tis worn by feet of mountain-flocks
That wander down to drink the tide

Never by cliff and gnarled tree
Wound fairy path so sweet to me
Yet of the native shepherds none
In open day and cheerful sun
Will tread its labyrinths alone
Far less, when evening's pensive hour
Hushes the bird and shuts the flower
And gives to Fancy majic power
O'er each familiar tone—

For round their hearths they'll tell the tale
And every listener Swears it true

92. *Text from B8*
14 its] <the>   21 cliff] <glen>   25+ *30–2 copied here and cancelled*

How wanders there a phantom pale
With spirit-eyes of dreamy blue—

It always walks with head declined
Its long curls move not in the wind
Its face is fair—devinely fair;
But brooding on that angel brow
Rests such a shade of deep dispair
As nought devine could ever know

How oft in twilight lingering lone
I've stood to whach that phantom rise
And seen in mist and moonlit stone
Its gleaming hair and solemn eyes

The ancient men in secret say
Tis the first chief of Aspin grey
That haunts his feudal home

But why—around that alien grave
Three thousand miles beyond the wave—
Where his exiled ashes lie
Under the cope of Englands sky—
Doth he not rather roam?

I've seen his picture in the hall;
It hangs upon an eastern wall
And often when the sun declines
That picture like an angel shines—

And when the moonbeam chill and blue
Streams the spectral windows through
That picture's like a spectre too—

The hall is full of portraits rare;
Beuty and mystry mingle there—
At his right hand an infant fair
Looks from its golden frame.

And just like his its ringlets bright
Its large dark eye of shadowy light
Its cheek's pure hue, its forehead white
And like its' noble name—

37 brooding] <lowering> 50 Under] <Beneath>

Daughter devine! and could his gaze
Fall coldly on thy peerless face?
And did he never smile to see
Himself restored to infancy?

Never part back that golden flow
Of curls—and kiss that pearly brow
And feel no other earthly bliss
Was equal to that parent's kiss?

No—turn towards the western side
There stands Sidonia's deity!
In all her glory, all her pride!
And truely like a god she seems

Some god—of wild enthusiast's dreams
And this is she for whom he died!
For whom his spirit unforgiven,
Wanders unsheltered shut from heaven
An out cast for eternity—

Those eyes are dust—those lips are clay—
That form is mouldered all away
Nor thought, nor sense, nor pulse, nor breath
The whole devoured and lost in death!

There is no worm however mean,
That living, is not nobler now
Than she—Lord Alfred's idol queen
So loved—so worshipped long ago—

O come away! the Norman door
Is silvered with a sudden shine—
Come leave these dreams oe'r things of yore
And turn to Nature's face devine—

O'er wood and wold, o'er flood and fell
O'er flashing lake and gleaming dell
The harvest moon looks down

And when heaven smiles with love and light
And earth looks back so dazzeling bright
In such a scene, on such a night
Earths children should not frown—

80 died!] *or* died?   82 unsheltered] <an exile>

93

October 23rd—42—Febuary 6th 1843

Self-Interrogation

The evening passes fast away,
Tis almost time to rest—
What thoughts has left the vanished day?
What feelings—in thy breast?

"The vanished day? it leaves a sense
"Of labour hardly done—
"Of little gained with vast expense—
"—A sense of greif alone—

"Time stands before the door of Death
"Upbraiding bitterly
"And Concience with exhaustless breath
"pours black reproach on me—

"And though I've said that Conscience lies
"And Time should Fate condemn
"Still, sad Repentance clouds my eyes
"And makes me yeild to them—"

Then art thou glad to seek repose?
—Art glad to leave the sea?
And anchor all thy weary woes
In calm Eternity?

Nothing regrets to see thee go—
Not one voice sobs, "farewell"
And where thy heart has suffered so
Canst thou desire to dwell?

"Alas! the countless links are strong
"That bind us to our clay;

93. *Text from A20, with substantive revisions of 1846 (for discussion of MS revisions, see commentary)*
Title 1846; not in A
Alternate lines indented in 1846
Quotation marks open each new stanza, closing at 24, 32, 36, 40, 48 in 1846
3 has] <have> 8 alone—] *ed.*; alone—" *A*; alone! *1846* 13 I've said] *1846*; <I think> I *?*say *A* 15 Still, sad] *1846*; <Yet> still weak *A* my] *1846*; <my> mine *A* 22 sobs] <says> 24 Canst thou desire to] <Say, would'st thou longer>

"The loving spirit lingers long
"And would not pass away—

"And rest is sweet, when laureled fame
"Will crown the soldiers crest;
"But a brave heart with a tarnished name
"Would rather fight, than rest."

Well, thou hast fought for many a year
—Hast fought thy whole life through—
—Hast humbled Falshood—trampled Fear—
What is there left to do?

" 'Tis true—this arm has hotly striven
"Has dared what few would dare
"Much have I done and freely given—
"But little learnt to bear—"

Look on the grave where thou must sleep
Thy last and strongest foe—
It is endurance not to weep
If that repose seem woe

The long war closing in defeat,
Defeat serenely borne—
Thy midnight rest may still be sweet—
And break in glorious morn—

94

Febuary 24th 1843

On the fall of Zalona.

All blue and bright, in glorious light
The morn comes marching on—
And now Zalona's steeples white
Glow golden in the sun—

33 Well, thou] *1846*; Well thou *A* 38 <How flowed this heart's blood dear> 39 done] <dared> 40 But] *1846*; <But> Yet *A* 41 Look] <*?*Long> 43 It is] *1846*; 'Twill be *A* 44 seem] *1846*; be *A* 45 war] *1846*; fight *A* 47 Thy midnight rest] *1846*; Thine eventide *A* (Doubt not *as alternative above*) 48 And break in] *1846*; Thy night, a *A*

94. *Text from B20*

This day might be a festal day;
The streets are crowded all,
And emerald flags stream broad and gay
From turret, tower and wall;

And hark! how music, evermore
Is sounding in the sky;
The deep bells boom—the cannon roar,
The trumpets sound on high—

The deep bells boom, the deep bells clash
Upon the reeling air:
The cannon, with unceasing crash
Make answer far and near—

What do those brazen tongues proclaim?
What joyous fête begun—
What offering to our country's fame—
What noble Victory won?

Go ask that Solitary Sire
Laid in his house alone;
His silent hearth without a fire—
His sons and daughters gone—

Go, ask those children, in the street
Beside their mother's door;
Waiting to hear the lingering feet
That they shall hear no more—

Ask those pale soldiers round the gates
With famine-kindled eye—
They'll say, "Zalona celebrates
The day that she must die!"

The charger, by his manger tied
Has rested many a day;
Yet ere the spur have touched his side,
Behold, he sinks away!

And hungry dogs, with wolf-like cry
UnBuried corpses tear;
While their gaunt masters gaze and sigh
And scearce the feast forbear—

32 die!"] *ed.*; die!

Now, look down from Zalona's wall—
There, war the unwearied foe:
If ranks before our cannon fall,
New ranks, for ever, grow—

And many a week, unbroken thus,
Their troops, our ramparts hem;
And for each man that fights for us
A hundred fight for them!

Courage and Right and Spotless Truth
Were pitched 'gainst traitrous crime
We offered all—our age, our youth—
Our brave men in their prime—

And all have failed! the fervant prayers,
The trust in heavenly aid,
Valour and faith and sealed tears
That would not mourn the dead—

Lips, that did breathe no murmering word;
Hearts, that did ne'er complain
Though vengeance held a sheathed sword
And martyrs bled in vain—

Alas, alas, the Myrtle bowers
By blighting blasts destroyed!
Alas, the Lily's withered flowers
That leave the garden void!

—Unfolds o'er tower, and waves o'er height,
A sheet of crimson sheen—
Is it the setting sun's red light
That stains our standard green?

Heaven help us in this awful hour!
For now might faith decay—
Now might we doubt God's gardian power
And curse, instead of pray—

He will not even let us die—
—Not let us die at home;
The foe must see our soldiers fly
As they had feared the tomb:

53 have] <has>

Because, we *dare* not stay to gain
Those longed for, glorious graves—
We dare not shrink from Slavery's chain
To leave our children Slaves!

But when this scene of awful woe
Has neared its final close
As God forsook our armies, so
May He forsake our foes!

95

April 13th 1843

How Clear She Shines

How clear she shines! How quietly
I lie beneath her gardian light
While Heaven and Earth are wispering me,
"Tomorrow wake—but dream to night"—

Yes—Fancy, come, my fairy love!
These throbbing temples, softly kiss.
And bend my lonely couch above
And bring me rest, and bring me bliss—

The world is going—Dark world adieu!
Grim world, conceal thee till the day;
The heart thou canst not all subdue
Must still resist if thou delay—

Thy love, I will not—will not share
Thy hatred only wakes a smile
Thy greifs may wound—thy wrongs may tear
But oh, thy lies shall ne'er beguile—

While gazing on the stars that glow
Above me in that stormless sea
I long to hope that all the woe
Creation knows, is held in thee!—

84 <h>He

95. *Text from A23, with substantive revisions of 1846*
Title 1846; not in A
Alternate lines indented in 1846
Stanza-breaks only at 8, 12, 20, 28 in 1846
2 gardian] *as alternative above* silver *A*; guardian *1846* 10 conceal] *1846*; go hide *A*
19 hope] <think>

And this shall be my dream to night—
I'll think the heaven of glorious spheres
Is rolling on its course of light
In endless bliss, through endless years—

I'll think, there's not one world above,
Far as these straining eyes can see,
Where Wisdom ever laughed at Love—
Or Virtue crouched to Infamy—

Where—writheing neath the strokes of Fate
The mangled wretch was forced to smile,
To match his patience 'gainst her hate,
His heart rebellious all the while—

Where Pleasure still will lead to wrong
And helpless Reason warn in vain
And Truth is weak, and Treachery strong
And Joy the surest path to pain—

And Peace the lethargy of greif—
And Hope a phantom of the soul—
And Life a labour void and breif—
And Death the despot of the whole—

96

May 1st 1843

To A S. 1830

Where beams the sun the brightest
In the noons of sweet July?
Where falls the snow the lightest
From bleak December's sky?

Where can the weary lay his head
And lay it *safe* the while
In a grave that never shuts its dead

22 the] <that> 30 was] *1846*; <was> is *A* 36 surest] <shortest> 40 whole] *1846*; while A

96. *Text from B26*
6 *safe*] *in sloping letters*

From heavens benignant smile?

Upon the earth in sunlight
Spring grass grows green and fair
But beneath the earth is midnight—
Eternal midnight there!

Then why lament that those we love
Escape Earth's dungeon Tomb?
As if the flowers that blow above
Could charm its undergloom—

From Morning's faintest dawning
Till Evening's deepest shade
Thou wilt not cease thy mourning
To know where she is laid;

But if to weep above her grave
Be such a priceless boon
Go, shed thy tears in Oacen's wave
And they will reach it soon.

Yet midst thy wild repining
Mad though that anguish be
Think heaven on her is shining
Even as it shines on thee—

With thy mind's vision peirce the Deep
Look how she rests below
And tell me, why such blessed sleep
Should cause such bitter woe?

97

E G. to M.R *May 4th 1843*

Thy Guardians are asleep
So I'm come to bid thee rise;
Thou hast a holy vow to keep
Ere yon crescent quit the skies:

Though clouds careering wide
Will hardly let her gleam
She's bright enough to be our guide
Accross the mountain stream.

26 though<t> 29 <d>Deep

97. *Text from B25*

O waken, Dearest, wake!
What means this long delay?
Say, wilt thou not for honour's sake
Chase idle Fears away?

Think not of future greif
Entailed on present joy;
An age of woe were only breif
Its memory to destroy—

And neither Hell nor Heaven
Though both conspire at last
Can take the bliss that has been given—
Can rob us of the past.

Then waken, Mary, wake
How canst thou linger now?
For true love's and Gleneden's sake
Arise and keep thy vow!

98

September 6th 1843

In the earth, the earth thou shalt be laid
A grey stone standing over thee;
Black mould beneath thee spread
And black mould to cover thee—

"Well, there is rest there
"So fast come thy prophecy—
"The time when my sunny hair
"Shall with grass roots twined be"

But cold, cold is that resting place
Shut out from Joy and Liberty
And all who loved thy living face
Will shrink from its gloom and thee

"Not so, *here* the world is chill
"And sworn friends fall from me

12 Fears] <sleep>

98. *Text from B27*
9 <">But

"But *there*, they'll own me still
"And prize my memory"

Farewell then, all that love
All that deep sympathy;
Sleep on, heaven laughs above—
Earth never misses thee

Turf-sod and tombstone drear
Part human company
One heart broke, only, there
That heart was worthy thee!—

99

December 18th 1843

Hope

Hope was but a timid Friend—
She sat without the grated den
Whaching how my fate would tend
Even as selfish-hearted men—

She was cruel in her fear—
Through the bars, one dreary day,
I looked out to see her there
And she turned her face away!

Like a false guard false whach keeping
Still in strife she wispered, peace
She would sing while I was weeping,
If I listened, she would cease—

False she was, and unrelenting,
When my last joys strewed the ground
Even Sorrow saw repenting
Those sad relics scattered round—

Hope—whose wisper would have given
Balm to all my frenzied pain—

99. *Text from A21, with substantive revisions of 1846*
Alternate lines indented in 1846
2 the] <my> 12 If] <When> 18 my] *1846*; that *A*

Stretched her wings and soared to heaven—
Went—and ne'er returned again!

100

Rodric Lesley. 1830 *Dec 18th 1843*

Lie down and rest—the fight is done
Thy comrades to the camp retire;
Gaze not so ernestly upon
The far gleam of the beacon fire.

Listen not to the wind-borne sounds
Of music and of soldiers cheer;
Thou canst not go—unnumbered wounds
Exhaust thy life and hold thee here

Had that hand power to raise the sword
Which since this morn laid hundreds low
Had that tongue strengh to speak the word
That urged thy followers on the foe

Were that warm blood within thy veins
Which now upon the earth is flowing
Splashing its sod with crimson stains
Reddening the pale heath round thee growing

Then Rodric, thou mightst still be Turning
With eager eye and anxious breast
To where those signal lights are burning—
To where thy monarch's legions rest—

But never more—look up and see
The twilight fading from the skies
That last dim beam that sets for thee,
Rodric, for thee shall never rise!

100. *Text from B38*
10 this] <the>

101

M G—For the U.S. *December 19th 1843*

T'was yesterday at early dawn
I whached the falling snow;
A drearier scene on winter morn
Was never streched below.

I could not see the mountains round
But I knew by the wind's wild roar
How every drift in their glens profound
Was deepening ever more—

And then I thought of Ula's bowers
Beyond the Southern Sea
Her tropic prairies bright with flowers
And rivers wandering free—

I thought of many a happy day
Spent in her Eden isle
With my dear comrades young and gay
All scattered now so far away
But not forgot the while!

Who that has breathed that heavenly air
To northern climes would come
To Gondals mists and moorlands drear
And sleet and frozen gloom?

Spring brings the swallow and the Lark
But what will winter bring?
Its twilight noons and evenings dark
To match the gifts of Spring?

No, look with me o'er that sullen main
If thy spirit's eye can see
There are brave ships floating back again
That no calm southern port could chain
From Gondal's stormy sea

O how the hearts of the voyagers beat
To feel the frost-wind blow!

101. *Text from B29*
16 scattered] <taken> 23 will] <can>

What flower in Ula's gardens sweet
Is worth one flake of snow?

The blast which almost rends their sail
Is welcome as a friend;
It brings them home, that thundering gale
Home to their journy's end;

Home to our souls whose wearying sighs
lament their absence drear
And feel how bright even winter skies
Would shine if they were here!

102

A S castle wood *Febuary 2 1844*

The day is done—the winter sun
Is setting in its sullen sky
And drear the course that as been run
And dim the beams that slowly die

No star will light my coming night
No moon of hope for me will shine
I mourn not heaven would blast my sight
And I never longed for harp devine

Through Life hard Task I did not ask
Celestial aid celestial cheer
I saw my fate without its mask
And met it too without a tear

The greif that prest my dreary breast
Was heavier far than Earth can be
And who would dread eternal rest
When labours hire was agony

102. *Text from E20*

1 The day] <My task> 4 dim] <cold> beams] <beams> <*?*rays> 5 will light my coming] <shall light the approaching> 6 for me will] <must ever> 7 I . . . blast] <Well> <But heaven would only take> 8 And] *in l.h. margin* never longed] <had no love> harp] *unclear* <joys> 11 my fate] <the earth> without its] *deleted in error* 12 it too] <my fate> 13 my dreary] <this dying> 14 Earth] <Clay> 15 would] <can> 16 When . . . was] <Worn down with ——> hire] <wage>

Dark falls the fear of this dispair
On hearts that drink of happiness
But I was brede the mate of care
The foster child of sore distress

No sighs for me no symathy
No wish to keep my soul below
The heart is dead since infancy
Unwept for let the body go

103

Febuary 10th 1844

My Comforter

Well hast thou spoken—and yet not taught
A feeling strange or new—
Thou hast but roused a latent thought,
A cloud-closed beam of sunshine brought
To gleam in open view—

Deep down—concealed within my soul
That light lies hid from men.
Yet glows unquenched—though shadows roll,
Its gentle ray can not control,
—About the sullen den—

Was I not vexed, in these gloomy ways
To walk alone so long?
Around me, wretches uttering praise
Or howling o'er their hopless days—
And each with Frenzy's tongue—

A Brotherhood of misery,
Their smiles as sad as sighs—
Whose madness daily maddened me,

17 fear] <glare> 18 <On dying hearts <<that>> with pleasure glad>; On hearts that <happiness can> drink of happiness (spirits born akin *as alternative*) 19 was brede] <have been> 20 sore] <*?*lone> 23 is] <was> 24 <Unmourned the body well may go>

103. *Text from A22, with substantive revisions of 1846*
Second and last line of each stanza indented in 1846
6 soul] <heart *or* breast> 9 ray] <light> 12] alone] *1846*; unlit *A* 17 Their] <With> 18 <Their madness daily maddening me>

Distorting into agony
The Bliss before my eyes—

So stood I—in Heavens glorious sun
And in the glare of Hell
My spirit drank a mingled tone
Of seraph's song and demon's moan,
—What my soul bore, my soul alone
Within its self may tell—

Like a soft air above a sea
tossed by the tempest's stir—
A thaw-wind, melting quietly
The snowdrift on some wintery lea
—No—what sweet thing resembles thee,
My thoughtful Comforter?

And yet a little longer speak
Calm this resentful mood
And while the savage heart grows meek,
For other token do not seek,
But let the tear upon my cheek
Evince my gratitude—

104

A.G.A. to A.S. *March 2d 1844*

This summer wind, with thee and me
Roams in the dawn of day;
But thou must be, where it shall be,
Ere Evening—far away—

The farewell's echo from thy soul
Should not depart, before
Hills rise and distant rivers roll
Between us evermore—

19 Distorting] *1846*; <And> Turning *A* (Distorting *as alternative above*) 24 moan] *1846*; <moan> ~ groan *A* 25 my . . . my] <the . . . the> 27 air above] <zephyre o'er> 28 tossed] <Vexed> 31 resembles] *1846*; can match with *A*

104. *Text from B5*
6 depart] <be gone>

I know that I have done thee wrong—
Have wronged both thee and Heaven—
And I may mourn my life time long
Yet may not be forgiven—

Repentant tears will vainly fall
To cancel deeds untrue;
But for no grief can I recall
The dreary word—Adieu—

Yet thou a future peace shalt win
Because thy soul is clear;
And I—who had the heart to sin
Will find a heart to bear—

Till far beyond earth's frenzied strife
That makes destruction joy
Thy perished faith shall spring to life
And my remorse shall die

105

March 5th 1844

A Day Dream

On a sunny brae alone I lay
One summer afternoon;
It was the marriage-time of May
With her young lover, June.

From her Mothers heart seemed loath to part
That queen of bridal charms;
But her Father smiled on the fairest child
He ever held in his arms

The Trees did wave their plumy crests,
The glad birds caroled clear
And I, of all the wedding guests,
Was only sullen there—

11 may] <might> 12 may] <could> 13 will] <would> 15 But for no grief] <Yet not for that> 17 Yet] <But> 19 And] <While> 21–4 *interlined with* <Yet ?Justice may grow tired of pouring | Her ?vials of wrath or woe | < <But> > And I'll not weary of enduring | My self cannot destroy>

105. *Text from A24, with substantive revisions of 1846*
Alternate lines indented in 1846

There was not one but wished to shun
My aspect void of cheer
The very grey roaks looking on
Asked, "what do you do here?"

And I could utter no reply—
In sooth I did not know
Why I had brought a clouded eye
To greet the general glow,—

So resting on a heathy bank
I took my heart to me
And we together sadly sank
Into a reverie

We thought—"When winter comes again
Where will these bright things be?
All vanished like a vision vain—
An unreal mockery!

The birds that now so blithly sing—
Through desarts frozen dry,
Poor Spectres of the perished Spring
In famished troops will fly

And why should we be glad at all?
The leaf is hardly green
Before a token of its fall
Is on the surface seen—"

Now whether it were really so
I never could be sure—
But as in fit of peevish woe
I stretched me on the moor

A thousand thousand gleaming fires
Seemed kindling in the air—
A thousand thousand silvery lyres
Resounded far and near

Methought the very breath I breathed
Was full of sparks devine

24 rever<y>ie 26 things] <hopes> 35 its] *1846*; the *A* 36 the] *1846*; its *A* 37 were] <was> 41 gleaming] *1846*; glancing *A* 44 far and near] <every where>

And all my heather couch was wreathed
By that celestial shine,—

And while the wide Earth echoeing rung
To their strange minstrelsy
The little glittering spirits sung
Or seemed to sing to me—

"O mortal, mortal, let them die—
"Let Time and Tears destroy
"That we may overflow the sky
"With universal joy—

"Let Greif distract the sufferer's brest
"And Night obscure his way
"They hasten him to endless rest
"And everlasting day

"To Thee the world is like a tomb—
"A desert's naked shore
"To us—in unimagined bloom
"It brightens more and more.

"And could we lift the veil and give
"One breif glimpse to thine eye
"Thou wouldst rejoice for those that live
"*Because* they live to die"—

The music ceased—the noon day Dream
Like dream of night withdrew
But Fancy still will sometimes deem
Her fond creation true—

106

E.W. to A.G.A. *March 11th 1844*

How few, of all the hearts that loved,
are greiveing for thee now!

49 rung] *1846*; rang *A* 51 sung] *1846*; sang *A* 60 everlasting] <?to ?eternal> 68 *Because*] *1846*; Because *A*

106. *Text from B23*
Title On a life perverted *added by ?CB*
2 greiveing] <mourning>

And why should mine, to night, be moved
With such a sense of woe?

Too often, thus, when left alone
Where none my thoughts can see,
Comes back a word, a passing tone
From thy strange history—

Sometimes I seem to see thee rise
A glorious child again—
All virtues beaming from thine eyes
That ever honoured men—

Courage and Truth, a generous breast
Where Love and Gladness lay;
A being whose very Memory blest
And made the mourner gay—

O, fairly spread thy early sail
And fresh and pure and free
Was the first impulse of the gale
That urged life's wave for thee!

Why did the pilot, too confiding
Dream oe'r that Oacens foam?
And trust in Pleasure's careless guiding
To bring his vessel home?

For, well, he knew what dangers frowned,
What mists would gather dim,
What roaks and shelves and sands lay round
Between his port and him—

The very brightness of the sun,
The splendor of the main,
The wind that bore him wildly on
Should not have warned in vain

An anxious gazer from the shore,
I marked the whitening wave
And wept above thy fate the more
Because I could not save—

14 Where] <?That> 15 Memory] <presence> 20 urged] <drove> 21 too] <so> 23 careless] <?heedless> 31 bore] <urged> 35 wept] <greived>

It recks not now, when all is over,
But, yet my heart will be
A mourner still, though freind and lover
Have both forgotten thee!

107

E W *May 1st 1844*

Song

The linnet in the rocky dells,
The moorlark in the air,
The bee among the heather bells
That hide my lady fair—

The wilddeer brouze above her breast;
The wildbirds raise their brood,
And they, her smiles of love carest,
Have left her solitude!

I ween, that when the graves dark wall
Did first her form retain
They thought their hearts could ne'er recall
The light of joy again—

They thought the tide of greif would flow
Unchecked through future years
But where is all their anguish now,
And where are all their tears?

Well, let them fight for Honour's breath
Or Pleasure's shade persue—
The Dweller in the land of Death
Is changed and carless too—

And if their eyes should whach and weep
Till sorrows' Source were dry
She would not in her tranquil sleep
Return a single Sigh—

107. *Text from B30, with substantive revisions of 1846*
Title 1846; not in B
E W *not in 1846*
Alternate lines indented in 1846
19 Dweller<s> 20 Is] <Are>

Blow, West wind, by the lonely mound
And murmer, Summer streams;
There is no need of other sound
To soothe my Lady's dreams—

108

September 3d 1844

To Imagination

When weary with the long day's care
And earthly change from pain to pain
And lost and ready to dispair
Thy kind voice calls me back again—
O my true friend, I am not lone
While thou canst speak with such a tone!

So hopeless is the world without
The world within I doubly prize
Thy world, where guile and hate and doubt
And cold suspicion never rise—
Where thou and I and Liberty
Have undisputed soveriegnty.

What matters it that all around
Danger and guilt and darkness lie
If but within our bosom's bound
We hold a bright untroubled sky
Warm with ten thousand mingled rays
Of suns that know no winter days—

Reason indeed may oft complain
For Nature's sad reality
And tell the suffering heart how vain
Its cherished dreams must always be
And Truth may rudely trample down
The flowers of fancy newly blown

108. *Text from A25, with substantive revisions of 1846*
Second and fourth line of each stanza indented in 1846
12 Have] <?Hold>   14 guilt] *1846*; greif *A*   16 untroubled] *1846*; unsullied *A*
21 tell] <teach>

But thou art ever there to bring
The hovering vision back and breathe
New glories oe'r the blighted Spring
And call a lovlier life from death
And whisper with a voice divine
Of real worlds as bright as thine

I trust not to thy phantom bliss
Yet still, in evening's quiet hour
With Never failing thankfulness
I welcome thee benignant power
Sure Solacer of human cares
And sweeter hope when hope dispairs—

109

D G C. to J.A. *October 2d 1844*

Come, the wind may never again
Blow as now it blows for us
And the stars may never again, shine as now, they shine;
Long before October returns
Seas of blood will have parted us
And you must crush the love in your heart and I, the love in mine!

For face to face will our Kindred stand
And as they are so we shall be
Forgetting how the same sweet earth has borne and nourished all—
One must fight for the people's power
And one for the rights of Royalty
And each be ready to give his life to work the other's fall—

The chance of war we cannot shun
Nor would we shrink from our father's cause
Nor dread Death more because the hand that gives it may be dear
We must bear to see Ambition rule

30 real] <other> 33 failing] <dying> 34 I] <A> 36 sweeter] *1846*; brighter *A*

109. *Text from B33*
6 heart | And

Over Love, with his iron laws;
Must yield our blood for a stranger's sake and refuse
ourselves a tear!

So, the wind may never again
Blow as now it blows for us
And the stars may never again shine as now they shine
Next October, the cannon's roar
From hostile ranks may be urging us—
Me to strike for your life's blood and you to strike for mine—

110

October 14th 1844

Plead for Me

O, thy bright eyes must answer now,
When Reason, with a scornful brow,
Is mocking at my overthrow;
O, thy sweet tongue must plead for me
And tell why I have chosen thee!

Stern Reason is to judgement come
Arrayed in all her forms of gloom;
Wilt thou my advocate be dumb?
No radiant angel, speak and say
Why I did cast the world away:

Why I have persevered to shun
The common paths that others run
And on a strange road journeyed on;
Heedless alike of Wealth and Power—
Of Glory's wreath and Pleasure's flower—

These once indeed seemed Beings devine
And they perchance heard vows of mine
And saw my offerings on their shrine—
But, careless gifts are seldom prized
And *mine* were worthily despised;

110. *Text from A26, with substantive revisions of 1846*
Title see commentary
10 did] <have> 16 Beings] <things> 20 *mine*] *1846*; mine *A*

So with a ready heart I swore
To seek their alter stone no more
And gave my spirit to adore
Thee, ever present, phantom thing,
My Slave, my Comrade and my King!

A Slave because I rule thee still
Incline thee to my changeful will
And make thy influence good or ill—
A Comrade—for by day and night
Thou art my intimate Delight—

My Darling Pain that wounds and sears
And wrings a blessing out from tears
By deadening me to earthly cares;
And yet a King—though prudence well
Have taught thy subject to rebel—

And am I wrong, to worship where
Faith cannot doubt, nor Hope dispair,
Since my own soul can grant my prayer?
Speak God of Visions, plead for me,
And tell why I have chosen thee!

III

I.M. to I G. *November 6th 1844*

Faith and Despondency

"The winter wind is loud and wild
"Come close to me my darling child!
"Forsake thy books and matless play
"And while the night is gathering grey
"We'll talk its pensive hours away—

21 ready] <willing> 33 earthly] *1846*; real *A* 34 a] <my>

III. *Text from B34, with substantive revisions and paragraph breaks of 1846*
I.M. to I G.] *not in 1846*
Title 1846; *not in B*
First line of each paragraph (apart from the first) indented in 1846
Indentation also at 56, 58, 64, 66, 68, 70 in 1846
Quotation marks open each paragraph, closing at 24, 62, 70 in 1846
Paragraph-breaks after 5, 9, 13, 17, 24, 27, 37, 44, 52, 62, 66 in B
4 gathering] *1846*; closing *B*

"Iernë, round our sheltered Hall
"November's gusts unheeded call
"Not one faint breath can enter here
"Enough to wave my daughter's hair.
"And I am glad to whach the blaze
"Glance from her eyes with mimic rays;
"To feel her cheek so softly pressed
"In happy quiet on my breast;

"But yet, even this tranquility
"Brings bitter, restless thoughts to me
"And in the red fire's cheerful glow
"I think of deep glens blocked with snow

"I dream of moor and misty hill
"Where evening closes dark and chill,
"For, lone among the mountains cold
"Lie those that I have loved of old
"And my heart aches in hopeless pain
"Exhausted with repinings vain
"That I shall greet them ne'er again!"

"Father, in early infancy
"When you were far beyond the sea
"Such Thoughts were tyrants over me—
"I often sat for hours together
"Through the long nights of angry weather
"Raised on my pillow to descry
"The dim moon struggling in the sky
"Or with strained ear to catch the shock
"Of roak with wave and wave with roak;
"So would I fearful vigil keep
"And, all for listening, never sleep;
"But this world's life has much to dread
"Not so, my father with the Dead.

"O, not for them should we dispair
"The grave is drear but they are not there;
"Their dust is mingled with the sod
"Their happy souls are gone to God!

7 gusts] *1846*; blasts *B* 8 faint] *1846*; fair *B* 19 closes] *1846*; gathers *B* 22 hopeless] *1846*; speechless *B* 24 greet] *1846*; see *B* 30 pillow] *1846*; ?pillows *B* 34 fearful] *1846*; fearful *or* tearful *B*

"You told me this, and yet you sigh
"And murmer that your friends must die
"Ah my dear father, tell me why?

"For if your former words were true
"How usless would such sorrow be!
"As wise to mourn the seed which grew
"Unnoticed on its parent tree

"Because it fell in fertile earth
"And sprang up to a glorious birth—
"Struck deep its root and lifted high
"Its green boughs in the breezy sky!

"But I'll not fear—I will not weep
"For those whose bodies rest in sleep:
"I know there is a blessed shore
"Opening its ports for me and mine
"And, gazing Time's wide waters oe'r
"I weary for that land devine
"Where we were born—where you and I
"Shall meet our Dearest when we die;
"From suffering and corruption free
"Restored into the Deity"—

Well hast thou spoken, sweet, trustful child!
And wiser than thy sire;
And worldly tempests, raging wild,
Shall strengthen thy desire—

Thy fervant hope, through storm and foam,
Through wind and Oacen's roar
To reach at last, the eternal home—
The steadfast, changless shore!—

112

From a Dungeon Wall in the Southern College— *Nov 11th 1844*
J B Sept. 1825

"Listen! when your hair like mine
"Takes a tint of silver grey,

51 root] *1846*; roots *B* 54 rest in sleep] *1846*; lie asleep *B* 60 <d>Dearest
65 worldly] *1846*; coming *B*

112. *Text from B31*

"When your eyes, with dimmer shine,
"Whach life's bubbles float away,

"When you, young man, have borne like me
"The weary weight of sixty three
"Then shall penance sore be paid
"For these hours so wildly squandered
"And the words that now fall dead
"On your ears be deeply pondered
"pondered and approved at last
"But their virtue will be past!

"Glorious is the prize of Duty
"Though she be a serious power
"Treacherous all the lures of Beauty
"Thorny bud and poisonous flower!

"Mirth is but a mad beguiling
"Of the golden gifted Time—
"Love—a demon meteor wiling
"Heedless feet to gulfs of crime—

"Those who follow earthly pleasure
"Heavenly knowledge will not lead
"Wisdom hides from them her treasure,
"Virtue bids them evil speed!

"Vainly may their hearts, repenting,
"Seek for aid in future years—
"Wisdom scorned knows no relenting—
"Virtue is not won by tears

"Fain would we your steps reclaim
"Waken fear and holy shame
"And to this end, our council well
"And kindly doomed you to a cell
"Whose darkness, may perchance, disclose
"A beacon-guide from sterner woes—"

So spake my Judge—then seized his lamp
And left me in the dungeon damp.
A vault-like place whose stagnant air
Suggests and nourishes dispair!

Rosina, this had never been
Except for you, my despot queen
Except for you the billowy sea
Would now be tossing under me
The winds' wild voice my bosom thrill
And my glad heart bound wilder still

Flying before the rapid gale
Those wonderous southern isles to hail
Which wait for my companions free
But thank your passion—not for me!

You know too well—and so do I
Your haughty beauty's soveriegnty
Yet have I read those falcon eyes—
Have dived into their mysteries—
Have studied long their glance and feel
It is not love those eyes reveal—

They Flash—they burn with lightening shine
But not with such fond fire as mine;
The tender star fades faint and wan
Before Ambition's scorching sun—
So deem I now—and Time will prove
If I have wronged Rosina's love—

113

M Douglas to E. R. Gleneden *November 21st 1844*

Honour's Martyr

The moon is full this winter night;
The stars are clear, though few
And every window glistens bright
With leaves of frozen dew—

The Sweet moon through your lattice gleams
And lights your room like day

40 queen<!> 50 beaut<i>y's

113. *Text from B35, with substantive revisions of 1846*
M Douglas to E. R. Gleneden] *not in 1846*
Title 1846; *not in B*
Alternate lines indented in 1846

And, there, you pass in happy dreams
The peaceful hours away;

While I, with effort hardly quelling
The anguish in my breast
Wander about the silent dwelling
And cannot think of rest.

The old clock in the gloomy hall
Ticks on from hour to hour
And every time, its measured call
Seems lingering slow and slower

And O how slow that keen-eyed star
Has tracked the chilly grey!
What whaching yet, how very far
The morning lies away!

Without your chamber door I stand
Love, are you slumbering still?
My cold heart underneath my hand
Has almost ceased to thrill

Bleak, bleak the east wind sobs and sighs
And drowns the turret bell
Whose sad note undistinguished, dies,
Unheard, like my farewell.

Tomorrow Scorn will blight my name
And Hate will trample me—
Will load me with a coward's shame
A Traitor's perjury!

False Friends will launch their covert sneers—
True Friends will wish me dead;
And I shall cause the bitterest tears
That you have ever shed!

The dark deeds of my out-lawed race
Will then like virtues shine;
And men will pardon their disgrace
Beside the guilt of mine;

19 yet, how] *B*; yet! how *1846* 21 Without] *1846*; Beside *B* 29 name] *1846*; <n>fame *B* 33 covert] *1846*; venomed *B*

For who forgives the accursed crime
Of dastard Treachery?
Rebellion in its chosen time
May Freedom's champion be—

Revenge may stain a righteous sword
It may be just to slay;
But, Traitor—Traitor—From *that* word
All true breasts shrink away!

O, I would give my heart to death
To keep my Honour Fair,
Yet I'll not give my inward faith
My Honour's *name* to spare.

Not even to keep your priceless love
Dare I, Beloved, deceive;
This treason should the Future prove
Gleneden, then believe!

I know the path I ought to go,
I follow fearlessly;
Enquiring not what deeper woe
Stern Duty stores for me—

So, Foes persue, and cold allies
Mistrust me, every one;
Let me be false in others' eyes
If faithful in my own—

114

From a D.W. in the N C. A G A. Sept. 1826. *Dec 2d 1844*

A Death-Scene

"O Day, He cannot die
"When thou so fair art shining.

47 *that*] *1846*; that *B* 52 *name*] *1846*; name *B* 56 Gleneden,] *B*; Then, only *1846*

114. *Text from B32, with substantive revisions of 1846* (*but see commentary*)
From a D.W. . . . 1826] *not in 1846*
Title 1846; *not in B*
Quotation marks open at 1 and close at 28 in 1846
2 When] <While>

"O sun, in such a glorious sky
"So tranquilly declining,

"He cannot leave thee now
"While fresh West winds are blowing
"And all around his youthful brow
"Thy cheerful light is glowing!

"Elbë awake, awake!
"The golden evening gleams
"Warm and bright on Elnor's lake.
"Arouse thee from thy dreams!

"Beside thee, on my knee
"My dearest friend, I pray
"That thou—to cross the eternal sea
"Wouldst yet—*one* hour delay!

"I hear its billows roar
"I see them foaming high
"But no glimpse of a further shore
"Has blessed my straining eye—

"Believe not what they urge
"Of Eden isles beyond
"Turn back from that tempestuous surge
"To thy own native land!

"It is not Death, but pain
"That struggles in thy breast
"Nay rally Elbë, rouse again
"I cannot let thee rest!"

One long look that sore reproved me
For the woe I could not bear—
One mute look of suffering moved me
To repent my usless prayer;

And with sudden check the heaving
Of distraction passed away;

3 glorious] <tranquil> 4 tranquilly] <gloriously> 9 Elbë] Edward *1846* 11 Warm] <*?* Clear> Elnor's] *ed.*; <?Elnor's> *?* Arden's *B*; Arden's *1846*; *see commentary* 13 *1846*; <Beside thee, on> <upon> my <bended> knee *B* 14 dearest] <own dear> 16 Wouldst] <Would> 22 Eden isles] <land> <port that lies> 24 own] <blest> <loved> 27 Nay] <Oh,> Elbë] <Dearest> *B*; Edward *1846* 33 And] <Then> 34 passed] <sank>

Not a sign of further greiving
Stirred my soul that aweful day

Paled at length the sweet sun setting
Sunk to peace the twilight breeze
Summer dews fell softly wetting
glen and glade and silent trees

Then his eyes began to weary
Weighed beneath a mortal sleep
And their orbs grew strangely dreary—
Clouded, even as they would weep

But they wept not, but they changed not—
Never moved and never closed—
Troubled still and still they ranged not
Wandered not nor yet reposed!

So I knew that he was dying,
Stooped and raised his languid head—
Felt no breath and heard no sighing—
So, I knew that he was dead—

115

Febuary 3d 1845

The Philosopher

"Enough of Thought, Philosopher,
Too long hast thou been dreaming
Unlightened, in this chamber drear
While summer's sun is beaming—

37–40 *interlined with* <Down behind the <<——>> gentle mountain | Sank the fervant sun of June | And above the moorland mounting | Slowly rose a <<cloudless>> golden moon> 37 length the] *1846*; last that *B* 38 Sunk] *1846*; sank *B* peace] <rest> twilight] <growing> 40 <misty glen and <<silent>> mountain bare> 41 began to] <grew weary,> 42 <Heavy with unearthly sleep> 43 orbs] *1846*; light *B* grew strangely] <was strange and>

115. *Text from A27, with substantive revisions of 1846*
Title 1846; The Philosopher's Conclusion *A*
Quotation marks open at 1–14, 27–40, and close at 14, 40 in B; *open at 1, 7, 15, 27, 41, and close at 14, 26, 40, 56 in 1846*
Indentation at 2, 4, 7–14, and alternate lines from 16 in 1846
No stanza-breaks at 10, 18, 22, 30, 44, 48, 52 in 1846
3 this] <thy>

Space-sweeping soul, what sad refrain
Concludes thy musings once again?"

"*O for the time when I shall sleep*
Without identity—
And never care how rain may steep
Or snow may cover me!

No promised Heaven, these wild Desires
Could all or half fulfill—
No threatened Hell—with quenchless fires
Subdue this quenchless will!

—So said I and still say the same,—
—Still to my Death will say—
Three Gods within this little frame
Are warring night and day—

Heaven could not hold them all, and yet
They all are held in me
And must be mine till I forget
My present entity—

O, for the time, when in my breast
Their struggles will be oe'r—
O for the day when I shall rest
And never suffer more!"

"I saw a Spirit standing, Man,
"Where thou dost stand—an hour ago,
"And round his feet, three rivers ran
"Of equal depth and equal flow—

"A Golden Stream, and one like blood
"and one like Sapphire, seemed to be
"But where they joined their triple flood
"It tumbled in an inky sea—

"The Spirit sent his dazzeling gaze
"Down through that Ocean's gloomy night
"Then—kindling all with sudden blaze

6 again?"] *ed.*; again? *A*, *1846* 7–14 *no italics in 1846* 11 <*d*>*Desires* 14 *will!*] *ed.*; *will!*" *A*; will!" *1846* 15 said I] *1846*; <said he> say I *A* 26 suffer] <waken> 28 dost] *1846*; doest *A* 31 <A>and 35 sent] *1846*; bent *A* 36 through] *1846*; on *A* night] <*?*tide> 37 kindling] <lighting>

"The Glad deep sparkled wide and bright
"White as the sun far, far more fair
"Than its devided sources were!"

"—And even for that Spirit, Seer,
Ive whached and sought my life time long
Sought Him in Heaven, Hell, Earth and Air
An endless search—and always wrong!

Had I but seen his glorious eye
Once light the clouds that wilder me,
I ne'er had raised this coward cry
To cease to think and cease to be—

I neer had called oblivion blest
Nor stretching eager hands to Death
Implored to change for senseless rest
This sentient soul, this living breath

O let me die that Power and Will
Their cruel strife may close
And conquered Good and conquering Ill
Be lost in one repose"

116

R Alcona to J Brenzaida. *March 3d 1845*

Remembrance

Cold in the earth and the deep snow piled above thee!
Far, far removed cold in the dreary grave!
Have I forgot, my Only Love, to love thee,
Severed at last by Time's all-severing wave?

Now, when alone, do my thoughts no longer hover
Over the mountains on Angora's shore:

38 <g>Glad deep] <waves> wide and bright] <far and wide> 40 its] <their> 51 Implored to change] <Offered to give> senseless] *1846*; <sensless *or* sunless> lifeless *A* 52+ <O for the lid that cannot weep— | The Breast that needs no breath— | The tomb that brings eternal sleep | —For Life's Deliverer, Death!> 53 O] <But> 54 strife] <*?*war> 55 conquered] *1846*; vanquished *A* and conquering] *1846*; victorious *A*

116. *Text from B36, with substantive revisions of 1846* (*but see commentary*)
R Alcona to J Brenzaida.] *not in 1846*
Title 1846; *not in B*
4 all-severing] *1846*; allwearing *B* 6 Angora's] *B*; that northern *1846*

Resting their wings where heath and firn-leaves cover
Thy noble heart for ever, ever more?

Cold in the earth, and fifteen wild Decembers
From those brown hills have melted into spring—
Faithful indeed is the spirit that remembers
After such years of change and suffering!

Sweet Love of youth, forgive if I forget thee
While the World's tide is bearing me along
Other desires and other Hopes beset me
Hopes which obscure but cannot do thee wrong—

No later light has lightened up my heaven:
No second morn has ever shone for me
All my life's bliss from thy dear life was given—
All my life's bliss is in the grave with thee

But when the days of golden dreams had perished
And even Dispair was powerless to destroy
Then did I learn how exsistance could be cherished
Strengthened and fed without the aid of joy

Then did I check the tears of usless passion,
Weaned my young soul from yearning after thine;
Sternly denied its burning wish to hasten
Down to that tomb already more than mine!

And even yet, I dare not let it languish,
Dare not indulge in Memory's rapturous pain
Once drinking deep of that devinest anguish
How could I seek the empty world again?

117

April 10th 1845

Death

Death, that struck when I was most confiding
In my certain Faith of Joy to be;

8 Thy] *1846*; <Thy> That *B* 15 Other] *1846*; Sterner *B* other] *1846*; darker *B* 17 later light] *1846*; other sun *B* 18 second morn] *1846*; other star *B* 20 thee] *1846*; me *B* 31 devinest] <delightful>

117. *Text from A29, with substantive revisions of 1846*
Title 1846; not in A

Strike again, Time's whithered branch deviding
From the fresh root of Eternity!

Leaves, upon Time's branch, were growing brightly
Full of sap and Full of silver dew;
Birds, beneath its shelter, gathered nightly;
Daily, round its flowers, the wild bees flew—

Sorrow passed and plucked the golden blossom;
Guilt stripped off the foliage in its pride;
But, within its parents kindly bosom
Flowed forever Life's restoring tide—

Little mourned I for the parted Gladness,
For the vacant nest and silent song;
Hope was there and laughed me out of sadness,
Whispering, "Winter will not linger long."

And behold, with tenfold increase blessing
Spring adorned the beauty-burdened Spray;
Wind and rain and fervant heat caressing
Lavished glory on that second May—

High it rose; no winged greif could sweep it;
Sin was scared to distance with its shine:
Love and its own life had power to keep it
From all wrong, from every blight but thine!

Cruel Death, the young leaves droop and languish!
Evenings gentle air may still restore—
No, the morning sunshine mocks my anguish—
Time for me must never blossom more!

Strike it down—that other boughs may flourish
Where that perished sapling used to be;
Thus at least, its mouldering corpse will nourish
That from which it sprung—Eternity—

20 that] *1846*; its *A*   23 it<'>s   25 Cruel] <Heartless>   31 will] <may>

118

April 14th 1845

Stars

Ah! why, because the dazzeling sun
Restord our earth to joy
Have you departed, every one,
And left a desert sky?

All through the night, your glorious eyes
Were gazing down in mine
And with a full hearts thankful sighs
I blessed that whach devine!

I was at peace—and drank your beams
As they were life to me
And revelled in my changeful dreams
Like petrel on the sea—

Thought followed thought—star followed star
Through boundless regions on
While one sweet influence, near and far,
Thrilled through and proved us one.

Why did the morning dawn to break
So great, so pure a spell,
And scorch with fire the tranquil cheek
Where your cool radiance fell?

Blood-red he rose, and arrow-straight
His fierce beams struck my brow
The soul of Nature sprang elate,
But *mine* sank sad and low!

My lids closed down—yet through their veil
I saw him blazing still;
And steep in gold the misty dale
And flash upon the hill—

118. *Text from A28, with substantive revisions of 1846*
Title 1846; unclear in A
Alternate lines indented in 1846
2 our] *1846*; <th>my *A* 17 dawn] *1846*; rise *A* 23 <n>Nature 24 *mine*] *1846*; mine *A* 27 steep] *1846*; bathe *A*

I turned me to the pillow then
To call back Night, and see
Your worlds of solemn light again
Throb with my heart and me!

It would not do—the pillow glowed
And glowed both roof and floor
And birds sang loudly in the wood
And fresh winds shook the door.

The curtains waved, the wakened flies
Were murmering round my room
Imprisoned there, till I should rise
And give them leave to roam—

O, Stars and Dreams and Gentle Night—
O, Night and Stars return!
And hide me from the hostile light
That does not warm, but burn—

That drains the blood of suffering men—
Drinks tears, instead of dew—
Let me sleep through his blinding reign
And only wake with you!

119

April 22d 1845

A thousand sounds of happiness
And only one of real distress;
One hardly uttered groan—
But that has hushed all vocal joy,
Eclipsed the glory of the sky
And made me think that misery
Rules in our world alone!

About his face the sunshine glows
And in his hair the south wind blows
And violet and wild woodrose
Are sweetly breathing near

41 <d>Dreams

119. *Text from B39*
4 hushed] <quenched>

Nothing without suggests dismay
If he could force his mind away
From tracking farther day by day
The desert of Dispair—

Too truely agonized to weep
His eyes are motionless as sleep,
His frequent sighs longdrawn and deep
Are anguish to my ear
And I would soothe—but can I call
The cold corpse from its funeral pall
And cause a gleam of hope to fall
With my consoling tear?

O, Death, so many spirits driven
Through this false world, their all had given
To win the everlasting haven
To sufferers so devine—
Why didst thou smite the loved the blest
The ardent and the happy breast
That full of Life desired not rest
And shrank appalled from thine?

At least, since thou wilt not restore
In mercy launch one arrow more
Life's conscious Death it wearies sore
It tortures worse than thee—
Enough of storms have bowed his head,
Grant him at last a quiet bed
Beside his early stricken Dead—
Even where he yearns to be!

120a

A.E. and R.C. *May 28th 1845*

Heavy hangs the raindrop
From the burdened spray;

24 spirits] <wanderers> 25 all] <life> 30 Life] <hope> 37 last] <length>

120a. *Text from B40*
1 raindrop <from>

Heavy broods the damp mist
On Uplands far away;

Heavy looms the dull sky,
Heavy rolls the sea—
And heavy beats the young heart
Beneath that lonely Tree—

Never has a blue streak
Cleft the clouds since morn—
Never has his grim Fate
Smiled since he was born—

Frowning on the infant,
Shadowing childhood's joy;
Gardian angel knows not
That melancholy boy.

Day is passing swiftly
Its sad and sombre prime;
Youth is fast invading
Sterner manhood's time—

All the flowers are praying
For sun before they close
And he prays too, unknowing,
That sunless human rose!

Blossems, that the westwind
Has never wooed to blow
Scentless are your petals,
Your dew as cold as snow—

Soul, where kindred kindness
No early promise woke
Barren is your beauty
As weed upon the roak—

Wither, Brothers, wither,
You were vainly given—
Earth reserves no blessing
For the unblessed of Heaven!

6 <And h>Heavy   18 sombre] <sunless>   25 Blossems] Blossem *?CB's revision*

120b

Child of Delight! with sunbright hair
And seablue, sea-deep eyes
Spirit of Bliss, what brings thee here
Beneath these sullen skies?

Thou shouldest live in eternal spring
Where endless day is never dim
Why, seraph, has thy erring wing
Borne thee down to weep with him?

"Ah, not from heaven am I decended
"And I do not come to mingle tears
"But sweet is day though with shadows blended
"And though clouded, sweet are youthful years—

"I, the image of light and gladness
"Saw and pitied that mournful boy
"And I swore to take his gloomy sadness
"And give to him my beamy joy—

"Heavy and dark the night is closing
"Heavy and dark may its biding be
"Better for all from greif reposing
"And better for all who whach like me—

"Guardian angel, he lacks no longer;
"Evil fortune he need not fear;
"Fate is strong—but Love is stronger
"And more unsleeping than angel's care—"

121

June 2d 1845

Anticipation

How beautiful the Earth is still
To thee, how full of Happiness;

120b. *Text from B41; no break after B40*
1 sunbright] <golden> 5 spring] <light> 23 but <my> Love
121. *Text from A30, with substantive revisions of 1846*
Title 1846; not in A
No stanza-breaks at 4, 22, 40 in 1846
Indentation at 10, 14, 18, 28, 32, 40, 44, 48, 52 in 1846

How little fraught with real ill
Or unreal phantoms of distress;

How spring can bring thee glory yet,
And summer win thee to forget
December's sullen time!
Why dost thou hold the treasure fast
Of youth's delight, when youth is past
And thou art near thy prime?

When those who were thy own compeers
Equals in fortune and in years
Have seen their morning melt in tears
To clouded, smileless day;
Blest, had they died untried and young
Before their hearts went wandering wrong
Poor slaves, subdued by passions strong
A weak and helpless prey!

"Because, I hoped while they enjoyed
"And by fulfilment, hope destroyed—
"As children hope, with trustful breast
"I waited Bliss and cherished Rest—

"A thoughtful Spirit taught me soon
"That we must long till life be done
"That every phase of earthly joy
"Must always fade and always cloy—

"This I forsaw; and would not chase
"The fleeting treacheries
"But with firm foot and tranquil face
"Held backward from that tempting race;
"Gazed oe'r the sands, the waves efface
"To the enduring seas—

"There cast my anchor of Desire
"Deep in unknown Eternity
"Nor ever let my spirit tire
"With looking for *What is to Be.*

4 unreal] *1846*; shadowy *A* 12 Equals in fortune] *1846*; Equal in fortunes *A* 14 clouded, smileless] *1846*; dull unlovely *A* 15 untried] *1846*; unproved *A* 16 went wandering wrong] *1846*; were wildly wrung *A* 21 trustful] <tranquil> 22 <b>Bliss . . . <r>Rest *A*; bliss . . . rest *1846* 26 Must] *1846*; Will *A* 35 Nor] <And> 36 With] *1846*; <With> <In> (*neither restored*) *A*

"It is Hope's Spell that glorifies
"Like youth to my maturer eyes
"All Natures million mysteries—
"The fearful and the fair—

"Hope soothes me in the greifs I know
"She lulls my pain for other's woe
"And makes me strong to undergo
"What I am born to bear.

"Glad comforter, Will I not brave
"Unawed, the darkness of the grave—
"Nay, Smile to hear Death's billows rave
"Sustained, my guide, by thee?
"The more unjust seems present fate
"The more my spirit swells elate
"Strong in thy strengh, to anticipate
"Rewarding Destiny!"

122

M.A. written on the Dungeon Wall—N C *August 1845*

I know that tonight, the wind is sighing,
The soft August wind, over forest and moor
While I in a grave-like chill am lying
On the damp black flags of my dungeon-floor—

I know that the Harvest Moon is shining;
She neither will wax nor wane for me,
Yet I weary, weary, with vain repining,
One gleam of her heaven-bright face to see!

For this constant darkness is wasting the gladness
Fast wasting the gladness of life away;
It gathers up thoughts akin to madness
That never would cloud the world of day—

I chide with my soul—I bid it cherish
The feelings it lived on when I was free,

41 in the] <for those> 48 Sustained, my guide] *1846*; My guide, sustained *A*
50 swells] *1846*; springs *A*

122. *Text from B42*
1 is] *ed.*; is is

But, shrinking it murmers, "Let Memory perish
Forget for thy Friends have forgotten thee!"

Alas, I did think that they were weeping
Such tears as I weep—it is not so!
Their carless young eyes are closed in sleeping;
Their brows are unshadowed, undimmed by woe—

Might I go to their beds, I'd rouse that slumber,
My spirit should startle their rest and tell
How hour after hour, I wakefully number
Deep buried from light in my lonely cell!

Yet let them dream on, though dreary dreaming
Would haunt my pillow if *they* were here
And *I* were laid warmly under the gleaming
Of that guardian moon and her comrade star—

Better that I my own fate mourning
Should pine alone in the prison-gloom
Than waken free on the summer morning
And feel they were suffering this aweful doom

123

Julian M —— and A. G. Rochelle— *October 9th 1845*

Silent is the House—all are laid asleep;
One, alone, looks out o'er the snow-wreaths deep;
Watching every cloud, dreading every breeze
That whirls the wildering drifts and bends the groaning trees—

Cheerful is the hearth, soft the matted floor
Not one shivering gust creeps through pane or door
The little lamp burns straight; its rays shoot strong and far
I trim it well to be the Wanderers guiding star—

Frown my haughty sire, chide my angry Dame;
Set your slaves to spy, threaten me with shame;
But neither sire nor dame, nor prying serf shall know
What angel nightly tracks that waste of winter snow.

16 th<e>y 30 prison<'s>-gloom

123. *Text from B43*

In the dungeon crypts idly did I stray
Reckless of the lives wasteing there away;
"Draw the ponderous bars, open Warder stern!"
He dare not say me nay—the hinges harshly turn—

"Our guests are darkly lodged" I whispered gazing through
The vault whose grated eye showed heaven more grey than
    blue;
(—This was when glad Spring laughed in awaking pride.)
"Aye, darkly lodged enough!" returned my sullen guide.

Then, God forgive my youth, forgive my careless tongue—!
I scoffed as the chill chains on the damp flagstones rung;
"Confined in triple walls, art thou so much to fear,
"That we must bind thee down and clench thy fetters here?"

The captive raised her face; it was as soft and mild
As sculptured marble saint or slumbering, unweaned child
It was so soft and mild, it was so sweet and fair
Pain could not trace a line nor greif a shadow there!

The captive raised her hand and pressed it to her brow
"I have been struck, she said, and I am suffering now
"Yet these are little worth, your bolts and irons strong
"And were they forged in steel they could not hold me long—"

Hoarse laughed the jailor grim, "Shall I be won to hear
"Doest think fond, dreaming wretch that *I* shall grant thy
    prayer?
"Or better still, wilt melt my master's heart with groans?
"Ah sooner might the sun thaw down these granite stones!—

"My master's voice is low, his aspect bland and kind
"But hard as hardest flint the soul that lurks behind:
"And I am rough and rude, yet, not more rough to see
"Than is the hidden ghost which has its home in me!"

About her lips there played a smile of almost scorn
"My friend, she gently said, you have not heard me mourn
"When you, my parent's lives—*my* lost life can restore
"Then may I weep and sue, but, never, Friend, before!"

Her head sank on her hands its fair curls swept the ground
The Dungeon seemed to swim in strange confusion round—

26 sculptured] <? slumbering>   40 which] <that>

"Is she so near to death?" I murmered half aloud
And kneeling, parted back the floating golden cloud

Alas, how former days upon my heart were borne,
How Memory mirrored then the prisoners joyous morn—
Too blithe, too loving child, too warmly, wildly gay!
Was that the wintry close of thy celestial May?

She knew me and she sighed "Lord Julian, can it be,
"Of all my playmates, you, alone, remember me?
"Nay start not at my words, unless you deem it shame
"To own from conquered foe, a once familiar name—

"I can not wonder now at aught the world will do
"And insult and contempt I lightly brook from you,
"Since those who vowed away their souls to win my love
"Around this living grave like utter strangers move!

"Nor has one voice been raised to plead that I might die
"Not buried under earth but in the open sky;
"By ball or speedy knife or headsman's skillful blow—
"A quick and welcome pang instead of lingering woe!

"Yet, tell them, Julian, all, I am not doomed to wear
"Year after year in gloom and desolate despair;
"A messenger of Hope comes every night to me
"And offers, for short life, eternal liberty—

"He comes with western winds, with evening's wandering airs,
"With that clear dusk of heaven that brings the thickest stars;
"Winds take a pensive tone and stars a tender fire
"And visions rise and change which kill me with desire—

"Desire for nothing known in my maturer years
"When joy grew mad with awe at counting future tears;
"When, if my spirit's sky was full of flashes warm,
"I knew not whence they came from sun or thunder storm;

"But first a hush of peace, a soundless calm descends;
"The struggle of distress and feirce impatience ends;
"Mute music sooths my breast—unuttered harmony
"That I could never dream till earth was lost to me.

51 warmly] <warm, too> 54 playmates] <comrades> 57 <o>aught
65 Yet . . . all] Still let my tyrants know *alternative*

"Then dawns the Invisible, the Unseen its truth reveals;
"My outward sense is gone, my inward essence feels—
"Its wings are almost free, its home, its harbour found;
"Measuring the gulf it stoops and dares the final bound!

"O, dreadful is the check—intense the agony
"When the ear begins to hear and the eye begins to see;
"When the pulse begins to throb, the brain to think again,
"The soul to feel the flesh and the flesh to feel the chain!

"Yet I would lose no sting, would wish no torture less;
"The more that anguish racks the earlier it will bless;
"And robed in fires of Hell, or bright with heavenly shine
"If it but herald Death, the vision is divine—"

She ceased to speak and I, unanswering watched her there
Not daring now to touch one lock of silken hair—
As I had knelt in scorn, on the dank floor I knelt still,
My fingers on the links of that iron hard and chill—

I heard and yet heard not the surly keeper growl;
I saw, yet did not see, the flagstones damp and foul;
The keeper, to and fro, paced by the bolted door
And shivered as he walked and as he shivered, swore—

While my cheek glowed in flame, I marked that he did rave
Of air that froze his blood and moisture like the grave—
"We have been Two hours good!" he muttered peevishly,
Then, losing off his belt the rusty dungeon key,

He said, "you may be pleased, Lord Julian, still to stay
"But duty will not let me linger here all day;
"If I might go, I'd leave this badge of mine with you
"Not doubting that you'd prove a jailor stern and true"

I took the proffered charge; the captive's drooping lid
Beneath its shady lash a sudden lightening hid
Earth's hope was not so dead heavens home was not so dear
I read it in that flash of longing quelled by fear

Then like a tender child whose hand did just enfold
Safe in its eager grasp a bird it wept to hold

83 Its . . . free] <Mute music soothes my> 86–8 *quotation-marks omitted* 88 feel the flesh] <feel its chain> 95 dank] *or* dark 96 on] *or* in 113 enfold] <enclose>

When peirced with one wild glance from the troubled hazle
eye
It gushes into tears and lets its treasure fly

Thus ruth and selfish love together striving tore
The heart all newly taught to pity and adore;
If I should break the chain I felt my bird would go
Yet I must break the chain or seal the prisoner's woe.

Short strife what rest could soothe—what peace could visit
me
While she lay pining there for Death to set her free?
"Rochelle, the dungeons teem with foes to gorge our hate—
"Thou art too young to die by such a bitter fate!"

With hurried blow on blow I struck the fetters through
Regardless how that deed my after hours might rue
Oh, I was over-blest by the warm unasked embrace—
By the smile of grateful joy that lit her angel face!

And I was overblest—aye, more than I could dream
When, faint, she turned aside from noon's unwonted beam;
When though the cage was wide—the heaven around it lay—
Its pinion would not waft my wounded dove away—

Through thirteen anxious weeks of terror-blent delight
I guarded her by day and guarded her by night
While foes were prowling near and Death gazed greedily
And only Hope remained a faithful friend to me—

Then oft with taunting smile, I heard my kindred tell
"How Julian loved his hearth and sheltering rooftree well;
"How the trumpet's voice might call the battle-standard wave
"But Julian had no heart to fill a patriot's grave."

And I, who am so quick to answer sneer with sneer;
So ready to condemn to scorn a coward's fear—
I held my peace like one whose conscience keeps him dumb
And saw my kinsmen go—and lingered still at home—

Another hand than mine, my rightful banner held
And gathered my renown on Freedom's crimson field
Yet I had no desire the glorious prize to gain—
It needed braver nerve to face the world's disdain—

124, 139–40 *opening quotation marks omitted*   147 Yet] <?But>

And by the patient strength that could that world defy;
By suffering with calm mind, contempt and calumny;
By never-doubting love, unswerving constancy,
Rochelle, I earned at last an equal love from thee!

124

The Prisoner

A Fragment

In the dungeon-crypts, idly did I stray,
Reckless of the lives wasting there away;
"Draw the ponderous bars! open, Warder stern!"
He dared not say me nay—the hinges harshly turn.

"Our guests are darkly lodged," I whisper'd, gazing through
The vault, whose grated eye showed heaven more grey than blue;
(This was when glad spring laughed in awaking pride;)
"Aye, darkly lodged enough!" returned my sullen guide.

Then, God forgive my youth; forgive my careless tongue;
I scoffed, as the chill chains on the damp flag-stones rung:
"Confined in triple walls, art thou so much to fear,
That we must bind thee down and clench thy fetters here?"

The captive raised her face, it was as soft and mild
As sculptured marble saint, or slumbering unwean'd child;
It was so soft and mild, it was so sweet and fair,
Pain could not trace a line, nor grief a shadow there!

The captive raised her hand and pressed it to her brow;
"I have been struck," she said, "and I am suffering now;
Yet these are little worth, your bolts and irons strong,
And, were they forged in steel, they could not hold me long."

Hoarse laughed the jailor grim: "Shall I be won to hear;
Dost think, fond, dreaming wretch, that *I* shall grant thy prayer?

151 unswerving] <and religious>

124. *Text from 1846, collated with lines 13–96 of B43* (*No. 123, above*)
Title 1846; *not in B*
4 dared] dare *B*

Or, better still, wilt melt my master's heart with groans?
Ah! sooner might the sun thaw down these granite stones.

"My master's voice is low, his aspect bland and kind,
But hard as hardest flint, the soul that lurks behind;
And I am rough and rude, yet not more rough to see
Than is the hidden ghost that has its home in me."

About her lips there played a smile of almost scorn,
"My friend," she gently said, "you have not heard me mourn;
When you my kindred's lives, *my* lost life, can restore,
Then may I weep and sue,—but never, friend, before!

Still, let my tyrants know, I am not doomed to wear
Year after year in gloom, and desolate despair;
A messenger of Hope, comes every night to me,
And offers for short life, eternal liberty.

He comes with western winds, with evening's wandering airs,
With that clear dusk of heaven that brings the thickest stars.
Winds take a pensive tone, and stars a tender fire,
And visions rise, and change, that kill me with desire.

Desire for nothing known in my maturer years,
When Joy grew mad with awe, at counting future tears.
When, if my spirit's sky was full of flashes warm,
I knew not whence they came, from sun, or thunder storm.

But, first, a hush of peace—a soundless calm descends;
The struggle of distress, and fierce impatience ends.
Mute music soothes my breast, unuttered harmony,
That I could never dream, till Earth was lost to me.

Then dawns the Invisible; the Unseen its truth reveals;
My outward sense is gone, my inward essence feels:
Its wings are almost free—its home, its harbour found,
Measuring the gulph, it stoops, and dares the final bound.

Oh, dreadful is the check—intense the agony—
When the ear begins to hear, and the eye begins to see;
When the pulse begins to throb, the brain to think again,
The soul to feel the flesh, and the flesh to feel the chain.

28 that] <that> which *B* 31 kindred's] parent's *B* 32+ *20 lines of B omitted*
33 Still . . . know] *1846*; *as alternative in B* (Yet, tell them, Julian, all *original reading in B*)
40 that] which *B*

Yet I would lose no sting, would wish no torture less,
The more that anguish racks, the earlier it will bless;
And robed in fires of hell, or bright with heavenly shine,
If it but herald death, the vision is divine!"

She ceased to speak, and we, unanswering, turned to go—
We had no further power to work the captive woe:
Her cheek, her gleaming eye, declared that man had given
A sentence, unapproved, and overruled by Heaven.

125

Jan 2d 1846

No coward soul is mine
No trembler in the world's storm troubled sphere
I see Heaven's glories shine
And Faith shines equal arming me from Fear

O God within my breast
Almighty ever-present Deity
Life, that in me hast rest
As I,—Undying Life, have power in thee

Vain are the thousand creeds
That move men's hearts, unutterably vain,
Worthless as withered weeds
Or idlest froth amid the boundless main

To waken doubt in one
Holding so fast by thy infinity
So surely anchored on
The steadfast rock of Immortality

With wide-embracing love
Thy Spirit animates eternal years
Pervades and broods above,
Changes, sustains, dissolves, creates and rears

61 we] I *B* turned to go] watched her there *B* 62–4 Not daring now to touch one lock of silken hair— | As I had knelt in scorn, on the dank [*or* dark] floor I knelt still, | My fingers on [*or* in] the links of that iron hard and chill *B*

125. *Text from A31*
Date Jan] <Dec>
2 trembler] <*?* shiverer> 8 power] <strength>

Though Earth and moon were gone
And suns and universes ceased to be
And Thou wert left alone
Every Exsistance would exsist in thee

There is not room for Death
Nor atom that his might could render void
Since Thou art Being and Breath
And what thou art may never be destroyed

126

14 September 1846

Why ask to know the date—the clime?
More than mere words they cannot be:
Men knelt to God and worshipped crime,
And crushed the helpless even as we

But, they had learnt from length of strife—
Of civil war and anarchy
To laugh at death, and look on life
With somewhat lighter sympathy.

It was the autumn of the year;
The time to labouring peasants, dear,
week after week, from noon to noon,
September shone as bright as June—
Still, never hand a sickle held;
The crops were garnered in the field—
Trod out, and ground by horses' feet
While every ear was milky sweet;
And kneaded on the threshing-floor
With mire of tears and human gore.

Some said, they thought that heaven's pure rain
Would hardly bless those fields again:

22 be] <shine> 24 thee] <thine> 27 Since] <For> <b>Being and <b>Breath 28 may] <shall>

126. *Text from B44*

1 ask] <seek> 4 <And trampled worms like thee and me> And crushed the <weak> <——> the helpless even <as> we 7 look on] <value> 8 <At somewhat lighter worth than we> 11 week after] <And week by> 13 a] <the> 18 human] <reeking> 19 Some] <?Men>

Not so—the all-benignant skies
Rebuked that fear of famished eyes—
July passed on with showers and dew,
And August glowed in showerless blue;
No harvest time could be more fair
Had harvest fruits but ripened there.

And I confess that hate of rest,
And thirst for things abandoned now,
Had weaned me from my country's breast
And brought me to that land of woe.

Enthusiast—in a name delighting;
My alien sword I drew to free
One race, beneath two standards fighting,
For loyalty, and liberty—

When kindred strive, God help the weak!
A brother's ruth 'tis vain to seek:
At first, it hurt my chivalry
To join them in their cruelty;
But I grew hard—I learnt to wear
An iron front to terror's prayer;
I learnt to turn my ears away
From torture's groans, as well as they.
By force I learnt—what power had I
To say the conquered should not die?
What heart, one trembling foe to save
When hundreds daily filled the grave?
Yet, there *were* faces that could move
A moments flash of human love;
And there were fates that made me feel
I was not to the centre, steel—

I've often witnessed wise men fear
To meet distress which they forsaw;
And sinning cowards nobly bear
A doom that thrilled the brave with awe:

Strange proofs I've seen, how hearts could hide
Their secret with a life-long pride,

27 And I confess] <And much I tell thee> (And *not clearly retained*) 43 By force] <Perforce> 52 meet <with> distress 53 sinning] <seeming> 54 A doom] <Anguish>

And then, reveal it as they died—
Strange courage, and strange weakness too,
In that last hour when most are true,
And timid natures strangely nerved
To deeds from which the desperate swerved—
These I may tell, but leave them now.
Go with me where my thoughts would go;
Now all today, and all last night
I've had one scene before my sight—

Wood-shadowed dales; a harvest moon
Unclouded in its glorious noon;
A solemn landscape, wide and still;
A red fire on a distant hill—
A line of fires, and deep below,
Another dusker, drearier glow—
Charred beams, and lime, and blackened stones
Self-piled in cairns oe'r burning bones
And lurid flames that licked the wood
Then quenched their glare in pools of blood—
But yestereve—ho!, never care;
Let street and suburb smoulder there—
Smoke-hidden, in the winding glen,
They lay too far to vex my ken.

Four score shot down—all veterans strong—
One prisoner spared, their leader young—
And he within his house was laid,
Wounded, and weak and nearly dead.
We gave him life against his will;
For he intreated us to kill—
But statue-like we saw his tears—
And coldly fell our captain's sneers!

"Now heaven forbid!" with scorn he said—
"That noble gore our hands should shed
Like common blood—retain thy breath
Or scheme, if thou canst purchase death—

60 timid] <*?*fearful> nerved] <*?*strung> 61 deeds . . . swerved] <desperate deeds that shamed the strong> the desperate] <the strongest> 62 I may tell] <may be told> 64 Now] <And> 83 weak] <bound> <s> <ill> 85 For] <How> 86 But] <How> saw] <heard> 87 coldly] <Fiend-like> harshly *alternative* 88 Now] <God> 91 thou<gh>

When men are poor we sometimes hear
And pitying grant that dastard prayer;
When men are rich, we make them buy
The pleasant privilege, to die—
O, we have castles reared for kings
Embattled towers and buttressed wings
Thrice three feet thick, and guarded well
With chain, and bolt, and sentinel!
We build our despots' dwellings sure;
Knowing they love to live secure—
And our respect for royalty
Extends to thy estate and thee!"

The suppliant groaned; his moistened eye
Swam wild and dim with agony—
The gentle blood could ill sustain
Degrading taunts, unhonoured pain.
Bold had he shown himself to lead;
Eager to smite and proud to bleed—
A man, amid the battle's storm;
An infant in the after calm.

Beyond the town his mansion stood
Girt round with pasture-land and wood;
And there our wounded soldiers lying
Enjoyed the ease of wealth in dying:
For him, no mortal more than he
Had softened life with luxury;
And truely did our priest declare
"Of good things he had had his share."

We lodged him in an empty place
The full moon beaming on his face
Through shivered glass, and ruins, made
Where shell and ball the fiercest played.
I watched his ghastly couch beside
Regardless if he lived or died—
Nay, muttering curses on the breast
Whose ceaseless moans denied me rest:

101 live] <sleep> 107 Degrad<ed>ing 108 Bold] <?Brave> 109 smite] <strike> 115 en<g>joyed 124 his] <him> ghastly] <?lonely>

'Twas hard, I know, 'twas harsh to say,
"Hell snatch thy worthless soul away!"
But then 'twas hard my lids to keep,
Night following night, estranged from sleep.
Captive and keeper, both outworn,
Each in his misery yearned for morn;
Even though returning morn should bring
Intenser toil and suffering.

Slow, slow it came! Our dreary room
Grew drearier with departing gloom;
Yet, as the west wind warmly blew
I felt my pulses bound anew,
And turned to him—nor breeze, nor ray
Revived that mould of shattered clay,
Scearce conscious of his pain he lay—
Scearce conscious that my hands removed
The glittering toys his lightness loved;
The jewelled rings, and locket fair
Where rival curls of silken hair,
Sable and brown, revealed to me
A tale of doubtful constancy.

"Forsake the world without regret;"
I murmered in contemptuous tone;
"The world, poor wretch, will soon forget
Thy noble name, when thou art gone!
Happy, if years of slothful shame
Could perish like a noble name—
If God did no account require
And being with breathing might expire!"
And words of such contempt I said
harsh insults oe'r a dying bed
Which as they darken memory now
disturb my pulse and flush my brow;
I know that Justice holds in store,

131 Night following] Through the long *alternative* 134 returning] <that laughing> 136 Our] <the> 138 west] <night> 144 lightness] <folly> 148 doubtful constancy] <past inconstancy> 149–54 *cancelled* 151 "The] *ed.*; The 154 name—] *ed.*; name—" 156 might] <may> expire!"] *ed.*; expire! 157 And . . . contempt] <But> <Nay ruder words than these> such] <cruel> 158 harsh] <Cold> 159 as] <when> 160 disturb my pulse] <Oppress> <Enchain my heart> (Oppress *restored as alternative*) 161 know that] <ask what>

Reprisals for those days of gore
Not for the blood, but for the sin
Of stifling mercy's voice within—
The blood spilt gives no pang at all;
It is my conscience haunting me,
telling how oft my lips shed gall
On many a thing too weak to be
Even in thought at enmity—
And whispering ever, when I pray,
"God will repay—God will repay!"

He does repay and soon and well
The deeds that turn his earth to hell
The wrongs that aim a venomed dart
Through nature at the Eternal heart
Surely my cruel tongue was cursed
I know my prisoner heard me speak
A transient gleam of feeling burst
And wandered o'er his haggard cheek
And from his quivering lids then stole
A look to melt a demon's soul
A silent prayer more powerful far
Than any breathed petitions are
Pleading in mortal agony
To mercy's source but not to me—
Now I recall that glance and groan
And wring my hands in vain distress
Then, I was adamantine stone
Nor felt one touch of tenderness

My plunder taan I left him there
To struggle with his last despair
Regardless of the wildered cry
Which wailed for death yet wailed to die
I left him there unwatched alone
And eager sought the court below

162 <What I have left to suffer more> 163 the blood] <blood spilt> 166 It is my] <Only that> 168 many a thing] <helpless things> 169 thought at enmity] <heart my enemy> 172–89 *cancelled* 176 tongue] <heart> 182 A] <That> 190 left him there] <watched him die> (die *uncancelled*) 190+ <With taunting tongue and brazen eye> 191 struggle . . . despair] <taste a> draw breath in the morning air *alternative* his] <the> 193 Which wailed] <Which prayed> 195 <And ran to drink the morning air> eager] <gladly>

Where o'er a trough of chizelled stone
An ice cold well did gurgling flow
The [ ] in its basin shed
A stranger tinge of gory red
I drank and scarcely marked the hue
My food was dyed with crimson too
As I went out a wretched child
With wasted cheek and ringlets wild
A shape of fear and misery
Raised up her trembling hands to me
And begged her fathers face to see
I spurned the piteous wretch away
Thy father's face is lifeless clay
As thou mayst be ere fall of day
Unless the truth be quickly told
Where they have hid thy father's gold
Yet in the intervals of pain
He heard my taunts and moaned again
And mocking moans did I reply
And asked him why he would not die
In noble agony uncomplaining
Was it not foul disgrace and shame
To thus disgrace his ancient name
Just then a comrade hurried in
Alas he cried sin gender sin.
For every soldier slain they've sworn
To hang up five [ ] ere morn
They've taan of stranglers sixty three
Full thirty from one company
And all thy father's family
And comrade thou hadst only one
They've taen thy all thy little son

196 trough] <well> 197 did gurgling] <?of ?water> 198 The <water> <——> in 199 stranger tinge of gory] <mingled shade of ?blood-sent> 202 As I went out] <Now I had marked> wretched] <haggard> 203 wasted] <haggard> <hollow> (wasted *also cancelled, less heavily*) 205 trembling hands] <——eyes> 206 dear *inserted above* face 207 I] <A> 208 dear *inserted above* face 211 they have] <thou hast> 212 <In intervals of wildering pain> (Through *alternative above* In) 216–17 *interlined with* <For I was angry and my eyes | Were weary of his ?agonies> 216 agony uncomplaining] <silent agony> 218 ancient] <noble> <lordly> 219 <While speaking one came hurrying in> (one came *uncancelled*) 221 every <prisoner> <soldier> slain 222 hang up] <murder> ere] *or* the morn <tomorrow> 224 Full] <And> 225 thy] *or* my

Down, at my captives feet I fell
I had no option in despair
As thou wouldst save thy soul from hell
My heart's one darling bid them spare
Or human hate and hate devine
Blight every orphan flower of thine
He raised his head from death beguiled
I lost last night my only child
Twice in my arms twice on my knee
You stabbed my child and laughed at me
And so with choking voice he said
I hope in God I trust she's dead
Yet not to thee not even to thee
would I return such misery
Fear not that aweful grief to know
I will not cause thee equal woe
Write that they yield him up to
[ ] that they harm no infant there
Write that it is my latest prayer
I wrote he signed and thus did save
My treasure from the gory grave
And I would freely gladly then
Have paid his saviour life again
But heedless of my gratitude
The silent corpse before me lay
And still methinks in gloomy mood
I see it fresh as yesterday
That sad face raised imploringly
To mercy's God and not to me
And mercy's God would [ ] die

228 captives] <prisoners> 231 o<w>ne 233 flower] <hope> 234 He wakened up he almost smiled *alternative* 237 You stabbed] <They pierced> 238 choking voice] <bursting heart> 239 I <pray to heaven> I <trust> she's dead (trust *restored below* pray; hope in God *written twice above line*) 239+ <But for the grief that I did bear | Whose bitterness would poison heaven> 240–1 *see commentary* 241 such] <that> 242 aweful] fearful *alternative* 243 thee] <that> 243+ <And as I hope to be forgiven> 244 yield . . . to] <——?hold ?my ?freind> 245 <Write> that harm] <kill> *above* 245+ <——will never——> 247 and thus did] <to slow to> 248 the] <his> 248+ And O <my stony heart> <soul with grief and tears> would <truely> (longed wildly *alternative above*) then | <Have> To give<n> his saviour <back> life again | And he was saved 249] <And then I felt an impulse ?warm> (then *uncancelled*) 250 Have paid] <To give> life] <back> 251 heedless of] <far beyond> 255 sad face] <grave look> 256 God] <source> 257 would] <was>

The last look of that glazing eye
I could not rescue him his child
I found alive and tended well
But she was full of anguish wild
And hated us like blackest hell
And weary with her savage woe
One moonless night I let her go

127

may 13th 1848

Why ask to know what date what clime
There dwelt our own humanity
power-worshippers from earliest time
Feet-kissers of triumphant crime
crushers of helpless misery
Crushing down Justice honouring Wrong
If That be feeble this be strong
Shedders of blood shedders of tears
Self-cursers avid of distress
yet mocking heaven with senseless prayers
For mercy on the merciless

It was the autumn of the year
When grain grows yellow in the ear
Day after day from noon to noon
That August, sun blazed bright as June
But we with unregarding eyes
Saw panting earth and glowing skies
No hand the reaper's sickle held
Nor bound the ripe sheaves in the field

258 look] <prayer> glazing] <liquid> <——less> 261+ <And shunned us mourning for her woe | And prayed all day for liberty> 262 us] <me> blackest] *unclear* 263 wear<ied>y savage] <gloomy>

127. *Text from B45*

1 Why ask to know] <Oh idle words!> what date what] <the date the> 3 power] <Gold> <Might> 4 Feet-kissers] <Kissing the feet> triumphant] <prosperous> 5 crushers of] <And trampling> helpless] <?righteous> 7+ <And mocking heaven with whyning prayers | for mercy when our —— hands> hears *uncancelled* 9 Self-cursers] <Restless to take> avid] <greedy> 10 senseless] <idiot> 15 That] <Did> <The> 16–17 <But we were <<careless>> heedless of the <<skies>> sky | Our ?nobler harvest-time was nigh>

Our corn was garnered months before
Threshed out and kneaded up with gore
Ground when the ears were milky sweet
With furious toil of hoofs and feet
I doubly cursed on foriegn sod
Fought neither for my home nor God

21 Threshed out] <And ground by>

UNDATED POEMS AND FRAGMENTS

128

Love is like the wild rose briar,
Friendship, like the holly tree
The holly is dark when the rose briar blooms,
But which will bloom most constantly?

The wild rose briar is sweet in spring,
Its summer blossems scent the air
yet wait till winter comes again
And who will call the wild-briar fair

Then scorn the silly rose-wreath now
And deck thee with the holly's sheen
That when December blights thy brow
He still may leave thy garland green—

129

Sympathy

There should be no dispair for you
While nightly stars are burning—
While evening pours its silent dew
And sunshine gilds the morning—

There should be no dispair—though tears
May flow down like a river—
Are not the best beloved of years
Around your heart forever?

128. *Text from A15*
3 rose] <wild>
129. *Text from A16, with substantive revisions of 1846*
Title 1846; not in A
No stanza-breaks in 1846 (page-break at 8)
Alternate lines indented in 1846
3 pours] *1846*; sheds *A* 4 And] *1846*; Or *A*

They weep—you weep—It must be so—
Winds sigh as you are sighing,
And winter sheds his greif in snow
Where Autums leaves are lying

Yet these revive—and from their fate
Your fate can not be parted
Then journey on, if not elate
Still, *never* broken-hearted—

130

To A.G.A.

"Thou standest in the green-wood now
"The place, the hour, the same—
"And here the fresh leaves gleam and glow
"And there, down in the lake below
"The tiney ripples flame—

"The breeze sings like a summer breeze
"Should sing in summer skies
"And tower-like roaks and tent-like trees
"In mingled glory rise.

"But where is he to day, to-day?"
"O question not with me—"
"I will not, Lady, only say
"Where may thy lover be?

"Is he upon some distant shore?
"Or is he on the sea?

11 sheds his] *1846*; pours its *A* 13 Yet] <But> these] *1846*; they *A* 14 can not] cannot *1846* 15 journey on, if] *1846*; man journy onward *A* 16 Still,] *1846*; But *A*

130. *Text from B4, collated with drafts of 1–27 in D3 and 26–33 in D8*
To A.G.A.] *not in D*
No quotation marks in D
1 Thou standest] I'm standing *D3* green-wood] forest *D3* 3 fresh] green *D3* gleam] <*?*glance> gleam *D3* 4 in the] on that *D3* 6 The breeze] The <wind> breeze *D3* 8 tower-like] <shadowy> towerlike *D3* tent-like] <shadowing> <shady> tentlike *D3* 9+ The murmer of their <branches> boughs and streams | Speaks pride as well as <joy> <*?*plea> bliss | And that blue heaven expanding seems | <The —— of god —— view> the circling hills to kiss *D3* 11 No wisper not to me— *D3* 12 Lady] dreamer *D3* 13 may] <can> may *D3*

"Or is the heart thou dost adore,
"A faithless heart to thee?"

"The heart I love, whate'er betide
"Is faithful as the grave
"And neither foriegn lands devide
"Nor yet the rolling wave—"

"Then why should sorrow cloud that brow,
"And tears those eyes bedim?
"Reply this once, is it that thou
"Hast faithless been to him?"

"I gazed upon the cloudless moon
"And loved her all the night
"Till morning came and ardent noon
"Then I forgot her light—

"No—not forgot, eternaly
"Remains its memory dear;
"But could the day seem dark to me
"Because the night was fair?

"I well may mourn that only one
"Can light my future sky.
"Even though by such a radiant sun
"My moon of life must die—"

131

Come, walk with me,
There's only thee
To bless my spirit now—
We used to love on winter nights
To wander through the snow;
Can we not woo back old delights?
The clouds rush dark and wild
They fleck with shade our mountain heights

18 whate'er betide] and you deride *D3* 19 faithful] changless *D3* 21 rolling] oacens *D3* 22 sorrow] trouble *D3* 24 Reply] <Answer> Reply *D3* 26–7 *B*, *D8*; I dreamt one dark and stormy night | When winter winds were wild *D3* 28 ardent] radiant *D8* 29 Then] And *D8*

131. *Text from B24*

The same as long ago
And on the horizon rest at last
In looming masses piled;
While moonbeams flash and fly so fast
We scearce can say they smiled.

Come walk with me, come walk with me;
We were not once so few
But Death has stolen our company
As sunshine steals the dew—
He took them one by one and we
Are left—the only two;
So closer would my feelings twine
Because they have no stay but thine—

"Nay call me not—it may not be
"Is human love so true?
"Can Freindship's flower droop on for years
"And then revive anew?
"No, though the soil be wet with tears
"How fair so e'er it grew
"The vital sap once perished
"Will never flow again
"And surer than that dwelling dread,
"The narrow dungeon of the Dead,
"Time parts the hearts of men—"

132

A A A

Sleep not dream not   this bright day
Willnot cannot last for aye
Bliss like thine is bought by years
Dark with torment and with tears

Sweeter far than placid pleasure
Purer higher beyond measure
Yet alas the sooner turning
Into hopless endless mourning

19 <W>Are

132. *Text from C12*

I love thee boy for all devine
All full of God thy features shine
Darling enthusiast holy child
Too good for this worlds warring wild
Too heavenly now but doomed to be
Helllike in heart and misery

And what shall change that angel brow
And quench that spirits glorious glow
Relentless laws that disallow
True virtue and true joy below

And blame me not if when the dread
Of suffering clouds thy youthful head
If when by crime and sorrow tossed
Thy wandering bark is wrecked and lost

I too depart I too decline
And make thy path no longer mine
'Tis thus that human minds will turn
All doomed alike to sin and mourn
Yet all with long gaze fixed afar
Adoring Virtues distant star

133

Alas that she
Would bid adieu
To all the hopes her childhood Knew

Hushed his the harp

134

Deep deep down in the silent grave
With none to mourn above

19 dread] *ed.*; dre (*leaf masked by stub*) 21 crime] <sin> tossed] *ed.*; tos (*leaf masked*) 22 and lost] *ed.*; an | los (*line tucked, leaf masked*)

133. *Text from D3*
 3–4 *short horizontal line below* Knew
134. *Text from D5*

135

Here with my knee upon thy stone
I bid adieu to feelings gone
I leave with thee my tears and pain
And rush into the world again

136

O come again what chains withhold
The steps that used so fleet to be
Come leave thy dwelling dark and cold
Once more to visit me

137

Was it with the feilds of green
Blowing flower and budding tree
With the summer heaven serene
That thou didst visit me?

No 'twas not the flowery plain
No twas not the fragrant air
Summer skies will come again
But *thou* wilt not be there—

138

How loud the Storm sounds round the Hall!
From arch to arch from door to door
Pillar and roof and granite wall
Rock like a cradle in its roar

That Elm tree by the haunted well
Greets no returning summer skies
Down with a rush the giant fell
And stretch athwart the path it lies

135. *Text from D5*
2 feelings] *ed.*; fellings D

136. *Text from D5*

137. *Text from D5*

138. *Text from D5*
1 sounds] <roars> 6 summer<ki>skies

Hardly had passed the funeral train
So long delayed by wind and snow
And how they'll reach the house again
To morrows sun perhaps will show

139

What use is it to slumber here,
Though the heart be sad and weary?
What use is it to slumber here
Though the day rise dark and dreary

For that mist may break when the sun is high
And this soul Forget its sorrow
And the rosey ray of the closeing day
May promise a brighter morrow

140

O evening why is thy light so sad?
Why is the suns last ray so cold
Hush our smile is—as ever Glad
but thy heart is growing old

141

Its over now Ive known it all
Ill hid it in my heart no more
But back again that night recall
And think the fearful vision o'er

The evening sun in cloudless shine
Had passd from summers heaven devine
And dark the shades of twilight grew
And stars were in the depth of blue

And in the heath on mountains far
From human eye and human care

139. *Text from D5*
5 may] <will>   6 this] <the>
140. *Text from D5*
141. *Text from D5*
3 th<e>at   recall] *ed.*; reall

With thoughtful heart and tearful eye
I sadly whached that solemn sky

142

O Hinder me by no delay
My horse is weary of the way
And still his breast must stem the tide
Whose waves are foaming far and wide
Leagues of I heard their thundering roar
As fast they burst upon the shore
A stronger steed than mine might dread
To brave them in their boiling bed

Thus spoke the traveller but in vain
The stranger would not turn away
Still clung she to his bridle rein
And still entreated him to stay

143

I'll come when thou art sadest
Hid alone in the darkend room
When the mad days mirth has vanishd
And the smile of joy is banished
From evenings chilly gloom

I ll come when the hearts rearl feeling
Has entire unbiassed sway
And my influence oer thee stealing
greif deepening joy congealing
Shall bear thy soul away

Listen 'tis just the hour
The awful time for thee
dost thou not feel upon thy soul
A Flood of strange sensations roll
Forunners of a sterner power
Heralds of me

142. *Text from D5*
143. *Text from D6*
2 Hid] *or* Laid 14 sen<t>sations

144

I would have touched the heavnly key
That spoke alike of bliss and thee
I would have woke the entrancing song
But its words died upon my tongue

And then I knew that hallowd strain
Could never speak of joy again
And then I felt

145

It was night and on the mountains
Fathoms deep the snowdrifts lay
Streams and waterfalls and fountains
Down in Darkness stole away

Long ago the hopless peasant
Left his sheep all buried there
Sheep that through the summer pleasant
He had whached with fondest care

Now no more a cheerful ranger
Following pathways known of yore
Sad he stood a wildered stranger
On his own unbounded moor

146

yes holy be thy resting place
wherever thou mayst lie
The sweetest winds breathe on thy face
The softest of the sky

And will not guardian Angels send
Kind dreams and thoughts of Love

144. *Text from D6*
5 strain] *ed.*; strai (*edge of leaf*)   6 <W>Could
145. *Text from D8*
4+ <Cold and wild the wind was blowing | Keen and clear the heaven above | But though countless stars were glowing | Absent was the star of love>
146. *Text from D8*
6 and thoughts of] <*?*of *?*hope *?*and>

Though I no more may whachful bend
Thy loved repose above

And will not heaven itself bestow
A beam of glorey there
That summers grass more green may grow
And summers flowers more fair

Farewell Farewell tis hard to part
yet loved one it must be
I would not rend another heart
Not even by blessing thee

Go we must break affections chain
Forget the hopes of years
Nay linger not wouldst thou remain
to waken wilder tears

This herald breeze with thee and me
Roved in the dawning day
And thou shouldest be where it shall be
ere evening far away

147

Lonly at her window sitting
While the evening stole away
Fitful winds forbodeing flitting
Through a sky of cloudy grey

148

There are two trees in a lonely feild
They breathe a spell to me
A dreary thought their dark boughs yeild
All waveing solemnly

8 loved] <long> 10 glorey] *ed.*; glrey 16 by] <with> 19 linger not] <nay ——> 21 herald] *unclear* breeze] <wind> 23 And] <But>

147. *Text from D10*
148. *Text from D10*

149

And the wind swept past her hopeless ear
Was nought on earth so wildly drear

150

What is that smoke that ever still
Comes rolling down the dark brown hill

151

Still as she looked the iron clouds
Would part and sunlight shone between
But drearly strange and pale and cold

152

Away away resign me now
To scenes of gloom and thoughts of fear
I trace the signal on my brow
Welcome at last though once so drear

153

It will not shine again
Its sad course is done
I have seen the last ray wane
Of the cold bright sun

154

None but one beheld him dying
Parting with the parting day

149. *Text from D10, heavily cancelled*
150. *Text from D10*
2 the] <that>
151. *Text from D10*
1 looked] <spoke>
152. *Text from D10*
3 my] *or* thy
153. *Text from D10*
154. *Text from D10*
1 one] *or* me

Winds of evening sadly sighing
Bore his soul from earth away

155

Coldly bleakly drearily
Evening died on Elbës shore
Winds were in the cloudy sky
Sighing mourning ever more

156

Old Hall of Time ruined lonly now
House to which the voice of life shall never more return
Chambers roofless desolate were weeds and ivy grow
Windows through whose broken arches the night winds sadly mourn
Home of the departed the long departed dead

157

Cold clear and blue the morning heaven
Expands its arch on high
Cold clear and blue Lake Wernas water
Reflects that winters sky

The moon has set but venus shines
A silent silvery star

158

Tell me tell me smileing child
What the past is like to thee?

155. *Text from D10*
2 El<d>bës
156. *Text from D10*
1 Time] <?Elbe>
157. *Text from D10*
158. *Text from D10*

An Autumn evening soft and mild
With a wind that sighs mournfuly

Tell me what is the present hour?
A green and flowery spray
Were a yong bird sits gathering its power
To mount and fly away

And what is the future happy one?
A sea beneath a cloudles sun
A mighty glorious dazzeling sea
Streching into infinity

159

The inspiring musics thrilling sound
The glory of the festal day
The glittering splendor rising round
Have past like all earths joys away

Forsaken by that Lady fair
She glides unheeding through them all
Covering her brow to hide the tear
That still though checked trembles to fall

She hurries through the outer Hall
And up the stairs through galleries dim
That murmer to the breezes call
The night-winds lonely Vesper hymn

160

Strong I stand though I have borne
Anger hate and bitter scorn
Strong I stand and laugh to see
How mankind have fought with me

Shade of mistry I contemn
All the puny ways of men

4+ <And what is the future>   7 <b> yong

159. *Text from D10*
160. *Text from D11*
5 mistry] *or* mastry

Free my heart my spirit free
Beckon and I'll follow thee

False and Foolish mortal know
If you scorn the worlds disdain
Your mean soul is far below
Other worms however vain

Thing of Dust—with boundless pride
Dare you ask me for a guide
With the humble I will be
Haughty men are naught to me

161

I paused on the threshold I turned to the sky
I looked on the heaven and the dark mountains round
The full moon sailed bright through that Oacen on high
And the wind murmered past with a wild eerie sound

And I entered the walls of my dark prison house
Misterious it rose from the billowy moor

162

O come with me thus ran the song
The moon is bright in Autumns sky
And thou hast toiled and laboured long
With acheing head and weary eye

163

Woods you need not frown on me
Specetral trees that so dolefuly
Shake your heads in the dreary sky
You need not mock so bitterly

10 dis<t>dain

161. *Text from D11*
2 dark] <wild>

162. *Text from D11*

163. *Text from D11*

164

How golden bright from earth and heaven
The Summer day declines
How gloriously o'er land and sea
The parting sun beam shines

There is a voice in the wind that waves
These bright rejoicing trees

165

Not a vapour had stained the breezless blue
Not a cloud had dimed the sun
From the time of mornings earliest dew
Till the summer day was done

And all as pure and all as bright
The beam of evening died
And purer still its parting light
Shone in Lake Elnors tide

Waveless and calm lies that silent deep
In its wilderness of moors
Solemn and soft the moonbeams sleep
Upon its heathy shores

The deer are gathered to their rest
The wildsheep seek the fold

166

Only some spires of bright green grass
Transparently in sunshine quivering

167

The sun has set and the long grass now
Waves drearily in the evening wind

164. *Text from D12*
2 Summer] <glor>
165. *Text from D12*
6 <*?* light> beam (beam *unclear*)
166. *Text from D12*
167. *Text from D12*

And the wildbird has flown from that old grey stone
In some warm knook a couch to find

In all the lonely landscape Round
I see no sight and hear no sound
Except the wind that far away
Comes sighing o'er the heathy sea

168

Lady in your palace Hall
Once perchance my face was seen
Can no memory now recall
Thought again to what has been

169

And first an hour of mournful museing
And then a gush of bitter tears
And then a dreary calm diffusing
Its deadly mist o'er joys and cares

And then a throb and then a lightning
And then a breathing from above
And then a star in heaven brightening
The star the glorious star of love

170

Wind sink to rest in the heather
Thy wild voice suits not me
I would have dreary weather
But all devoid of thee—

Sun set from that evening heaven
Thy glad smile wins not mine

168. *Text from D12*
2 Once] <One> 4 again] <to days>
169. *Text from D12*
170. *Text from D12*
6 smile] <sky>

If light at all is given
O give me Cynthias shine

171

Long neglect has worn away
Half the sweet enchanting smile
Time has turned the bloom to grey
Mould and damp the face defile

But that lock of silky hair
Still beneath the picture twined
Tells what once those features were
paints their image on the mind

Fair the hand that traced that line
"Dearest ever deem me true"
Swiftly flew the fingers fine
When the pen that motto drew

172

Awaking morning laughs from heaven
On golden summers forests green
And what a gush of song is given
To welcome in that light serene

A fresh wind waves the clustering roses
And through the open window sighs
Around the couch were she reposes
The lady with the dovelike eyes

With dovelike eyes and shineing hair
And velvet cheek so sweetly moulded
And hands so white and soft and fair
Above her snowy bosom folded

171. *Text from D12*
2 enchanting] *or* the hanting
172. *Text from D12*

173

Her sisters and her brothers feet
Are brushing off the scented dew
And she springs up in haste to greet
The grass and flowers and sunshine too

174

O Harold while the darkness falls
So lone and drear

175

Tis evening now the sun descends
In Golden glory down the sky
The citys murmer softly blends
With Zephers breathing gently by

And yet it seems a dreary morn
A dark October morn to me
And black the piles of rain clouds borne
Athwart heavens Stormy canopy

176

We wander on we have no rest
It is a dreary way

177

What Shadow is it
That ever moves before my eyes
It has a brow of ghostly whitness

173. *Text from D12*
174. *Text from D12*
175. *Text from E2*
5 morn] *unclear* 7 borne] *ed.*; *?*bord
176. *Text from E3*
177. *Text from E3*
1 is it <th> 2 my] <mine>

178

There let thy bleeding branch atone
For every torturing tear
Shall my young sins my sins alone
Be everlasting here?

Who bade thee keep that cursed name
a pledge for memory
As if Oblivion ever came
To breathe its bliss on me

As if through all the wildering maze
Of mad hours left behind
I once forgot the early days
That thou wouldst call to mind

179

Upon her aching breast
She lulled her little child
A winter sunset in the West
A dreary glory smiled

180

I gazed within thine ernest eyes
And read the sorrow brooding there
I heard thy young breast heave with sighs
And envied such dispair

Go to the grave in youths [ ] woe
That doom was written long ago

181

All hushed and still within the house
Without—all wind and driving rain

178. *Text from E4*
2 tortur<ed>ing 6 a pledge for] <That seal of> 8–9 *no stanza-break* 9 through] <in> 11 forgot] *or* forget
179. *Text from E6*
180. *Text from E6*
2 sorrow] <spirit> 3, 5 *unclear; see commentary*
181. *Text from E8*

But something wispers to my mind
through rain and hail and wailing wind
—Never again
Never again? Why not again?
Memory has power as real as thine

182

Iernës eyes were glazed and dim
When the castle clock tolled one
She looked around her dungeon grim
the grating cast a doubtful gleam
from one cloud saddened cold moon-beam
Iernë gazed as in a dream
And thought she saw the sun
She thought it was the break of day
The night had been so long

183

When days of Beauty deck the earth
Or stormy nights descend
How well my spirit knows the path
On which it ought to wend

It seeks the consecrated spot
Beloved in childhoods years
The space between is all forgot
Its sufferings and its tears

184

Still beside that dreary water
Stood he neath the cold moon ray

3 wispers . . . mind] <speaks ?of ?woe and ?pain> 3+ <Some thing I ——> fear to <——> 4 hail] *unclear* 5 Never] <?Again>

182. *Text from E8, where these lines are cancelled*
1 were] <?waxed> 2 clock] <bell> 3 looked] <gazed> 3+ <The pale moon shone her moving gleam> stream *uncancelled* 4+ <A pale ?ray —— ——paler gleam> 5 from] <Of>

183. *Text from E12*

184. *Text from E12*

Thinking on the deed of slaughter
On his heart that darkly lay

Soft the voice that broke his dreaming
Stealing through the silent air
yet before the ravens screaming
He had heard regardless there

Once his name was sweetly uttered
Then the echo died away
But each pulse in horror fluttered
as the life would pass away

185

There swept adown that dreary glen
A Wilder sound than mountain wind
The thrilling shouts of fighting men
With something sadder far behind

The thrilling shouts they died away
Before the night came greyly down
But closed not with the closing day
the choking sob the tortured moan

down in a hollow sunk in shade
Where dark heath waved in secret gloom
A weary bleeding form was laid
Waiting the death that was to come

186

Arthr Ex To marcius

In dungeons dark I cannot sing
In sorrows thrawl tis hard to smile
What bird can soar with broken wing
What heart can bleed and joy the while

185. *Text from E12*
1 swept] *ed.*; spwept 2 A] *added in l.h. margin* 3 <s>thrilling 4–5 *no stanza-break* 10 in secret gloom] <against the sky> 11 weary] *unclear*
186. *Text from E12*
Heading Arthr Ex | To [*wavy line*] marcius *to right, by head of poem*

187

I'm happiest when most away
I can bear my soul from its home of clay
On a windy night when the moon is bright
And the eye can wander through worlds of light

When I am not and none beside
Nor earth nor sea nor cloudless sky
But only spirit wandering wide
Through infinite imensity

188

M A A—

Methinks this heart should rest a while
So stilly round the evening falls
The veiled sun sheds no parting smile
Nor mirth nor music wakes my Halls

I have sat lonely all the day
Whaching the drizzly mist descend
And first conceal the hills in grey
And then along the valleys wend

And I have sat and whached the trees
And the sad flowers how drear they blow
Those flowers were formed to feel the breeze
Wave their light leaves in summers glow

Yet their life past in gloomy woe
And hopless comes its dark decline
And I lament because I know
That cold departure pictures mine

187. *Text from E13*

2 bear] *or* tear

188. *Text from E15, collated with cancelled draft of 9–10 in D10*

3 sheds] *ed.*; shade *or* shede   9 have sat and whached the trees] could sit and whach the clouds *D*   12 leaves] <heads>   13 life] <lives>   16 cold] <sad>

189

That dreary lake that midnight sky
That wan moon struggling through the cloud
That sullen murmer wispering by
As if it dared not speak aloud
Fall on my heart so sadly now
Wither my joy so lonly
Touch them not they bloom and smile
But their roots are withering all the while
Ah

190

His land may burst the galling chain
His people may be free again
For them a thousand hopes remain
But hope is dead for him

Soft falls the moonlight on the sea
Whose wild waves play at liberty
And Gondals wind sings solemnly
Its tireless midnight hymn

Around his prison walls it sings
His heart is stirred through all its strings
Because that sound remembrance brings
Of scenes that once have been

His soul has left the storm below
And reached a realm of sunless snow
The region of unchanging woe
Made voicless by dispair

And Geralds land may burst its chain
His subjects may be free again
For them a thousand hopes remain
But hope is dead for him

189. *Text from E16*
3 murmer wispering] <?moaning ?rustling>
190. *Text from E17*
1 may] <might> 2 may] <might> 2+ <His subjects <<shall>> still the strife maintain | And they may ——> 8 <holey> tireless (tireless *unclear*) midnight] <evening> 9 sings] <sighs> 10 <Waking a thousand memories> 12 scenes] <what> have] <has> 14 sunless] drear *alternative*

Set is his sun of liberty
Fixed is his earthly destiny
A few years of captivity
And then a captives tomb

191

it is not pride it is not shame
That makes her leave the gorgeous hall
And though neglect her heart might tame
She mourns not for her sudden fall

'Tis true she stands among the crowd
An unmarked and an unloved child
While each yong comrade blithe and proud
glides through the maze of pleasure wild

And all do homage to their will
And all seem glad that voice to hear
She heeds not that but hardly still
her eye can hold the quivering tear

What made her weep what made her glide
Out to the park this dreary day
And cast her jeweled chains aside
And seek a rough and lonely way

and down beneath a cedar shade
On the wet grass regardless lie
With nothing but its gloomy head
Between her and the showery sky

I saw her stand in the gallery long
whaching two little children there
As they were playing the pillars among
And bounding down the marble stair

191. *Text from E18*
3 might] <may> 6 unmarked] <unloved> unloved] <unbl> 10 that] <the> 16 seek] <then> 17 shade] <tree> 19 nothing] <only> <*?*naught> 21 I] <A> 22 whaching] <I saw>

192

She dried her tears and they did smile
To see her cheeks returning glow
A fond delusion—all the while
that full heart throbbed to overflow

With that sweet look and lively tone
And bright eye shining all the day
They could not guess at midnight lone
How she would weep the time away

193

But the hearts that once adored me
Have long forgot their vow
And the freinds that mustered round me
Have all forsaken now

T'was in a dream revealed to me
But not a dream of sleep
A dream of whachful agony
of greif that would not weep

Now do not harshly turn away

194

Start not upon the minster wall
Sunshine is shed in holey calm
And lonely though thy footsteps fall
The saints shall shelter thee from harm

Shrink not if it be Summer noon
This shadow should right welcome be
These stairs are steep but landed soon
We'll rest us long and quietly

192. *Text from E19*
1 She . . . they] <I've dried my tears and then> 3 a fond delusion—] <How little dreaming> 4 overflow] <let *?*o'erflow> 7 could not] <cannot> 8 would] ~ <had> <will>
193. *Text from F2. A tenth line beginning* B *has been cancelled*
194. *Text from T3*

What though our path be o'er the dead
They slumber soundly in the tombe
And why should mortals fear to tread
The pathway to their future home?

195

My heart is not enrapturd now
My eyes are full of tears
And constant sorrow on my brow
Has done the work of years

It was not hope that wrecked at once
The spirits oacen storm
But a long life of solitude
Hopes quenched and riseing thoughts subdued
A bleak novembers calm

196

What woke it then? a little child
Strayed from its fathers cottage door
And in the hour of moonlight mild
Laid lonely on the desert moor

197

I heard it then you heard it too
And seraph sweet it sang to you
But like the shreik of misery
That wild wild music wailed to me

198

Through the hours of yester night
Hall and gallery blazed with light

9 be] <is>   10 the<y>   12 pathway to] <— — of>

195. *Text from T3*
1 <i>enraptured
196. *Text from T3*
197. *Text from T3*
198. *Text from T3*

Every lamp its lustre showerd
On the adorer and the adored
None were sad that entered their
All were loved and all were fair
Some were dazzeling like the sun
Shineing down at summer noon
Some were sweet as amber even
Dieing in the depth of heaven
Some were soft and kind and gay
Mornings face not more devine
Some were like Diana's day
Midnight moonlights holy shine

199

Harp of wild and dream like Strain
When I touch thy strings
Why dost thou repeat again
Long forgotten things?

Harp in other earlier days
I could sing to thee
And not one of all thy lays
Vexed my memory

But now if I awake a note
That gave me joy before
Sounds of sorrow from thee float
Changeing ever more

Yet still steeped in mournful dyes
They come sailing on
Darkening all my summer skys
Shutting out my sun

200

All day I've toiled but not with pain
In learnings golden mine

199. *Text from T3*
7 thy] *or* my; *see introduction, p. 20*
200. *Text from T5*

And now at eventide again
The moonbeams softly shine

There is no snow upon the ground
No frost on wood or wave
The south wind blew with gentlest sound
And broke their icy grave

Tis sweet to wander here at night
To whach the winter die
With heart as summer sunshine light
And warm as summers sky

O may I never lose the peace
That lulls me lonely now
Though time should change my youthful face
And years should shade my brow

True to myself and true to all
May I be heedfull still
And turn away from passions call
And curb my own wild will

201

Stanzas

Often rebuked, yet always back returning
  To those first feelings that were born with me,
And leaving busy chase of wealth and learning
  For idle dreams of things which cannot be:

To-day, I will seek not the shadowy region,
  Its unsustaining vastness waxes drear;
And visions rising, legion after legion,
  Bring the unreal world too strangely near.

I'll walk, but not in old heroic traces,
  And not in paths of high morality,
And not among the half-distinguished faces,
  The clouded forms of long-past history.

5 ground] <grass>   6 frost] <ice>   18 be heedfull] <remember>   19 And] <To>

201. *Text from 1850*

I'll walk where my own nature would be leading:
  It vexes me to choose another guide:
Where the grey flocks in ferny glens are feeding;
  Where the wild wind blows on the mountain side.

What have those lonely mountains worth revealing?
  More glory and more grief than I can tell:
The earth that wakes *one* human heart to feeling
  Can centre both the worlds of Heaven and Hell.

COMMENTARY

For symbols and abbreviations see pp. xiii–xvi. For descriptions of the manuscripts see introduction, pp. 13–22. The commentary records all personal signatures by EB. Composition dates, Gondal dates and Gondal headings are included in the text.

Works cited are published at London unless otherwise specified. Biblical references are to the Authorized Version. Shakespeare quotations are from the Cambridge edition of 1891–3 by William Aldis Wright *et al.*, whose lineation is followed in the one-volume edition by Peter Alexander (1951). Quotations from Sir Walter Scott are taken from the 'magnum opus' edition of the *Waverley Novels* (48 vols., Edinburgh, 1830–3) and the companion editions of his *Poetical Works* (12 vols., 1833–4) and *Prose Works* (28 vols., 1834–6). Epictetus is quoted from the translation by Elizabeth Carter in *All the Works of Epictetus* (1758), reprinted in the Everyman Library as *Moral Discourses, Enchiridion and Fragments* (1910).

1. First published in *1902*, prefaced by **157**, which immediately precedes it in D10. *GQ* (pp. 47–9) reads the poem as a prophecy made before the birth of A.G.A., which on this view took place in a storm. The contrast of weathers in stanzas 2 and 4 recurs in **41**. 1–8 and in *WH*, pp. 301–2.

10–14 Cf. BB's Angrian 'Life of Percy' (1834), in which stormy weather at Percy's birth portends an unhappy life (Collins, p.12).

2. First published in *1902* as one poem with **163**, which follows it in D11. For the exhilarating effect of a storm at night, cf. and contrast **85**. A very high south-west wind with much rain was recorded at Keighley, near Haworth, on the day the piece was written (see Dingle). *Wind*, with homonyms like *breeze* and *blast*, occurs in more than half of EB's poems and fragments, seventeen times in the first line. The metre is not used elsewhere by EB, but for a similar metrical experiment see *Poems of AB*, 21.

3. First published in *1910*, and until now printed as the first stanza of one poem or sequence which went on to include **195**, **196**, and **197**. These pieces follow one another on T3 but are separated by horizontal strokes (see introduction, pp. 19, 26).

4. The first poem copied by EB in February 1844 into B, the notebook headed 'Emily Jane Brontë . . . Gondal Poems'; she may have transcribed it from pages of C that she later tore out (see introduction, pp. 17–18). First published (as a facsimile, with printed extracts) in Virginia Moore, *The Life and Eager Death of Emily Brontë* (1936); included in *1938*. Facsimiles of the first page appear in *1941* (frontispiece), Gérin (p. 183), Lloyd-Evans (p. 64), and Wilks (p. 113).

Here A.G.A. recalls the death of Alexander, Lord of Elbë, her lover or (in Paden, pp. 37–9) her husband. More than seven years later EB wrote another version of the scene, likewise related by A.G.A. (see 114).

1 *noon of night*: the phrase occurs in the 'eve of Waterloo' passage of *Childe Harold* (III. xxvi) and elsewhere in Byron; cf. also Thomas Warton, 'The Pleasures of Melancholy', 50–1.

20 *brow of pride*: cf. Scott, *Lord of the Isles*, II. ix. 3.

23 *gold*: EB began to write 'light'.

41–2 These lines suggest that Elbë Hall is in Gaaldine, whose 'soft, sunny, southern skies' are often contrasted with those of Gondal. But 8 seems to locate Elbë in Gondal; and other references to weather at Elbë (8. 2, 155) are consistent with Gondal's harsher climate.

63 *Augusta*: Elsewhere this name appears only in 81. 254, and in a reference to 'Agustus-Almedas life' in EB's record paper of 26 June 1837 (see appendix V).

5. Signed 'E. J. Brontë' at head below date in D. First published in *1902*. *1923*, *1934*, *1941* print 47–58 as a separate poem; but no break occurs in D, though these lines are slightly indented to mark the shift within the 'dream visitation' (Hewish, p. 43) to the speech or song of the royal ghost. The death that the ghost laments may be his or her own, or another's; that of Julius Brenzaida (Hinkley, p. 276; *GQ*, pp. 96–8), or Brenzaida's victims (Paden, pp. 22–3). For the stanza-form of this poem and 114 cf. Charles Wesley's hymn 'Soldiers of Christ, arise', and (with simplified rhyming) John Keble's hymn, 'Blest are the pure in heart'.

23 *ranny*: 'uncanny' in *1902*; first corrected in *1941*. Answering an enquiry by C. W. Hatfield, G. M. Hort wrote in the *Sunday Times* on 6 May 1934: 'The adjective *ranny* is, in North-Eastern England, applied to anything sharp or shrewish. "The air was ranny" would, therefore, be quite intelligible to Yorkshire ears.' The sense seems derived from *ranny* as a noun, meaning a shrew (*English Dialect Dictionary*, ed. Joseph Wright (1898–1905)).

47–8 *Regina*: 'The capital of Gondal' (*GGG*, and cf. 'Regina's towers', *Poems of AB*, 15. 2). As a personal name, 'Regina' occurs in a list of fictional characters made by EB (see appendix VI).

6. First published in *1902*. 'Fernando' in 28 seems to identify the doomed child as Fernando De Samara, who after a love affair with A.G.A. was first imprisoned, and then banished by her, and committed suicide (see 37, 72; also 17. 38 and comment).

13 *child of dust*: not directly scriptural, though *dust* is a common biblical metaphor for mortality. Cf. 'Frail children of dust', in Sir Robert Grant's hymn 'O worship the King', 22, printed in Edward Bickersteth's *Christian Psalmody* (1833) and Henry Venn Elliott's *Psalms and Hymns for Public, Private and Social Worship* (1835).

28 *Fernando*: previously read as 'For'. The name features in Wellington's Peninsular campaigns—e.g. Sir William Napier's *History of the War in the Peninsula* (1828–40) refers to 'the great fortress of Fernando de Figueras'

(bk. XIII, ch. 4; cf. comment on 'Almeda' in 18). Also, Fernando Po in West Africa provided the real-life site for Glasstown, centre of the Brontës' earlier game: see Christine Alexander, *The Early Writings of Charlotte Brontë* (Oxford, 1983), p. 30.

29–30 Cf. Scott, *Lady of the Lake*, V. x. 1–2, 'to his heart | The life-blood thrilled with sudden start'; *Rokeby*, I. iii. 13–14, 'a sudden start | Impelled the life-blood from the heart'.

49 *cut away*: possibly EB intended to write 'cast away', but unintentionally repeated 'cut' from 48.

7. Signed 'E J B' at head below date in D. First published in *1902*. The text may have been one of a series of fair copies made between late 1838 and early 1839 (see introduction, p. 19). *GQ* (p. 63) and Paden (p. 40) identify the speaker as A.G.A., who finds snow drifting into her prison in 18 as the present speaker does in 35–6, though with different reactions. For the dungeon theme see introduction, p. 11.

26 *my . . . my*: in EB's 'Brontë script' *my* and *thy* can look exactly alike, since the first crown of the *m* is often tall and spiky and the *t* in *thy* is often uncrossed. The reading given here is that of all previous editions and follows the probable sense of the passage.

35–6 Cf. Byron, *Prisoner of Chillon*, 119–20: 'And I have felt the winter's spray | Wash through the bars when winds were high.'

44 *scearce*: see appendix I, p. 278

49 *my*: previous editions read 'thy'; but the word could be either (see comment on 26), and it is not clear that another person is addressed.

8. Signed 'E' at head before date in B. First published in *1902* from the D text. A.G.A., who speaks the poem, is standing in the heather on Elbë hill, from which she can see the lights of Elbë Hall among the woods below; the place to which she will return (13) may also be Elbë.

In the D text, the earliest surviving version, nothing suggests that Elbë is dead: he is 'on the desolate sea' longing for Gondal, Elbë, and A.G.A. After copying the poem into the C notebook, EB apparently decided to relocate it in a period after Elbë's death (described by A.G.A. in 4, written more than five months earlier), and rewrote these lines accordingly. Thus 'the desolate sea' became 'a desolate sea'—a metaphor for death, made explicit in the revised last line. After recopying the revised poem into B, EB tore out of C the leaf on which 1–15 had been written, but left the leaf containing 16–20 and the still-uncopied 18.

2 For Elbë weather, see commentary on 4. 41–2.

9. First published in *1902*. The earliest datable poem that may deal with EB's own experience as a writer; **144** may be related to it.

10. First published in *1902*, followed under the same poem number by other fragments from D12 (164–8). *GQ* (pp. 55–7) takes **10** and **164–7** to refer to a battle in which Elbë was killed (see 4, 114). There were probably many battles in Gondal, but the scenery and time of day are right.

11. Signed 'E J B' at head on left, opposite date. First published in *1910*. EB may have meant to go on to introduce the anguished survivor (37–40), and to explain the narrator's reference to 'what had been before' (41–4); but the fragment ends on T2^{v}, more than half of which is left blank.

4 *Tyndarum*: not referred to elsewhere by EB or AB. Tyndrum in Perth is mentioned by Scott as 'wild Teyndrum', 'Teyndrum's dread rout' (*Lord of the Isles*, II. xii. 13, IV. xix. 16), and 'Teinedrum' (*Legend of Montrose*, ch. 17).

21–2 EB first copied 25–6 here, then sponged them out and wrote these lines over what remained.

25–32 For a similar scene see **126**. 120–4. The snow, shattered glass, branches, 'wandering moan', and dream feeling come together again in *WH*, pp. 30–1.

51–2 Cf. Byron, *Giaour*, 1130, 'The Morning-star of Memory'; Thomas Moore, 'The Fire-Worshippers', in *Lalla Rookh* (1817), 'His heart's pure planet, shining yet | Above the waste of memory' (*Poetical Works* (1841), vi. 311–12).

12. First published in *1910*. For the theme and journey metaphor, cf. **129**.

1 *land of rest*: Canaan, the place of rest promised to the Israelites after their forty years' wandering in the wilderness (Deuteronomy 3: 20, 12: 9–10), became in Christian teaching a type of spiritual repose (Matthew 11: 28–9) and of heaven (Hebrews 3: 17–18; 4 *passim*).

13. The last of nine pieces copied on to T3. Space remained for another four lines, but a row of crosses shows that at the copying date EB had no thought of adding to the fragment. First published in *1910*.

14. First published in *1902*. Hinkley (p. 279) and *GQ* (p. 133) conjecture that this poem is spoken by Fernando De Samara to his childhood sweetheart (see **17**); Paden (p. 58 n. 30) that Julius Brenzaida speaks it to Geraldine S. (see **34**, **35**).

1 *breast*: previously read as 'heart'; but EB changed 'heart' by overwriting, to avoid a threefold repetition.

13–16 Cf. Scott, *Marmion*, III. introd. 137–51.

15. First published in *1902*. Various places have been found for this episode in the story of A.G.A. For the stanza form, with its effective two-stress fourth line, cf. **77**.

In *Confessions of an English Opium Eater* (1822) Thomas De Quincey describes a shadowy tormenting sleep-world in which the imagery of 'faces, imploring, wrathful, despairing' alternates with that of 'weltering waves' (see *Works*, ed. David Masson (Edinburgh, 1896–7), iii. 441). Hewish (pp. 27, 35–6) notes a possible influence of De Quincey on the Brontës, and points out that CB sent him a copy of *1846* 'in acknowledgement of the pleasure and profit we have often and long derived from your works' (*LL*, ii. 136).

1 EB probably began to write 'rest', as in 5.

10 EB probably began to write 'deepest'.

21–2 Gezari compares *Macbeth*, II. ii. 37, 'Sleep that knits up the ravell'd sleave of care'.

16. First published in *1902*. For comment on this mysteriously powerful poem see Grove, pp. 45–6.

17. First published in *1902*. The 'Fernando' named in 38 is probably Fernando De Samara, a lover of A.G.A. (**37**, **72**); for her sake he 'betray[ed] the faith of yesterday', while still young (**72**. 62, 69–72). It has been assumed that this poem begins to tell how 'ten years after his departure the [earlier] sweetheart dies of his desertion' (Hinkley, p. 279). But by 67 she has gained 'power for copeing' with his absence and silence, and EB still has about nine years of poem-time in hand. Probably EB meant to add more events, which may not have been fully planned.

The most famous Victorian poem spoken to a mother by a daughter who confesses love troubles as her death approaches is the section of Tennyson's 'The May Queen' called 'New-Year's Eve'. A version had appeared in his *Poems* (1832), and EB may have seen a copy; but Tennyson's fame was not established until 1842, and the *Quarterly Review* and *Blackwood's Magazine* had ignored this poem.

9 *Twice twelve short years*: EB is likely to have been exact about dates in her poems, as she was in *WH*. If the speaker is now twenty-four, she must when Fernando left (37–8) have been fourteen—like the idyllic lovers in 'Alexander and Zenobia' (*Poems of AB*, **2**. 9, 109).

27 Cf. 'Nay, nay, you must not weep, nor let your grief be wild' (Tennyson, 'New-Year's Eve', 35).

33–4 Cf. CB's 'A Leaf from an Unopened Volume' (1834), where Sofala is deserted by Zamorna and 'decay began to fade her cheek and dim her eye' (*CBEW*, ii/I. 376).

38 *his home and you*: from this and 'hearts together nourished' in 47, it has been deduced that Fernando is the speaker's foster-brother (Hinkley, p. 279; *GQ*, p. 133).

45 *Areons Forest*: 'Areon' clearly recurs only in **63**, where the speaker, who once lived at 'Areon Hall' and may be Fernando, imagines the fate of a woman now living there who may be his former sweetheart.

18. The signature 'Emily Jane Brontë' appears with the date at the foot of the C text. The fragments on E13 seem to be the remains of a draft later copied into C: '~~O transient v~~' appears on one side of the leaf inverted to the other texts, among which (overleaf) are **18**. 22–8. First published in *1910*.

A.G.A. was imprisoned after the death of Alexander Elbë, which she records in another prison poem (**114**) and which explains her 'mourning brow' in 6; 'rebel' in 7 may mean that her own royal power has been lost to her captors. For the dungeon theme see introduction, p. 11.

Wreath of snow: a chiefly Scottish expression which usually means a snowdrift, capable of blocking rivers (Burns, 'A Winter Night', 9) or burying sheep (Scott, *Black Dwarf*, last paragraph). But here and in **21**. 5–6 EB seems to have imagined something light and graceful, wafted into the dungeon as in **7**. 35–6. She may have inferred this meaning from the motto to *Black Dwarf*, ch. 10 (quoted in commentary on **21**). AB includes 'wreathed snow' among childhood delights, like flowers and sparkling frosts, in 'Memory' (*Poems of AB*, 32. 34).

A G Almeda: the one occurrence of 'Almeda' in surviving poems; elsewhere it appears in EB's record paper of 26 June 1837 (see appendix V), and as a single word upside-down in the margin of E15. Almeida, a Portuguese city, features in the Peninsular campaigns of 1810–11 by CB's hero the Duke of Wellington (cf. comment on 'Fernando' in **6**. 28).

17–24 For the Gondals' love of their climate and of snow, cf. **101**, esp. 33–4.

19 *Shining through darkness*: perhaps an echo of New Testament phrases (John 1: 5, 2 Corinthians 4: 6) which gave the title 'Light Shining out of Darkness' to Cowper's hymn beginning 'God moves in a mysterious way'.

19. First published in *1910*. Perhaps a Gondal poem; Paden (p. 40) assigns it to the dying Alfred S. In metre, diction, and feeling the poem resembles many hymns.

5–16 For the nautical metaphor, cf. one of John Wesley's hymns, under 'Describing Death':

> Our brother the haven hath gained,
> Out-flying the tempest and wind,
> His rest he hath sooner obtained,
> And left his companions behind,
> Still tossed on a sea of distress,
> Hard toiling to make the blest shore,
> Where all is assurance and peace,
> And sorrow and sin are no more.

(*A Collection of Hymns for the Use of the People called Methodists*, ed. Franz Hildebrandt and Oliver A. Beckerlegge, in *Works of John Wesley*, vii (Oxford, 1983), 140.) The debt is generic. With 'that dark Oecan', cf. also the 'darker wave' of **15**. 16.

20. First published in *1902* (from D). The song celebrates a victory by Julius Brenzaida (for whom see introduction, pp. 12–13) over Zalona, a city and a kingdom in Gaaldine (see **94**).

Julius Angora: 'Angora' is apparently one of Brenzaida's territorial titles, from the mountainous region (probably in Gondal) where he was later to be buried (**116**. 6).

11–12 Julius's crimson flag appears in **88**. 14; a 'sheet of crimson sheen' is contrasted with the 'emerald flags' of Zalona in **94**. 7, 66–8.

15 *Almedore*: another kingdom in Gaaldine (*GGG*), used like Angora as a territorial title for Brenzaida (**88**. 27).

21. The line of crosses which separates this poem from **33**, which precedes it in E12^{v}, is interrupted by two capital A's, thus: 'x x A x x A x x x'. First published in *1910*. For critical comment see Grove, pp. 57–8.

5–6 Cf. Scott, *Black Dwarf*, motto to ch. 10: 'I left my ladye's bower last night— | It was clad in wreaths of snaw,— | I'll seek it when the sun is bright, | And sweet the roses blaw.' See also comment on title of **18**.

22. First published in *1910*.

Febuary H G 1838. It is not clear whether these are Gondal initials, which do not elsewhere occur in the middle of a composition date. A 'Gleneden' (forename unknown, also imprisoned) speaks **26**, written three months later.

1 *Weaned*: detached, alienated; cf. **116**. 26.

23. First published in *1902* as one poem with **141** and **142**, which precede and follow it in D5. The poem describes in retrospect the oath of alliance between Julius Brenzaida and Gerald Exina (see introduction, p. 12). The solemnities may reflect the approaching coronation of Queen Victoria (28 June 1838). With this poem cf. **64**.

20 *bitter smile*: signifying treachery, as in Byron, *The Corsair*, 229–30, 'Love shows all changes—Hate, Ambition, Guile | Betray no further than the bitter smile'; cf. also *Giaour*, 848–9.

22 *Geralds hand*: this monarch can be identified with the 'Gerald Exina' who occurs in two lists of Gondal names by AB (see appendix VI), and with the 'Gerald' of **190**, imprisoned (presumably by the treacherous Julius) while Gondal endures a 'galling chain'. Either he or another Exina makes war against Julius in the weeks before Julius is assassinated (**88**. 59).

24. First published in *1902*. With 9 comes what seems a complete change of subject, and 9–20 may be a separate poem, as Paden (p. 15) believes. (Both parts show uncertainty about metre.) But there is no dividing line or extra space in D, and the two themes may be connected in Gondal history. Interpretations differ widely.

1 Hinkley (pp. 277–8) identifies the 'lone green dell' with the dell in which the speaker of **55** apparently abandons her child Alexandria.

5 Cf. Scott, *Lady of the Lake*, III. v. 3–6: 'deep within a dreary glen, | Where scatter'd lay the bones of men, | In some forgotten battle slain, | And bleach'd by drifting wind and rain.'

9 *Noble foe*: cf. Shakespeare, *Troilus and Cressida*, I. iii. 309; Scott, *Lord of the Isles*, III. vi. 15.

19 *the gilded vapours fly*: a compressed version of the metaphor in **74**. 5–8: illusions evaporate like morning mists gilded by the early sun.

25. Presumably copied from C into B shortly after EB began this later transcript book in February 1844. First published in *1902*.

A.G.A. to A.S.: A.G.A. speaks at least two other poems to her lover A.S., usually identified with Alfred ?Sidonia of **92** (see introduction, p. 12). The grouping of poems in B suggests that after she left him (**104**), he 'failed' (**48**) and died. The signs of spring in **25** need not mean that he died out of doors.

13–16 Cf. AB's 'The Captive's Dream', written four months earlier: 'He was so changed from what he used to be, | There was no redness on his woe-worn cheek, | No sunny smile upon his ashy lips, | His hollow wandering eyes looked wild and fierce' (*Poems of AB*, 4. 2–5).

17 *Can Death*—: the sentence broken off would presumably have ended 'have claimed thee?', or words to that effect. The reading 'Call Death', said

to appear 'in a transcript by A. B. Nicholls' (*1934*, p. 57 n.), was adopted in *1910*, *1923*, and *1941*.

26. Signed 'E —' at head on right, before date. EB has written '1' boldly in ink above the title—presumably to show that this poem should be taken before **45**, copied immediately before it, over which she has written '2'. First published in Shorter, pp. 154–7. 'Gleneden' may be Arthur Gleneden (**45**), or the 'H G' of **22**. The assassination of which he dreams resembles that of Julius Brenzaida (cf. **46**, 88). *GQ* (pp. 106–8) interprets the dream as prophetic of that event. With the period of tyranny in Gondal described here, cf. **190**.

14 *southwinds*: cf. 'northwind's', 37. 3.

28 *Patriot*: particularly, one who fights for his country's freedom; cf. Scott, *Lord of the Isles*, III. xxvii. 3–4.

bloody tombs: tombs of those who have died by execution or other violence: cf. Scott, *Lay of the Last Minstrel*, introd. 44, 'Monmouth's bloody tomb'.

27. Copied from D into C, but not into B, the main copy-book for Gondal poems. First published in *1902*. The voyage over stormy waters in a small boat suggests flight, across the lake and then downstream to the sea.

A A: Paden (pp. 46–7) interprets this as 'Alexandria Augusta'— the daughter, in his reconstruction, of A.G.A., abandoned in a snowstorm by her mother (55) but rescued by Blanche, a friend or attendant. Another possibility is that the song belongs to an early episode in the life of A.G.A. herself. Her initials are not found elsewhere without the 'G.', but eleven months earlier EB had been writing 'Agustus-Almedas life' (for record paper, see appendix V).

Blanche (in D title): either the mother or a nurse; the name recurs only in **29**, written in the following month.

4 *dark haird*: dark hair is not often described as 'bright' (D reading), and EB may have changed the word to make it consistent with other descriptions. (A.G.A. has 'black resplendant hair', 37. 17.)

6 *Elderns lake*: the lake was in or near Angora (88. 13–15), apparently a province in the mountainous northern part of Gondal (**116**. 6, and cf. **72**. 60). For an 'Eldurn's shore' among uninhabited woods and mountains, see Thomas Campbell, 'Lines on Leaving a Scene in Bavaria', 21, 33.

8 *fair-browed*: the child may be dark-haired and pale-skinned, like several of EB's Byronic characters; and like the boy whose 'Soft raven curls hung clustering round | A brow of marble white' in 'Alexander and Zenobia' (*Poems of AB*, 2. 11–12).

28. First published in *1910*. An example of EB's tendency to hoard short passages of verse: these lines have been copied on to a slip with eight other pieces, one dated February 1839, another October 1837. They may refer to the time of Gondal tyranny described in **26** and **190**.

29. First published in *1910*. For the other occurrence of 'Blanche', see **27** (collation and comment). 'We may suppose that Blanche and her ward were at first welcomed in a Gaaldinian court, and that later . . . Blanche was forced to flee again' (Paden, p. 47).

5 *my sunburnt neck*: a tan, associated with outdoor labour and low status, was still thought to detract from women's beauty: cf. Scott, *Lady of the Lake*, I. xviii. 4–5.

7 *red of noble birth*: the red of rosy cheeks in contrast with white skin.

9 *care as quenched*: perhaps a clue to EB's pronunciation (see appendix I).

19–20 Cf. Scott, *Lay of the Last Minstrel*, introd. 15–16: 'No longer courted and caress'd, | High placed in hall, a welcome guest'.

30. First published in *1902*.

31. First published in *1902*, as two poems dividing after 8. The 'Song' tells of the escape of the outlaw Douglas from riders eager to avenge their 'soveriegn's gore' (59). Since at the close of **81** Lord Eldred sends men in pursuit of a Douglas, apparently outlawed (35–40), who has killed his 'royal foe' A.G.A. (220), it seems likely that this is the sequel. If so, EB, who did not begin writing **81** until 1841, had become uncertain about Douglas's fate: in that poem he is wounded by A.G.A. in their struggle and Angelica watches 'his last hopless agony' (259)—though he manages to leave the scene on foot (288–95). Hinkley (p. 276) believes that in **31** Douglas is escaping after having assassinated Julius Brenzaida. 'Douglas' occurs only in **31** and **81**; 'M. Douglas' in **113**. In fifteenth- and sixteenth-century Scotland the powerful clan of Douglas was involved in contests with royal power, and members were frequently banished (Scott, *Tales of a Grandfather*, *passim*). The outlawed Douglas in Scott's *Lady of the Lake* is an imaginary person.

1–8 The device of framing a 'song of troubled times' in a more recent setting had been used by Scott, e.g. in *Lay of the Last Minstrel*, *Marmion*, and *Tales of My Landlord*. EB uses the device in this poem and **92**; a more subtle framing is achieved in *WH*.

2 *organ's . . . sound*: 'music's', CB in B. An organ had been installed in Haworth Church in May 1835. For drawing-room use, EB may have had in mind one of the prototypes of the harmonium.

5 *window's velvet veil*: the furnishings recall those of Thrushcross Grange (where the curtains are 'looped up': *WH*, p. 62) as perceived by Catherine and Heathcliff.

8+ *Song*: what follows is EB's most successful attempt at a literary ballad, using traditional devices like repetition, question and answer, and the impersonal witness ('I saw . . .', 13). There seem to be echoes of BB's 'How fast that courser fleeted by' (1835; *Poems of BB*, pp. 99–114, 379–96).

13 Cf. 'How fast that courser', 5: 'I saw his Riders darkned form'. 67 *wildbeast*: to hyphenate after 'wild' was common practice, indicating in verse a 'rhythmic stress on the adjective' (*OED*). To make one word of adjective and noun was less common, but cf. 'wildswan' in Tennyson, *Princess*, IV. 414. EB does so here and in **60**, **107**, **165**, **167**; elsewhere (e.g. **40**) she writes them separately. CB apparently stresses the adjective in the line 'The desert wild deer's tread' ('A Leaf from an Unopened Volume' (1834), in *CBEW*, ii/I. 349).

69–70 Cf. 'How fast that courser', 49–50: 'why smiled he, when that far off light | Again broke twinkling on his sight'. 71 ff. In Scott's *Old Mortality*, ch. 43, the outlaw Burley's cavern is approached by 'an old oak-tree, flung across the chasm in a manner that seemed accidental, [which] formed a bridge of fearfully narrow dimensions and uncertain footing'. Burley's defence is to send it crashing down with 'one spurn of my foot'.

32. Signed 'E.' at head on right, before date. First published in *1850*. Hinkley (p. 279), *GQ* (p. 128), and Paden (p. 44) identify A.G.A.'s former lover with Fernando De Samara, whose singing she enjoyed (72. 65–72) before she 'ceased to care'. EB copied this poem into B immediately before 72 and 37, in which Fernando looks back on his affair with A.G.A. At this stage EB was grouping the B poems by story and character. A guitar is personified and a tree felled in P. B. Shelley's 'With a Guitar, to Jane', which is spoken by 'Ferdinand'; the poem appeared in the *Athenæum*, 20 October 1832, and in *Fraser's Magazine*, January 1833.

Title: 'The Lady to her guitar', CB in A and *1850*.

1 *foreign string*: the guitar had enjoyed an increasing vogue in England since the mid-eighteenth century, but kept its exotic associations. In Ann Radcliffe's fiction 'peculiarly romantic instruments appear to be the lute, guitar, French horn and oboe' (Eino Railo, *The Haunted Castle* (1927), p. 53).

7 'When clouds of storm, or shades of night' *1850*.

9–10 *glassy brook . . . willows*: cf. *Hamlet*, IV. vii. 167.

12 *gleaming*: 'dryad', CB in B and *1850* ('Dryad-hair').

13–16 In Scott, *Legend of Montrose*, ch. 10, a listener thanks a harpist 'for having opened a fountain [of tears] which hath been dry for many a year'.

14 *woke*: 'waked' restored by CB in B and *1850*.

15 *flow*: 'moan' *1850*.

33. Centred over the head of the poem in E is what may be '9', 'I', or 'J' (perhaps a false start for 'Julius Brenzaida', who heads the following poem), with a few decorative pen-strokes. First published in *1910*.

The period EB spent as a teacher in Miss Patchett's school at Law Hill, near Halifax, seems to have begun late in September 1838 and ended about six months later (see Edward Chitham and Tom Winnifrith, *Brontë Facts and Brontë Problems* (1983), pp. 21–9; Jennifer Cox, 'Emily at Law Hill, 1838: Corroborative Evidence', *BST*, 18/94 (1984), 267–70). This may be her first surviving poem of that period, which was surprisingly fertile.

2 *low green hills*: visible from the back of Law Hill school; see photograph in Wilks, p. 88.

10 *azure flowers*: cf. 'azure moss and flowers', in P. B. Shelley, 'Ode to the West Wind', 35.

34. Signed 'E.' at head on left. First published in *1902*. For Julius Brenzaida see introduction, pp. 12–13; the other poems linking him with

Geraldine are 35, 87. Visick (pp. 30–2) suggests that the pictures of happiness on the moors, in all weathers, anticipate *WH*. But the courtly opening and close of Julius's song imply a different world from that of Catherine and Heathcliff.

4 *Ushered*: EB may have begun to write 'Heralded'.

35. Signed 'E.' at head on left. Facsimile of MS in Moore, *The Life and Eager Death of Emily Brontë*. First published in *1850*. One of the few lyrics by EB whose cadence recalls Cavalier poetry.

Title: 'Love's Farewell' added in B, almost certainly by CB; 'Last Words' *1850*.

1–4 Visick (pp. 31–2, 84) draws a parallel with 'Heathcliff reproaching Catherine' for deserting him (*WH*, p. 138), and finds here part of a 'sketch' of the main relationships of the novel. But the tone is quite different, and in 87 it is Geraldine who appears the deserted partner.

4 *slighted heart*: 'lips or heart' *1850*.

5 *moorside*: 'hill-side', CB in B and *1850*.

10 *rosey*: 'falsest', CB's alternative in B, *1850*.

13–14 Phrasing and rhythm may echo Lovelace, 'To Althea, from Prison', 25–6.

14 *prison*: 'castle', CB in B; 'strongest' *1850*.

17–24 As a young prince or nobleman, Julius loved the ambitious Rosina [Alcona], which led to his imprisonment in the 'Southern College' (**112**). The easiest explanation of these lines is that, his affair with Geraldine being ended, he intends to return to Rosina, with whom he was closely tied later during his wars, and who was in his palace when he died (**88**).

19 *eyes, whose lightening shine*: Rosina's 'falcon eyes' 'burn with lightening shine' (**112**. 51, 55).

36. 'A G A' appears on right, under date. First published in *1902*, with two fragments which follow in D11 (**161**, **162**) added under the same poem number but after rows of periods.

4–6 'I spy comfort in that stranger's countenance; I know not why it should be so, but I am well persuaded he is a friend' (Mary Queen of Scots to Roland Graeme in Scott, *Abbot*, ch. 35).

9–12 Evidently some relationship unknown to A.G.A. links her with the Byronic stranger and gives rise to these feelings. Cf. the effect produced on Sir Duncan Campbell by Annot Lyle, his unknown, long-lost daughter (Scott, *Legend of Montrose*, ch. 9); also CB's parodic 'The Enfant', written in 1829, in which 'M. Hanghimself . . . felt a love for the poor little Enfant, for which he could by no means account', and the 'Enfant' proves to be his own stolen child (*CBEW*, i. 35–6). Paden (pp. 32–49) identifies the stranger as Henry Angora, son of Julius Brenzaida by Geraldine S., who in Paden's reconstruction was the sister of A.G.A.'s lover Alfred.

37. Signed 'E.' at head on right, before date. First published in *1902*. The poem presents the closing act in the story of Fernando De Samara: see introduction, p. 12. The poem begins with two four-foot lines, but by 12 has settled into iambic hexameter, used by EB only here and in **123**.

3 *northwind's*: cf. 'southwinds', **26**. 14.

15 *alone*: EB began to write 'only'.

38. Cancelled in C after having been copied into A; the earliest poem in the 'non-Gondal' notebook. For problems of interpreting the group among which it appears, see introduction, pp. 4–5. Facsimile of A text in *1934*, p. 311. First published in *1902*.

4 *decay*: fade. Cf. Scott, *Lord of the Isles*, I. introd. 41, 'on Coolin's hills the lights decay'.

15 *'tis enough for me*: either 'It is enough to have had the vision in the past', or 'It is a satisfaction to know the vision cannot come again, since its memory can yield me nought but care.'

39. The first poem entered into MS A, headed on left 'E J B.' and on right 'Transcribed Febuary 1844.' Facsimile of MS in *1934*, pp. 301–2. First published in *1850*.

CB's prefatory note presents **39**, **40**, and **42** as 'three little poems of my sister Emily's, written in her sixteenth year . . . composed at twilight, in the schoolroom, when the leisure of the evening play-hour brought back in full tide the thoughts of home' (*1850*, pp. 471–3; for a longer extract see *WH*, pp. 445–6). The composition dates show that EB was twenty when she wrote these poems, during her period of teaching at Law Hill in 1838–9. CB may have confused this period with EB's spell as a pupil at Roe Head in 1835 (though EB's dates are plainly visible); or she may have felt that these poems would be more acceptable if offered as the work of a schoolgirl. No doubt EB suffered in both places from the homesickness and sense of confinement on which CB dwells, and these poems are easier to relate to her life than **38**. But even here there are fictional elements: in **39** the 'highlands' and 'glens' (21, 34) suggest Scotland (which EB never saw) or Gondal rather than the hills around Haworth; and 69–70 seem to add a conventional love interest, though they could refer to EB's family.

In *1850* CB made verbal alterations in twenty lines of this poem, some of which remove fictional touches. Unlike her revisions of **40**, these are not written into A.

Date: the earlier MS does not give the day of the month, which EB may have worked out, or guessed, later. On 11 November the weather at Keighley, twelve miles from Law Hill, was cold but windless (Dingle).

2 *the waned autumnal*: 'th' autumnal' *1850*.

4 *stormy winters*: 'of winter' *1850*.

6 'Did my exiled spirit grieve' *1850*.

7 *Sighed . . . sighed*: 'Grieved . . . grieved' *1850*.

11 This line and 35 apparently quote words from a poem or song which 'awakened a spell'.

for: 'and' *1850*.

19–22 'Awaken, o'er all my dear moorland, | West-wind, in thy glory and pride! | O! call me from valley and lowland, | To walk by the hill-torrent's side!' *1850*.

25 *darker waves round*: 'sullenly waves' *1850*.

27 *yellow-stars*: celandines; cf. 'golden star and heatherbell', *Poems of AB*, **32**. 32.

mountain: see commentary on **40**. 32.

30 *wintery*: 'wintry' *1850*.

32 *scarlet*: 'vermeil' *1850*.

33 *slopes*: 'heights' *1850*.

34 *glens*: 'crags' *1850*.

35 No quotation-marks in *1850*.

36 *that*: 'it' *1850*.

39–42 For the joys of a remembered freer life, cf. ''Tis strange to think' (*Poems of AB*, **26**), esp. 25–8.

39 *dusk heaven*: 'dawn-heaven' *1850*.

42 *While*: 'As' *1850*.

43–6 'My sister Emily loved the moors. Flowers brighter than the rose bloomed in the blackest of the heath for her; out of a sullen hollow in a livid hill-side her mind could make an Eden. She found in the bleak solitude many and dear delights; and not the least and best loved was—liberty' (CB in *1850*, p. 472). Moors were not wanting at Law Hill, which had 'commanding views in three directions of almost uninterrupted moorland' (Gérin, p. 73).

52 *That*: 'Which' *1850*.

59–60 *the loved music*: the *ranz des vaches*, a melody varying from district to district, played on the alpenhorn to bring the cows home for milking. Boswell calls it 'that air, which instantly and irresistibly excites in the Swiss, when in a foreign land, the *maladie du pais*' (*Life of Johnson*, ed. G. B. Hill, rev. L. F. Powell (Oxford, 1934–50), iii. 198). The belief that it was forbidden to play it in the hearing of Swiss troops for fear of causing desertion, or even death, had been current since 1710 (ibid., pp. 510–11). Cf. Wordsworth, 'On Hearing the "Ranz des Vaches" on the Top of the Pass of St Gothard' (1822), in *Poetical Works*, ed. E. de Selincourt (Oxford, 1940–9), iii. 178.

62 'Than, for me, in that blighted heath lay' *1850*.

63 *that*: 'which' *1850*.

40. The second poem entered into A; facsimile of MS in *1934*, pp. 303–4. First published in *1850*. Like **39**, the poem may express homesickness at Law Hill, but with touches that suggest a longing for Scotland or Gondal rather than Haworth ('chain of mountains', 'wandering deer'). CB revised it before publication, noting most of her intended revisions in A, and removed the deer, undignified weeds, and dungeon bars.

1–4 For CB's misdated summary of a letter from EB, now lost, describing the long hours and short breaks at Miss Patchett's school, see *LL*, i. 162. CB's revision in 2 accords with her presentation of the poem as the work of a schoolgirl, not a teacher (see comment on **39**).

2 *noisy crowd are barred*: 'weary task is put', CB in A, *1850*.

4 *A little*: 'Alike,' *1850* (perhaps a misreading).

6 *Full many a land*: 'What thought, what scene', CB in A, *1850*.

7 *And places near, and*: 'What spot, or near and', CB in A; 'What spot, or near or' *1850*.

8 *Have*: 'Has' *1850*.

14 'Moonless above bends twilight's dome' *1850*.

19 *garden-walk with weeds*: 'gable grey, the walk', CB in A; 'thorn-trees gaunt, the walks' *1850*. Cf. AB's 'Home', written at Thorp Green *c.*1843–4: 'Restore to me that little spot, | With gray walls compassed round, | Where knotted grass neglected lies, | And weeds usurp the ground' (*Poems of AB*, **30**. 21–4).

21–4 Omitted in *1850*.

22 *Another clime*: usually interpreted as Gondal, whose scenery (like that of 31–40) is that of the Scottish highlands. Cf. AB's lines of January 1845: 'To our beloved land I'll flee, | Our land of thought and soul' (*Poems of AB*, **36**. 5–6), where Gondal is meant. EB's two 'climes' are not clearly contrasted: the 'little . . . green lane' could belong to either, and 'familiar . . . accents' seem to be heard in both. In *1850* CB combines them.

25 *Yes*: 'Still', CB in A, *1850*.

26 *flickering*: 'alien' *1850*.

32 *mountains*: 'moorland', CB's alternative in A. *1850* retains 'mountains' here and 'mountain' at **39**. 27. The word was used for 'elevations of moderate altitude' (*OED*), and usage varied with locality. Mrs Margaret Smith points out to me that CB refers to 'our mountains' round Haworth, e.g. when writing to Ellen Nussey on 20 June 1833 (*LL*, i. 109), and similar usage can be found in Nussey's letters and Gaskell's *Life of Charlotte Brontë*.

37 *That*: italicized in *1850*.

38 *pathways far and near*: 'turfy pathway's sweep', CB in A, *1850*.

40 *deer*: 'sheep', CB in A, *1850*.

43–8 The painful interruption of fantasy by the demands of school life is also recorded in CB's poem 'We wove a web in childhood' and in the prose she appended to it: see *Poems of Charlotte Brontë*, ed. Victor A. Neufeldt (New York, 1985), pp. 165–70.

44 'Restraint & heavy task recoil', CB in A, *1850*.

48 'And brought back labour, task & tear', CB in A ('~~pain & fear~~', CB in margin); 'And back came labour, bondage, care' *1850*.

41. Facsimile of MS in *1934*, pp. 304–5. First published in *1902*. The contrast of 'still' and 'breezy' weather in 1–8, expressing mood or temperament, reappears in *WH*, pp. 301–2; cf. also **1**. The Keighley weather record shows 7 December 1838 as a fine day with little wind (Dingle).

2 *scearce*: the spelling, like the rhyme at 6 and 8, may represent EB's pronunciation; see appendix I.

30 *July's golden beam*: the old pronunciation of *July* to rhyme with *truly* (as in Wordsworth, 'Goody Blake and Harry Gill', 9) lingered in the north of England and Scotland; cf. **55**. 1. But EB later rhymes it with 'sky' (**96**. 2).

32 Cf. Byron, *Oscar of Alva*, xlvi: 'The blue flames curdle o'er the hearth.'

42. Facsimile of MS in *1934*, pp. 305–6. First published in *1850*, with the title 'The Bluebell' and revisions by CB. The 'bluebell' of the Brontës was not the wild hyacinth but *campanula rotundifolia*, known farther south as the harebell. For the effect of this flower, cf. AB's 'The Bluebell', written at Thorp Green in August 1840:

> Whence came that rising in my throat,
> That dimness in my eye[s]?
> Why did those burning drops distil—
> Those bitter feelings rise?
>
> O, that lone flower recalled to me
> My happy childhood's hours
> When bluebells seemed like fairy gifts
> A prize among the flowers,
>
> Those sunny days of merriment
> When heart and soul were free,
> And when I dwelt with kindred hearts
> That loved and cared for me.
>
> (*Poems of AB*, 10. 29–40)

For another poem on this flower by EB, see 48.

3 *mightest*: previous editions read 'mightiest'.

12 *its*: 'her' *1850*.

13–16 18 December 1838 was frosty (Dingle).

13 *glancing*: 'flashing' or (in Scottish usage) 'shining' (*OED*).

21 *heather-bell*: 'sweet Bluebell' *1850*.

25–40 Omitted in *1850*.

41 'Yet oh when chill the sunbeams fall', CB in A; 'For, oh! when chill the sunbeams fall' *1850*.

42 *the*: 'that' *1850*.

43 *the*: 'yon' *1850*.

45 *yearn*: 'weep' *1850*. It is not clear which way the revision went in A, but as EB often removed repetitions, it seems likely that she changed what would have been the third 'weep' in nine lines.

43. First published in *1902*. Several nature spirits associated with storms and the care of animals are listed in K. M. Briggs, *The Fairies in Tradition and Literature* (1967), pp. 40–1. The theme of supernatural punishment for cruelty to animals had become prominent in the late eighteenth century with G. A. Bürger's *Der wilde Jäger* (translated by Scott) and Coleridge's *Ancient Mariner*. A Border folk tale tells of a hunter confronted by the 'wee brown man' of the moors, who 'considered the wild animals as his subjects', denounced him for destroying them, and punished him after a second offence. John Leyden makes use of this legend in his ballad 'The Coût of Keeldar', included by Scott in *Minstrelsy of the Scottish Border* (1802–3). A fuller version appears in Scott's note to *Lady of the Lake*, IV. xiii. 12. In the preceding note but one, EB found the ballad that Nelly Dean sings to Hareton in *WH*, p. 95. Scott repeats the tale in a note to *Black Dwarf*, ch. 1. The name 'Keeldar' reappears in CB's *Shirley*.

7 *menace*: previous editions read 'morsel'.

21 *the middle night*: midnight (dialect, chiefly Scottish).

27–8 Cf. Byron, *Giaour*, 500–1, where Leila's 'feet | Gleamed whiter than the mountain sleet'.

58 Cf. Proverbs 3: 3: 'Let not mercy and truth forsake thee.'

61–2 For the severity of the punishment cf. *The Ancient Mariner*.

44. First published in *1910*. Hinkley (p. 281) and *GQ* (p. 128) agree that the crime revealed was committed by A.G.A.; Hinkley believes it was that of leaving her baby daughter to die (see **55** and comment).

Date: the year is unclear: *1910* gives '1832'; Gezari agrees ('clearly dated 1832'), though she includes **44** among undated poems; *1923* and *1934* give '?1842'; *1941*, '1839'. Either 1832 or 1839 may be read, but 1832 is less likely: it would mean that the poem was written when EB was thirteen, preceding other dated work by nearly four years and other appearances of A.G.A. by five.

3 *that spectre ring*: Hinkley interprets: 'the little circle of greener grass where a body has been absorbed into the vegetation'. This presumably takes 'beneath . . . ring' as a modifier and 'A . . . crime' (meaning the body) as the subject of 'lay'; but to separate verb and subject by a stanza-break would be unusual in EB. *GQ* interprets it as jewellery ('a long-lost ring recovered from overgrowing grass'), taking 'ring' as the subject of 'lay' with 'A . . . crime' in apposition.

45. 'E' before date in B. The last of the poems in C, as they appear in that notebook, to be copied into B. The leaf of C carrying 4–33 has been torn out, and the rest of the C text cancelled. In B, EB has written '2' boldly in ink above the title, presumably to show that this poem would be better placed after the next (**26**, which has '1' above the title). First published in *1902* with the title 'The Absent One'. The person mourned in **45** may be the 'Gleneden' who was in prison in **26**, though the speaker believes him to have 'fallen' in battle (25).

6 *April rain*: the Keighley weather record shows a wet morning on 17 April 1839 (Dingle).

17 *One is absent*: AB had left Haworth on 8 April 1839, eight days before this poem was written, to become governess at Blake Hall (*LL*, i. 174–5).

21–4 'Arthur, brother' may apostrophize the person mourned, as supposed by Hinkley (p. 277) and *GQ* (p. 113), who identify him with the 'Arthr Ex[ina]' imprisoned in **186**. In that case, 'Desmond' (not mentioned elsewhere) may be the family home. Alternatively, 'Arthur, brother' is the person to whom the lines are spoken, in which case 'Desmond' is the person 'lost and mourned' and addressed in 25–6.

33–4 Cf. Scott, *Marmion*, IV. introd. 71–3: 'To leave the hearth his dogs repine; | Whistling, and cheering them to aid . . .'. Later in this Epistle Scott mentions two dogs named 'Pandour and Camp'; cf. 35 in C.

44 *One being absent*: C and unrevised B may reflect EB's pronunciation, 'been'; see appendix I.

46. First published in *1910*. Neither this poem nor its companion-piece **20** was copied from C into B, the later transcript book for Gondal poems. For King Julius, i.e. Julius Brenzaida, see introduction, pp. 12–13.

1 *the south country*: one of Julius's titles is 'Almedore', the name of 'a kingdom in Gaaldine' (*GGG*).

5 *the triumphal hymn*: EB's record paper of 26 June 1837 reports 'the Emperors and Empresses of Gondal and Gaaldine preparing to depart from Gaaldine to Gondal to prepare for the coronation which will be on the 12th of July' (appendix V). Possibly Julius was to have been crowned emperor. But *GQ* (p. 99) takes the coronation to have been an earlier occasion on which Julius falsely swore union with Gerald Exina (**23**).

13–16 These lines suggest a scene from the Dance of Death. EB may have seen a version of the woodcuts of 1538 attributed to Holbein, which were well known in this period: at least a dozen different pictorial works based ultimately on these woodcuts were published in Britain between 1788 and 1849. In plate 7 of *The Dance of Death . . . with a Dissertation* (1833) by Francis Douce, Death as a mocking skeleton discrowns the Emperor in the act of giving audience. In plate 31 Death transfixes the Knight with his own lance; in plate 32 a 'daggered Death' beats the Count with his own breastplate (Death's dagger is sheathed at his belt). Douce's frontispiece shows elaborate designs for the sheath of a dagger, with similar motifs.

17 In Wenzel Hollar's engravings of the Dance of Death, Death points a spear or long arrow at the Soldier, a detail that does not occur in the Holbein woodcuts on which Hollar's series is based.

19–20 The assassination of Julius in his palace is reported by an eyewitness in **88**. 65–72.

47. The last poem in C; though apparently a Gondal piece, it was never transcribed into B. First published in *1910*. *GQ* finds no place in Gondal history for the poem; Hinkley (p. 275) identifies the 'iron man' with Julius Brenzaida. He is the earliest known version by EB of the figure known as the 'Byronic hero' (though its main features were established long before Byron, especially in Gothic fiction): the 'stern and swarthy brow' (10) and criminal past are typical. Similar figures are the stranger guest in **56** and Douglas in **81**. Heathcliff in *WH* owes something to the type.

48. 'E.' before date in B. First published in *1902*. *GQ* (p. 127) and Paden (p. 45) suppose that A.G.A. is haunted by the memory of a child she left to die from exposure. From the position of the poem in B, following **76**, **130**, **104** and **25**, and preceding **92**, it is more likely that the dead 'darling' is Alfred ?Sidonia, whom she has seen 'fail' in **25**. At this stage EB was copying poems into B in related groups. Cf. also Hinkley, p. 280.

49. First published in *1910*, correctly dated; redated 'May 17, 1837' in *1941*, for which *1910* supplied the text. Hatfield probably took 7–8 as an autobiographical statement and knew that EB's *7* and *9* could be confused; but the holograph (not available to Hatfield) shows the year plainly as 1839. (Unusually for EB, the date is centred over the poem and written in cursive.)

Much criticism has been based on the erroneous date, which made the poem seem to be a personal statement. That the speaker's age is not EB's shows that the poem has a dramatic cast, like many others which cannot clearly be assigned to Gondal; and the facts of EB's life at Haworth contradict a literal reading of 1–8. Nevertheless, isolation is a recurrent theme in EB's poetry (the words 'lonely', 'lone', and 'alone' occur ninety-three times in the poems), and the misanthropy of 19–24 is not confined to this poem (cf. her Brussels *devoir* 'Le Chat', reprinted in Gérin, pp. 266–7).

7 *after 18 years*: at the time of writing, EB was twenty years and ten months old.

22 EB first wrote 'All hollow lying insincere'. She then deleted the first two adjectives (and the 'll' of 'All'), wrote 'searvile' above the cancelled 'lying', and added 'Deceitful' in the left-hand margin. 'Deceitful' was later heavily deleted.

50. 'E J Brontë' at foot of poem. First published in *1910*. Like 49, written eight days earlier, the poem seems to be spoken by a fictional character and describes a situation of which no details are known.

25–8 Cf. AB's Gondal poem 'The Captive's Dream', written 24 January 1838: 'I could bear | My deadly fate with calmness if there were | No kindred hearts to bleed and break for me!' (*Poems of AB*, 4. 25–7).

51. First published in *1910*. 'Claudia' does not appear in other writings by EB or AB. How the speaker's situation is read turns on the relation of 15–16 to 17–18: either 'My body lay exiled in England while my spirit wandered in my own country,' or 'It seemed that both body and spirit returned from exile to visit my own country, England.' On the first reading, which is supported by 11–12 and the contrast of verbs in 15 and 17, Claudia's own country may be Gondal. (The links between Gondal and England are uncertain: cf. 92, cancelled 42 of 80.) On the second, Claudia is an Englishwoman banished during the Interregnum and a supporter of Charles I. Paden (pp. 51, 69) suggests that '"Gondal's royal race" were Stuarts', arguing from the frequent Scottish motifs and the presence of 'Marcellus St[e]wart' and 'Ronald St[e]wart' in a list of Gondal names by EB. Miles (pp. 81–2) discusses the intricate rhyme scheme.

52. First published in *1910*.

53. 'E. J.' in left-hand margin opposite title in B. For a facsimile of the first seven stanzas, see *GQ*, facing p. 17. First published in *1902*; the second E draft of 1–5 is also printed separately in *1910*, p. 303, where the date is given as 'June 3, 1831' (no such date appears in E). In Gondal history, *GQ* (pp. 113–19) and, tentatively, Visick (p. 84) assign this poem to the period after the overthrow of Julius Brenzaida; Hinkley (p. 282) to the close of the Royalist–Republican wars. With this poem cf. 45.

P. of I: Palace of Instruction, in which the royalty and nobility were educated: a feature of Brontë games which goes back to June 1828 (*CBEW*, i. 22–5). The Gondal version comprised a Northern and a Southern College, each equipped with dungeons (cf. 112, 114, 122 of EB, and 35 in *Poems of AB*). In July 1845 EB and AB 'were' young persons 'escaping from the palaces of Instruction to join the Royalists who are hard driven at present by the victorious Republicans' (see EB's record paper in appendix V).

10th of January 1827: 'Gondal dates' are few: for a list, see appendix VI. In April 1826 Alexander [Hybernia] was in 'a Dungeon in the Southern P of I' (*Poems of AB*, 35), and in September 1826 A.G.A. was writing on 'a D.W. in the N C.' (114).

54. First published in *1910*. This is an easier poem than most to read as a straightforward personal statement by EB, though the resolution in 3–4 had no lasting effect.

Date: so in *1910*, where it may derive from T8 when in a better condition than at present. From T it is not now possible to be certain of the year: what looks at first like the top of '9' coincides with the torn upper edge of the leaf. The lower part of the figure lacks the curve that is usual, but not invariable, in EB's *9*.

2 *a dreary strain*: the words 'drear', 'dreary', 'drearier', and 'drearily' occur in seventy-one of EB's poems, often more than once.

8 this *my soul is day*: the event most likely to cause EB's spirits to rise in the first half of 1839 would have been the resignation of her teaching post at Law Hill.

55. 'E. J.' on left below title. First published in the *Cornhill Magazine*, 1 (May 1860), 616, with the title 'The Outcast Mother'; probably sent to the editor, Thackeray, by CB's widower A. B. Nicholls. First collected in *1923*. There is no evidence as to who speaks this poem: Hinkley (p. 277), Visick (p. 84), and *GQ* (pp. 120–4) suppose it to be A.G.A.

Alexandria: as a personal name this does not occur elsewhere in EB's writings. 'Alexandria Zenobia Hybernia' appears in a list of Gondal characters by AB, and may be identical with 'Alexandrina Zenobia', who speaks four of AB's poems (see appendix VI). 'Child of love' (28) and 'unblessed' (35) need not mean that the child is illegitimate, but here they probably do.

1 *July's shine*: see commentary for **41**. 30.

7–10 Elsewhere EB mentions the song of the skylark, the linnet, and the 'moorlark' (**39**. 47–50, **107**. 1–2). Lapwings are remembered in *WH*, p. 150.

12 Before 'dew' CB has added in pencil 'might', using a caret.

56. 'E J Brontë' at head on left, in a cursive hand. First published in *1902*. The shepherd's guest is one of the most obviously 'Byronic' figures in EB's poetry. Helen Brown ('The Influence of Byron on Emily Brontë', *MLR*, 34 (1939), 377–8) aptly compares him with the Giaour at the monastery (*Giaour*, 832–915). *GQ* (p. 156) identifies him with Douglas, who has escaped pursuit after murdering A.G.A. The poem gives no means of identifying the figure, and may (like *The Giaour*) have been designed as 'a fragment'.

9–14 Cf. the arrival of Bertram at Oswald's castle in Scott, *Rokeby*, I. vi: disdaining Oswald's 'anxious courtesy', he removes helmet and cloak,

> And, turning to the genial board,
> Without a health, or pledge, or word

Of meet and social reverence said,
Deeply he drank, and fiercely fed;
As free from ceremony's sway,
As famish'd wolf that tears his prey.

(For Bertram's 'Byronic' appearance and manner see viii.)

23–4 With the long dark hair and pale brow cf. *Giaour*, 894–900.

31–46. Cf. *Giaour*, 832–45:

Dark and unearthly is the scowl
That glares beneath his dusky cowl . . .
For in it lurks that nameless spell,
Which speaks, itself unspeakable,
A spirit yet unquelled and high,
That claims and keeps ascendancy;
And like the bird whose pinions quake,
But cannot fly the gazing snake,
Will others quail beneath his look,
Nor 'scape the glance they scarce can brook.

42 *a <spectre's> spirit's look*: The curse pronounced upon the Giaour by Hassan's mother is that he should become a vampire: 'Go—and with Gouls and Afrits rave; | Till these in horror shrink away | From Spectre more accursed than they!' (*Giaour*, 784–6).

46 *basilisk charm*: The basilisk, a serpent mentioned in the Bible and classical authors, combined the snake's power of fascinating its prey with that of killing by its eye. Heathcliff has 'basilisk eyes' (*WH*, p. 122). The Giaour is also compared to one of the Gorgons, whose glance turned victims to stone (*Giaour*, 896–8).

57. 'Emily Jane Brontë' is written upside-down below the text. Repeated revisions make this a difficult MS, especially from 25. First published in *1902*; facsimile of MS in Romer Wilson, *All Alone* (1928), p. 172. Neither of the speakers can be identified and, like **56**, it may be an independent 'fragment'. The story of the musician's initiation resembles that of Cædmon as told by Bede.

6 *Ula's hall*: Ula was a region of Gaaldine; at one stage 'a kingdom . . . governed by 4 Sovereigns' (*GGG*, and cf. **80**. 36, **101**. 9–12, 33–4).

25 *vioce*: 'note' *1941*, Gezari.

30 'Then died away, nor came again' *1902*; 'Then died, nor lived ever again' *1941*, Gezari. The line is obscured by a cancelled earlier version, most of which is indecipherable.

58. First published in *1910*. The dead man cannot be identified and may be imaginary, as the speaker may be. The logic of the poem seems to run: 'Do not mourn this man, whom Heaven mourns' (1–8). 'But Heaven does not mourn for the death of good men' (9–16). 'A man who has rejected God's grace during his life cannot expect mercy, but eternal punishment' (17–32). Much of the poem uses in a straight-faced way the language of certain kinds of hymn; but it seems clear by the end that the views expressed have been distanced. EB, CB, and AB developed a strong resistance to the doctrine, orthodox for most Christians at this time, of eternal punishment for the damned. See *Poems of AB*, **22**; *Jane Eyre*, pp. 66–7; commentary to both. EB was interested in the idea of a purgatorial function for earthly suffering, and quite possibly she came to reject the traditional notion of hell altogether. See Tom Winnifrith, *The Brontës and their Background* (1973; repr. 1988), chs. 3, 4.

6 *sweeping*: EB's mistake in 'spweeping', which she corrected here, reappears in 'spwept', **185**. 1.

14 *golden harp-strings*: for a perhaps derisory reference to this traditional image of heaven, see **102**. 8.

16–20 Cf. the vessel on the 'sea of gloom' in **19**. 5–12.

59. When EB drew a stroke under 4 she may have thought of the first stanza as a separate fragment; it is impossible to say whether she had already written the lines which follow. First published in *1910*. The poem captures a moment of life at Haworth, but slightly fictionalizes it in 8.

3 *the day has wept its fill*: the Keighley weather record shows 27 July as a windless day with 'much rain' following a wet night (Dingle).

60. D14 (decorated by a winged serpent and other doodles) shows more alterations than usual, and may be the original draft. For a photograph see *Life*, facing p. 161. First published in *1902*. The speakers are not identified; apart from a few illegible words, the poem seems complete and independent.

7 New speeches begin here and at 13, 27.

10 *dream*: editions from *1902* to *1934* read 'thought', probably from confusion with overwritten 'ghost'.

19 For the seventh word I can neither accept previous readings nor establish a new one. Editions from *1902* to *1934* read 'mountain'; *1941* and Gezari, 'heaven'. Two successive words have been deleted here, one of which seems to be 'shadowy'. It is possible that the final word is meant for 'lawn', though I have not seen this misspelling elsewhere.

22–3 *leaves . . . sweet*: MS 'leave . . . sweets' probably results from a hasty correction in which 's' was added to the wrong word.

24 *wildbirds*: cf. **31**. 67 and comment.

35 *Regive*: perhaps because she felt uncertain of this word, EB has written 'regive' and 'regive him' six times at the foot of the poem.

61. First printed in *1910* from T, with **191** following it as one poem. The speaker is apparently a soothsayer, and it has been conjectured that he is addressing A.G.A., whom the bird will guide to the dying Elbë (Hinkley, p. 278; Paden, pp. 29, 39). But this could hardly be 'the wishedfor boon' promised in the E text, nor an answer to the prayers encouraged in T.

Date: the T date, added in the left-hand margin, is the one example found of EB giving a new composition date after rewriting a poem.

3 *a bird with sable wing*: probably a raven, usually a bird of ill omen (*Macbeth*, I. v. 35–7; *CBEW*, i. 29). In one of CB's 1829 'Tales of the Islanders' the 'dull flapping of wings and . . . ominous croak' of a raven is heard as two heroes keep a nocturnal appointment with their enemies on

the Great Moor (*CBEW*, i. 30). EB figures as a character in this story, and may have had a share in inventing it. Here, however, the raven is apparently a guide and oracle. A supernatural bird gives 'comfort' to the heroine in 'Sadak and Kalasrade', *Tales of the Genii*, ii. 71–2, 142.

9 *Futur*: previous editions read 'fortune'.

62. Facsimile of MS in *1934*, pp. 306–7. Before copying this poem into the A notebook, EB first wrote and deleted the opening of 84. First published in *1902*. When this poem was written, AB had been a governess with the Inghams since April. In the same month BB had been in Liverpool, and CB had been planning a holiday with Ellen Nussey.

1–2 Interlined with cancelled opening of 84.

5 *The old tower*: the tower of Haworth church stood to the north-east of the Parsonage, and would catch the evening sun.

9–12 In November 1834 EB and AB 'want to go out to play' after noon, but there are beds to be made, potatoes to be peeled, and lessons to be done. Soon after 4 p.m. on 26 June 1837 they 'agreed to go out 1st to make sure' of their outing (see record papers in appendix V).

11 *labours tyrant power*: 'some light labour's task', CB in A.

17–24 In A these lines have been lightly cancelled, probably by CB.

24 *sun blinks*: 'gleams of sunshine'; 'moments of joy' (*OED*).

25 *Ah no*: 'Be still', CB in A.

27 *When . . . their*: 'Think . . . its', CB in A.

63. Faintly written in pencil on card. First printed by Helen Brown and Joan Mott in 'The Gondal Saga', *BST*, 9/48 (1938), 155–72.

Since this poem concerns a man and woman who live or have lived at 'Areon Hall', Hinkley (p. 279) and *GQ* (pp. 136–8) connect it with 17, which mentions 'Areons Forest' (45). They take the speaker of 63 to be Fernando, in love now with A.G.A. but imagining his deserted foster-sister, his childhood sweetheart, still at Areon. This reading, if correct, would go far towards identifying A.G.A. with Rosina Alcona, to whom the poem is addressed (see *GQ*, p. 27). Brown and Mott (p. 160) and Paden (p. 23) suppose the speaker to be Julius Brenzaida.

1 *Alcona*: usually identified with the 'R Alcona' of 116, who in turn is identified with the 'Rosina' linked with Julius Brenzaida in 88, 112.

9–13 *Areon*: Brown and Mott read 'Arvon'.

12 *my home*: 'thy home' is given as an alternative in *BST*, *1941*, Gezari.

30 Overwriting has made the first word or words illegible. *BST* prints 'Unheard at'; *1941* 'Unm[ark]edst', where the bracketed letters are conjectured (but there does not seem room enough for this reading); Gezari 'Unm[ark]dst' (which does not scan). Sense and metre require something like 'A priestess' or 'Unwearied'.

33–44 Cf. AB's 'The lady of Alzerno's hall', written on 10 July 1838, in which Eliza has waited three years for her lord to return. Alexandrina Zenobia tells her that Alzorno is faithful but must be dead; then confides to the reader that 'when he drew his parting breath | His head was pillowed on my knee' (*Poems of AB*, 7).

35 *faith in him*: if the speaker means himself, 'faith in me' would have been more natural; but cf. **72**. 64–71.

40 Two successive words have been deleted here, but none substituted or reinstated. *BST* gives 'spreading'; *1941* takes 'spreading' to be cancelled, but restores it.

41–2 'Even if she does see a horseman hastening by, it no longer fills her with hope and excitement.'

64. Apparently unfinished. First published in *1910*. Hinkley (p. 276) and *GQ* (p. 125) interpret the poem as a meditation at the tomb of Julius Brenzaida; though as Hinkley notices, Julius is later said to have been buried under the heath and fern 'on Angora's shore' (**116**. 6–8). For another conjecture, see Paden (p. 62 n. 41). With this poem cf. **23**.

Date: the year has previously been given as 1837, but the last digit looks more like a *9*.

65. First published in *1910*. Paden (p. 58 n. 30) reads the poem as 'another appeal by Julius to Geraldine'. In spite of the lyric form and romantic touches, it shows more grasp of the complexities of emotional relationships than most Gondal poems. Miles (p. 71) sees this poem and **67** as marking the development in EB of 'a rather down-hearted pragmatism'.

1 *distress and pleasure*: the sad speaker (also represented by 'woe' in 14) and the joyous friend or lover, whose spirits are repressed (the speaker fears) in the effort to feel or show sympathy.

3–4 Not 'It is useless to try for friendship once love is over,' but 'It is useless for wretched persons with no other joys to try to keep those of friendship.'

19 *dissemble*: probably 'put on a feigned or false appearance of' (*OED*), though the opposite sense, 'conceal', was the dominant one.

66. Facsimile of MS in *1934*, p. 312. First published in *1902*. On this group of A poems see introduction, pp. 4–5.

12 Cf. **38**. 3–4, where the light 'decays' at source; here it weakens as it plays on the recipient.

24 Probably 'And another love might brighten my soul', though as Gezari points out, other readings are possible: 'My soul might gild (i.e. glorify) another love', or simply 'My soul might love another.'

67. First published in *1910*. See Miles, quoted on **65**.

4 *defye*: apparently intransitive, meaning 'to utter defiance', though this sense had long been obsolete (*OED*).

5 *in the days of ardent youth*: EB's twenty-first birthday had been two or three months before.

68. Facsimile of MS in *1934*, p. 314. The earliest of EB's poems to be included in *1846*. Its inclusion in A counts against 'that wretche' (6) being a Gondal figure; but the boundaries between the A and B notebooks may not be rigid (see introduction, pp. 4–5), and the poem may have had its origins in Gondal. Or it may be a self-contained piece of fiction, like Thomas Moore's 'When First I Met Thee' (in *Irish Melodies*), which presents a comparable situation. This is not to deny any element from EB's own experience. Though BB's death was still nine years away, mixed feelings about him may have given EB the impulse for the poem, and conceivably the 'one word' (7) was opium, which he had recently begun to take. Or the poem may deal with some figure known to EB from her reading; see Chitham, 'Emily Brontë and Shelley', in *Brontë Facts and Brontë Problems*, ed. Chitham and Tom Winnifrith (1983), pp. 69–70. Whatever the nature of this figure, EB uses him to dramatize and resolve an important conflict in her own attitudes, between contempt for the weak and a belief that, among humans as among animals, all must act according to their innate characteristics, which makes moralizing futile. See Stevie Davies, *Emily Brontë: Heretic* (1994), pp. 128–9.

69. Written in EB's angular cursive hand, not 'Brontë script'. Below these lines is a calculation involving six dates. First published in *1910*, followed under the same poem number by a stanza made up of **176** and **177** (which follow **69** on E3).

70. Written in pencil. First published in *1902*.

1–2 For EB's responsiveness to the wind, see **2** and comment. This poem was written on a windless day (Dingle).

71. 'A' seems to have been written in the left-hand margin at head, then cancelled and the date written round it. First published in *1910*, with **179** and **180** from E6 under the same poem number. This poem or fragment does not fit easily into what we know of Gondal, but Paden (p. 75 n. 96) suggests that A.G.A. may have spoken it 'in contemplation of the deaths of Alfred and Fernando'.

72. Signed 'E.' at head on right, before date. First published by Clement Shorter in 'Relics of Emily Brontë', *The Woman at Home* (August 1897), pp. 906–12. First collected in *1902*. The speaker, F. De Samara, also speaks **37**, is probably the 'Fernando' of **6** and **17**, and may be the speaker of **63**; see introduction, p. 12.

Gaaldine prison caves: the only reference to Gaaldine in EB's poems, though the Gaaldine kingdoms of Ula and Almedore are mentioned more often. Gothic fiction had many cave-like dungeons, and Byron's Chillon, where prisoners die and are buried in 'the cold earth of our cave' (*Prisoner of Chillon*, 151), supplied a historical counterpart.

7–18 Cf. **58**. 25–32 and comment. To a rejection of eternal damnation EB now adds the idea of the redemptive power of earthly suffering, to be extended in her Brussels *devoir* 'Le Papillon' (Gérin, pp. 271–2; Winnifrith, *Brontës and their Background*, p. 63).

9 Cf. Byron, *Manfred*, III. iv. 125–6: 'Thou hast no power upon me, *that* I feel' (spoken to a spirit who comes to take Manfred to hell).

26 *grim concave*: the vault of heaven, source of the tempests and lightnings; cf. P. B. Shelley, *Queen Mab*, I. 232.

28 Despite Fernando's condemnation of A.G.A. in this poem, his 'priceless joy' seems more likely to be her love than that of his former sweetheart; cf. **37**. 41–4.

29 *They*: the lightnings.

60 *Elderno's shores*: cf. **27**. 6, **88**. 15.

73. Facsimile of MS in *1934*, pp. 314–15. First published in *1902*. As with **68**, the inclusion of this poem in A counts against its being a Gondal poem, but it may have had its origins in Gondal. (It might well have been spoken after Fernando De Samara's death by his early sweetheart: see Roper, 'Emily Brontë's Lover', *BST*, 21/1 (1993), 24–30.) Alternatively, the poem may concern some figure from the past whose fate EB had contemplated; as with **68**, P. B. Shelley has been suggested.

9 *blighted name*: cf. Byron, *Giaour*, 1227; the phrase occurs in four other poems by Byron.

17–18 'Then the Lord rained upon Sodom and upon Gomorrah brimstone and fire' (Genesis 19: 24).

23 *doom*: EB may have begun to write 'grave'.

74. Facsimile of MS in *1934*, pp. 311–12. First published in *1902*. With this poem, cf. **38**, **66**, and see introduction, p. 4.

3 *lit my brow*: for similar phrases in contexts of a lost or rejected vision, see **38**. 3–4, **66**. 11–12.

5–8 For the comparison of illusions to mists gilded by the early sun, which evaporate as the sun mounts, cf. **24**. 19–20. Hardy (p. 115) notes that here the metaphor 'combines barrenness and radiance' and finds that 'the poem moves from the strongly asserted refusal to dream to the weaker expression of gratitude for past dreaming.'

75. Facsimile of MS in *1934*, p. 310. First published in *1846*. So far as is known, no one close to EB was expected to die at this time, and the poem belongs to the group in MS A which seem to be non-Gondal fiction (see introduction, pp. 3–4), though content and feeling may remind us of Gondal. The scene from a story most of which remains untold was an accepted nineteenth-century genre, and in EB's poetry death and parting are favourite themes for such scenes (cf. **65**, **77**).

76. Signed 'E.' at head on right, before dates. First published in *1902*. Other poems spoken by A.G.A. to A[lfred] S. are **25**, **104**; for other occurrences of an 'A.S.', see appendix VI. On the strength of his forename and blue eyes, Alfred S. has been identified with 'Lord Alfred' in **92**, in which case his surname is probably 'Sidonia' (**92**. 76, 90). Visick (pp. 20–32, 83) argues that the relationship of A.G.A. to Alfred S. foreshadows that of Catherine Earnshaw to Edgar Linton, with Julius Brenzaida taking the part of Heathcliff; she compares the feeling of this poem with Catherine's 'almost over fond' feeling for Edgar early in their marriage (*WH*, p. 113). But Visick's antithesis between 'Julius the sun-man and Alfred the moon-lover' (p. 42) is hard to sustain in view of **76**. 25–33. Brenzaida is not clearly linked with Alfred or with A.G.A. in any poem.

1 Cf. Scott, *Rokeby*, II. xi. 19: 'In such a spot, at such an hour'.

2 *made of light*: it seems almost certain that this is literally, as well as metaphorically, a scene of 'summer noon' (32), when the fact that night must come (4) is recognized but not felt.

10–14 Visick (p. 56) interprets: 'the gentle lover is religious, and even converts A.G.A. by his love to "adore" a spiritual heaven as well as the blue heaven of the natural world'. This reading is supported by 33–4, where 'heaven's sun' shining in Alfred is distinguished from 'earths sun'. But A.G.A.'s main concern is not to distinguish between the natural and spiritual, but to oppose a bright world of love to a 'drear' world of non-love: the soul's purity belongs to the bright world, religious asceticism to the drear.

15–29 'Though the joys of heaven will be brighter, this does not make the sunshine of earthly love less precious or reconcile us to its absence.'

77. Facsimile of MS in *1934*, pp. 310–11. First published in *1902*; titled 'The Appeal' in *1923*, *1934*. One of the group of fictional poems in A that do not belong to Gondal, though they may have originated there (see introduction, pp. 4–5). Miles (p. 76) calls it 'a perfect illustration of [EB's] Gondal manner. A brilliant, haunting lament of betrayal, whose pain . . . recalls that of Shakespeare in the *Sonnets*—yet it is plainly not personal in the way that Shakespeare's poems are, nor could we say with any conviction which of Emily Brontë's *dramatis personae* it properly belongs to.' Gezari follows Margaret Homans (*Woman Writers and Poetic Identity*, Princeton, NJ, 1980) in interpreting the poem as an appeal to the imagination. See also Roper, 'Emily Brontë's Lover', esp. p. 28.

78. Decorated in MS by a pen-and-ink doodle suggesting a winged snake. First published in *1910*. So far as is known, this beginning was never continued, and it bears no clear relation to other narratives by EB.

2 After finally settling on 'soft' for the first adjective, EB went back from 'soft' to her first choice, 'still', for the second.

79. Facsimile of MS in *1934*, pp. 308–9, where the title is faint; it is clear in BPM photographs, and may have been added by either EB or CB. First published in *1850*. Above the separating rules at the head of the text, '1' has been written boldly in ink, presumably to show that this poem should be taken before the preceding poem in A (84), over which '2' has been written. EB's revisions in 9, 33–6 may have been made when the poem was being considered for inclusion in *1846*. Those in 25, 29, 31, which passed into *1850*, look like CB's work, but even from the excellent photographs at BPM it is hard to be sure. In *1850* this poem followed 84, to which CB's introductory sentences refer: 'Here again is the same mind in converse with a like abstraction. The Night-Wind, breathing through an open window, has visited an ear which discerned language in its whispers.' On 11 September 1840 EB could have seen a full moon from the 'parlour', or dining-room, of the parsonage; the day had been warm, with a moderate wind and a little rain (Dingle).

1 *summer's . . . midnight*: elsewhere EB thinks of September, and even August, as autumn (**126**. 9–12, **127**. 12–15).

12 *the woods*: the valleys near Haworth were then well wooded. The woods of the poem have their archetypal power to represent what is primitive, untamed, even (cf. 23) unhuman.

25 *leave*: 'heed', CB in A, *1850*.

29 'Were we not friends from childhood', CB in A, *1850*.

31 *hast loved the night*: 'the solemn night', CB in A, *1850*.

34 *churcheyard*: 'church-aisle' *1850*. EB was buried in the family vault under the chancel in Haworth Church.

35, 36 'I' and 'thou' are italicized in *1850*.

80. Signed 'E J B—' at head on left. First published in *1910*, omitting the last four stanzas. Complete facsimile in *Wuthering Heights*, ed. Clement K. Shorter (1911), p. 443. The last four stanzas were printed by Helen Brown and Joan Mott in 'The Gondal Saga', *BST*, 9/48 (1938), 155–72.

For the Gleneden group see introduction, p. 13. They are involved several times in sea adventures, and here some of them are sailing to join companions in Gaaldine; but the scene of dreaming around the fire (17–20) suggests that EB did not imagine life on board a sailing ship, in rough weather, in any detail.

R. Gleneden: the name is written in sloping letters and is not easy to read.

25 *Edmunds*: this may well be the E. Gleneden of **97**, who begs Mary R. to run away with him.

35–6 *GGG* identifies Zedora as 'a large Provence in Gaaldine', and Ula as 'a kingdom in Gaaldine'.

37 *Mary and flora*: Mary may be the Mary R. of **97**, now Edmund's wife. Flora does not appear elsewhere in EB's poems, but see appendix VI.

42 The cancelled line gives one of the few glimpses of connections with Britain, much less frequent in what we know of the Gondal world than in Angria.

81. 'E.J.' on left of title in B. First published in *1902*. As the double date shows, EB returned to this poem at least twice over three years. It is her longest poem and the most complex in narrative, making much use (like *WH*) of analepsis and ellipsis. It also gives a full display of the contradictions of A.G.A.'s character, though she is on stage only briefly and says little. The supporting cast is larger than usual. Angelica (29), Surry (143), and Lord Eldred (290) do not occur under these names in any other writings of EB or AB. ('Lady Serena Surry' appears in CB's story 'The Silver Cup', *CBEW*, i. 73.) Douglas (93) appears only in this poem and **31**, though 'M. Douglas' is the speaker of **113** and 'Helen Douglas' is one of a list of Gondal characters made by AB (see appendix VI). The Lord Lesley (164) of this poem may be related to the Rodric Lesley of **100**.

9 *a woman tall and fair*: *GQ* (pp. 71, 143) and Paden (p. 41) conjecture that Angelica is the fair-haired daughter of Lord Alfred of Aspin (**92**), and was brought up by A.G.A. as a stepdaughter.

35–44 What Douglas's crimes have been is not known. Hinkley (pp. 275–6) and *GQ* (pp. 102–6) believe he was one of the assassins of Julius Brenzaida.

63–80 Philippa Tristram compares this all-absorbing childhood relationship, later betrayed, with that of the young Catherine and Heathcliff

('"Divided Sources"', in *The Art of Emily Brontë*, ed. Anne Smith (1976), pp. 196–7).

73 *Majian devotee*: the Magi of Persia were believed to have worshipped the sun, called 'their worshipp'd planet' in *Lalla Rookh* ('The Fire-Worshippers', *Poetical Works of Thomas Moore* (1841), vi. 246 and n.); *devotee* suggests extreme or superstitious adoration.

102–4 Angelica's past crimes, like Douglas's, are obscure. In Ratchford's reconstruction (*GQ*, p. 101) she has already revenged herself upon A.G.A. by taking a leading part in the assassination of Brenzaida. Ratchford takes 'We' in 104 to mean Angelica and Amedeus; but the other person may have been Douglas, who already knows (103) what Angelica is telling him.

138–9 A broken line appears between these lines of text in B, but no space to suggest that EB planned to fill in the narrative ellipsis—in which, presumably, Douglas mortally wounds Lesley and Surry.

139 ff. With the setting and the feeling of this death-scene, cf. **114**, written six or seven months after EB completed **81**.

141 *dying bed*: deathbed. Cf., Scott, *Abbot*, ch. 37, '"the field of battle was my cradle." "Beware it be not thy dying bed."'

163–6 Here EB comes closer than usual to the effect of a traditional ballad.

197–8 For death as a sea passage, cf. **8**, **19**, **114**. 14–24.

259 *his last hopless agony*: EB may have been undecided about Douglas's fate; at 288–93 we learn that he has fled bleeding across the moors, and in **31** a Douglas escapes from pursuers eager to avenge their 'soveriegn's gore'. But **31** was written more than two years before EB began work on **81**.

261–2 Again no space is left in B for filling this gap in the narrative, during which Angelica apparently escapes and Lord Eldred arrives on the scene.

275 *all deadly fair*: cf. Byron, *Giaour*, 92, 'so deadly fair'.

290 *Lord Eldred*: it has been supposed that this reflective commentator also speaks **96**, **106**, and **107**.

303 *of wail*: of mourning: cf. Byron, *Bride of Abydos*, 1103, 'a voice of wail'.

82. First published in *1910*, followed as if in one poem by **188**. The title 'The Caged Bird' was added by A. C. Benson in *Brontë Poems* (1915). No cage is mentioned in the poem. EB may have had in mind the hawk Nero, kept as a pet by the Brontës. In her record paper of 30 July 1841 (see appendix V) she notes 'Nero [is] in his cage', which seems to imply that he was sometimes out of it; if so, he would have been chained to a perch, like the bird of the poem. At BPM is a water-colour by EB, dated 27 October 1841, of a merlin hawk (perched on a bough) which closely resembles an engraving in Bewick's *British Birds* (Gérin, p. 116); also reproduced in Moore, *The Life and Eager Death of Emily Brontë*, frontispiece; Wilks, p. 64.

Juliet Barker writes: 'Emily's identification with the bird in the poem is total; like it she is alone, longing for liberty and freedom on the moors, but knowing that for both the only release will be the eternal one of death' (*The Brontës: selected poems* (1985), p. 131). This identification is imaginative and metaphorical, as EB was not in any ordinary sense 'wholey lone'; the moors were close at hand, and she could have released Nero at any moment. In AB's 'The Captive Dove', a poem often compared with **82**, the emphasis falls on the bird's lack of a mate: 'The heart that nature formed to love | Must pine neglected and alone' (*Poems of AB*, **24**).

5 *me*: it appears that EB first wrote 'her'; then remembered the neuter pronouns of 2–3 and changed 'her' to 'us'; then decided that the hills were for the speaker rather than the bird, and wrote 'me'. Their 'equal prayer' is for the speaker to be free on the hills, and the bird in 'heavens blue sea'.

7–8 Here EB switched from singular into plural and back again, but forgot to change 'hearts' into 'heart'.

83. Facsimile of MS in *1934*, p. 309. First published in *1846*. EB was attracted to Stoicism and may have known some of the writings of Epictetus in the translation of Elizabeth Carter (1758); see Margaret Maison, 'Emily Brontë and Epictetus', *Notes & Queries*, 223 (1978), 230–1.

Title: Cf. 'An Epicurean's song', the title given by BB to an Angrian poem when revising it for the *Halifax Guardian* (*Poems of BB*, pp. 227, 460–1). 11 *a chainless soul*: 'Fortune is an evil chain to the body, and vice to the soul. For he whose body is unbound, and whose soul is chained, is a slave. On the contrary, he whose body is chained, and his soul unbound, is free' (Epictetus, *Fragments*, vii).

84. Facsimile of MS in *1934*, p. 307. Above the text, '2' has been boldly written in ink by EB, probably to show that this poem should be read after **79**, which follows it in A and is marked '1'. First published in *1850*, with a prefatory sentence by CB: 'The following little piece has no title; but in it the Genius of a solitary region seems to address his wandering and wayward votary, and to recall within his influence the proud mind which rebelled at times even against what it most loved.' The speaker seems in fact to be Earth, or Nature.

21–4 These lines crystallize a central paradox of EB. Juliet Barker compares them with Catherine Earnshaw's dream, in which 'heaven did not seem to be my home; and I broke my heart with weeping to come back to earth' (*The Brontës: selected poems*, p. 132; cf. *WH*, pp. 99–100).

23 *none*: 'few' *1850*.

24 *the*: 'this' *1850*.

85. Facsimile of MS in *1934*, pp. 309–10. First published in *1850* following **79**, with some rewriting by CB and an introductory sentence: 'In these stanzas a louder gale has roused the sleeper on her pillow: the wakened soul struggles to blend with the storm by which it is swayed.' The speaker is not necessarily in bed, and a basic problem is to decide who is speaking and to whom. CB presents 1–4 as spoken by EB, 5–24 as spoken to her by a being such as the Night Wind in **79**, or Earth or Nature in **84**. It is easier to read the poem as one speech: conceivably addressed by EB to some real or imagined person sharing her response to the wind, but more likely addressed to an EB figure, either by this person or by a spirit of nature (cf. 84). For comment see Grove, pp. 51–3.

1 *it*: the glorious wind : see commentary on 2.

2–4 'Deep feelings I thought dead; | Strong in the blast—quick gathering light— | The heart's flame kindles red' *1850*.

5–end Placed in quotation marks in *1850*.

5 *And*: 'Now' *1850*.

6 *thy kindled*: 'thine eyes' full' *1850*.

9–12 What is swept aside is the world in its 'mundane' and restrictive aspects, as opposed to the tempest, of which the person addressed becomes a part.

12 *foam-bells*: bubbles in the foam: cf. James Hogg, *Queen's Wake* (1813), 307, 'Light as the . . . foam-bells floating on the brine'; also *CBEW*, i. 152. The simile recurs as 'idlest froth' in 125. 12.

13–16 This merging with nature resembles that claimed for Keats in P. B. Shelley's *Adonais*, xlii–xliii, and in a sense anticipates the death predicted in 21–4. The divine nature of the universe, and the reabsorption of the soul in it after death, were beliefs of the Stoics.

15 *essence*: 'thunder' *1850*.

16 'The whisper of its fall:' *1850*.

18 Perhaps: 'Free from the limiting effects of your own individuality'. *1850* removes EB's capital, which is probably not significant, from 'Thine'.

24 After EB's final line *1850* adds, without a stanza-break: 'Nature's deep being, thine shall hold, | Her spirit all thy spirit fold, | Her breath absorb thy sighs. | Mortal! though soon life's tale is told; | Who once lives, never dies!' For differences in style and meaning between these lines and EB's, see Stevie Davies, *Emily Brontë* (1988), pp. 26–7.

86. Facsimile of MS in *1934*, pp. 315–16. First published in *1902*. Cf. 84. 21–4 for the combination of pessimism about human life with intense love of, and a sense of kinship with, the natural world, 'perceived as being *like ourselves* in vulnerability' (Davies, *Emily Brontë*, pp. 38–9). Davies sees the poem as a rejection of heaven in favour of earth, and of the divine father in favour of a maternal principle, attitudes which she also finds in *WH*.

1 <*pillars*> *tombstones*: some tombstones at Haworth dating from before 1841 are between five and six feet tall and closely ranked. From a point outside the church, looking up the slope towards the Parsonage, they can resemble pillars.

18–19 Cf. Byron, 'Elegy on Newstead Abbey', xxix: 'The gloomy tenants, Newstead! of thy cells.'

27 *cursless*: Earth will not curse Heaven by wishing its inhabitants to resume their sufferings. *1902-1923* read 'tearless'; later editions, 'careless'.

31–2 Cf. Wordsworth, *Ode: Intimations of Immortality*, 77–85. EB reverses Wordsworth's attitude: in her poem heaven is the distant relation, earth the true mother.

87. 'E.' at head of text in B, on right and immediately before date. The last stanza has been squeezed into B after copying of the next poem had already begun. First published in *1902*. The other poems referring to the love of Julius Brenzaida and Geraldine S. are **34** and **35**. The identity of the narrator is unknown (and may never have been definite), and Geraldine's child is not clearly referred to elsewhere. *GQ* (p. 120), identifying Geraldine with both A.G.A. and Rosina Alcona, supposes that the ambitious mother is planning to rid herself of 'the hampering care of the little one'.

22 *Zedora*: listed in *GGG* as 'a large Provence in Gaaldine, Governed by a Viceroy'. This agrees with the subtropical scenery of 9; cf. also **80**. 35.

88. 'E' above text and to left of title in B. First published in *1902*. For Rosina, Brenzaida, and the Exina family, see introduction, pp. 12–13. Other poems bearing upon his death are **46** and **116**.

13 *Angora's hills*: Angora was a mountainous region of northern Gondal associated with Brenzaida, sometimes known as Julius Angora (see **20**, **116**).

14 *crimson flag*: Brenzaida's standard (cf. **20**. 11).

15 *Elderno's waves*: cf. 'Elderns lake', **27**. 6; 'Elderno's shores', **72**. 60.

27 *Almedore*: 'A kingdom in Gaaldine' (*GGG*). Brenzaida ruled it for a time (**20**. 15) and is referred to here by its name.

40 *my lonely halls*: though 'this palace dome' is Brenzaida's home (65–7). Hinkley (p. 274) suggests that after the death of Geraldine, Brenzaida married Rosina.

43 *dark Ambitions thwarted pride*: EB was consistent about this trait of Rosina's: cf. **112**. 55–60, written three years later but referring to a much earlier period in the story.

59 *Exina's arms*: for 'Gerald Exina' and 'Arthur Exina', see appendix VI.

73–4 Cf. **116**. 5–8.

76 *mental shade*: a memory, a ghost haunting people's minds. Previously read as 'mortal shade'.

89. A title, 'encourgement', added to B in pencil in a cursive hand, is probably by CB; the revision in 14, done in pencil and in small print, could be by either sister. The poem may have been considered for inclusion in *1846*. First published in *1850*, without Gondal heading and with CB's title. Mrs Brontë had died when CB was five years old, EB three.

A S to G S: for occurrences of 'A.S.', see appendix VI; the initials are often ascribed to Alfred ?Sidonia, the Lord Alfred of Aspin Castle. 'G[erald] S.' occurs only here. Paden (pp. 22–3) deduces that Alfred, Gerald, and Geraldine were siblings of the reigning Exina family.

5 *brow*: there may be a tiny 's' at the end in B, but 'brow' is more likely: in EB's poems 'brow' occurs thirty-eight times, 'brows' only three times and always in early poems.

14 *Gerald*: 'sister' *1850*.

21 *knowst*: 'knowest' *1850*.

well: 'thou' *1850*.

22 *we*: italicized in *1850*.

90. The earliest of three pieces begun during EB's stay in Brussels. CB's alterations are in pencil, except for a few in the margin. First published in *1902*. The unidentified speaker of this poem sees two lovers who resemble, except for their exchange of colouring, two lovers known years before. Of that pair the man died, or was killed, and was buried away from Gondal; the woman wept over his body. A possibly related poem is **120**. The theme of love repeated over two generations, the first time tragically, with differences expressed by the colouring of hair, recalls *WH* (Visick, pp. 19–20; Inga-Stina Ewbank in *WH*, p. 485).

In colouring the earlier pair correspond to the fair-haired Alfred ?Sidonia and the black-haired A.G.A. The speaker may be A.G.A. herself, who loved Alfred (**76**), acknowledged she had wronged him (**104**), and saw him die (**25**); later his ghost returned (**92**; cf. **90**. 33–6). Her third-person narrative might be explained by the fact that the memory now seems to her a dream.

H.A. and A.S: presumably the lovers now observed. 'H.A.' does not occur elsewhere, though one of the young Gondal royalists listed by EB in her record paper of July 1945 is named Henry Angora (appendix VI). 'A.S.' often indicates A.G.A.'s fair-haired lover Alfred S., but he can be neither the dark man nor the fair woman. Hinkley, *GQ*, and Paden identify this A.S. with Alfred's unnamed fair-haired daughter (**92**). *GQ* (pp. 76–7) further identifies her with Angelica of **81**; on this view, 'H.A.' may be her early lover [H.] Amedeus (**81**. 110). Paden (pp. 45–9) believes this A.S. to be the daughter of Alfred by A.G.A. He identifies her as the rescued Alexandria (**55**) and her lover as Henry Angora, 'the child born by Geraldine to Julius Brenzaida in a cave in far Zedora' (**87**).

6–8 CB wrote alternative lines into the margin of B: 'who now has raven hair | And those eyes rival dark of night | Were all as morning fair'.

9 *I've dreamt*: presumably, 'I remember—though now it seems a dream'; so in 13.

12 *verdure of the heart*: cf. Keats, *Endymion*, III. 187–8, 'a surpris'd start | Frosted the springing verdure of his heart'.

22 *beats so*: 'once beat', CB in B.

23 'Where her heart found a living nest', CB in B.

24 *And move*: 'That moved', CB in B.

27–8 Cf. **92**. 47–52. Over each line CB has written 'English' as an alternative to *Gondal's*.

33 *for her woe*: because of her woe (as the woman is brought from the dead by her lover's grief in the ballad 'The Unquiet Grave').

36+ CB wrote into the margin of B: 'Whose then the arms and whose the eyes | That clasp and watch her now'.

37–48 The wrong seems to have been done to one of the younger lovers, and may be the injury that A.G.A. did to Lord Alfred's daughter by estranging her father from her: cf. **92**.

91. EB began D8^r by writing **145** in ink; cancelled its original second stanza; turned the page round and wrote a list of Gondal characters, then **91** with the date at its foot, and finally a draft of **130**. 26–33, all inverted to **145** and the last two items in pencil. First published in *1902*, followed as if in one poem by the draft for **130**.

92. Begun in Brussels, finished at Haworth. For a facsimile of the first page of MS see *1941*, facing p. 176. First published in *1902*. It is clear from 47–51 that Aspin is in Gondal, though references to the 'Norman door' and the 'first chief of Aspin grey' with his 'feudal home' suggest a tale of medieval Scotland. Gondal and Angria could accommodate such anomalies: cf. the 'feudal residence' of the Marquis of Charlesworth, with its 'tall, arched windows' and 'pillared Norman gateways', built by the colonists of Glasstown (*CBEW*, ii/I. 157–8). These castles would have been contemporary with Scott's Abbotsford. Aspin is not mentioned in other poems. Interpreters agree that 'Lord Alfred' (the ghost, named at 90) is a lover of A.G.A. named elsewhere as 'A[lfred] S.' (see commentary on **90**). The figures match in their fair hair, blue eyes, spiritual looks, culpable love affair, and distant grave.

23–33 For this traditional framing device, cf. Scott, *Rokeby*, II. x.

61–6 Dorothy Van Ghent takes this to be a picture of 'the woman for whom [Lord Alfred] died' (*The English Novel: Form and Function* (New York, 1953; repr. 1961), p. 167). It is in fact a portrait of his daughter, whose fair hair (71–2) and innocence are contrasted with the 'black resplendant hair' (37. 17) and stormy pride of A.G.A. in the other picture.

76 *Sidonia's deity*: Hinkley (pp. 279–80) reasonably infers that Alfred's surname or title is Sidonia and that he idolized his beloved: cf. 90–1. The Brontës would have read of the Duke of Medina Sidonia, commander of the Spanish Armada in 1588, and enjoyed using such names: cf. *Alcona*, *Almeda*, *Zenobia*. In 1844 Disraeli took the name for a figure in *Coningsby*.

79 *wild enthusiast's dreams*: cf. **126**. 31.

101 Cf. **76**. 1, 'At such a time, in such a spot'. That poem about the love of A.S. and A.G.A. may have been in EB's mind as she completed **92**, which puts the affair in a different perspective.

93. Begun in Brussels two weeks before EB left; completed at Haworth on the same day as **92**. Facsimile of MS in *1934*, pp. 316–17. First published in *1846*. Though 5–8 may be a comment on EB's experiences at Brussels, the poem declines (as usual) to be read as straightforward autobiography: the known facts scarcely explain 21–2 or 33–8. There are general and specific resemblances between this poem and AB's 'Self-Communion' (*Poems of AB*, 57), written after 'Self-Interrogation' had been printed.

5–8 Cf. 'Self-Communion', 299–300.

13–14 *that Conscience . . . condemn*: 'that self-reproach is unjustified, and circumstances are to blame if time has passed unprofitably.' The successive revisions in 13–16 are discussed by Roper, pp. 164–5.

33–6 Cf. 'Self-Communion', 280–4, 297–8.

41–8 Cf. ibid. 306–13.

94. 'E.J.' at head of text, left of title, in B. First published in *1902*. 'Zalona' does not occur in other poems, but *GGG* includes 'ZELONA, a kingdom in Gaaldine'. The besieging forces are those of Julius Brenzaida, as in **20**. 11–12, where the victory of his 'crimson ensign' over the 'sea-green Standard' of Zalona is celebrated. In **94** EB comes closer than previously to the miseries of war.

61–4 The myrtle (scared to Venus) was a traditional emblem of love; the lily of innocence.

67–8 *stains our standard green*: stains our green standard, prophetically transforming it to the enemy's crimson flag over the city.

73–80 'We long to die fighting, but our children would survive to be enslaved; we must protect them while we can, even though we shall be enslaved ourselves.'

95. Facsimile of MS in *1934*, pp. 319–20. First published in *1846*. Gérin comments (p. 151): 'The note of pity struck here was new in her poetry, but from then on it constantly recurs.' See also Hardy, pp. 111–12.

1–4 The night of 13 April 1843 was frosty, with a full moon (Dingle). With the role of the moon here, cf. that of the stars in **118**. 'Some of her greatest poems are nocturnals, reflecting a night-journey, and exchanging the solar light by which the world reads and transacts its business for a feminine lunar light disclosing an alternative dimension of vision' (Stevie Davies, *Emily Brontë* (1988), p. 155).

2 *gardian*: only the downstroke of the 'g' is visible in the *1934* facsimile, but the word can be seen in photographs at BPM and is recorded in the transcript made by Davidson Cook; see Roper, p. 167. Cf. BB's 'Ode to the Polar Star' (1832), 73: 'His Guardian in the sky'.

36 *surest*: visible in BPM photographs, and recorded by Davidson Cook.

40 Three people in EB's life had died late in 1842, in each case after much suffering: her aunt Elizabeth, her friend Martha Taylor, and the well-liked curate William Weightman. On 29 October 1842 BB wrote to F. H. Grundy: 'Death only has made me neglectful of your kindness, and I have lately had so much experience with him, that your sister would *not now* blame me for indulging in gloomy visions either of this world or another' (Grundy, *Pictures of the Past* (1879), p. 84). CB wrote on 10 November: 'Aunt—Martha Taylor—Mr Weightman are now all gone—how dreary & void everything seems' (*LL*, i. 282, corrected from Harvard MS by the kind assistance of Mrs Margaret Smith).

96. 'E' above text in B, immediately before composition date. '1830' is one of six surviving Gondal dates, shared with **100**. First published in *1902* with a title supplied by A. B. Nicholls, 'Grave in the Ocean'.

To A S.: 'A.S.' is usually, but not always, Alfred ?Sidonia; see appendix VI, and commentary to **89**, **92**. The poem does not fit easily into any Gondal reconstruction, but see Hinkley, p. 274; Paden, p. 31.

9–16 Cf. **98**, written four months later.

97. 'E' above text in B immediately before date. 'Octr 18' appears in ink in the left-hand margin. Below the Gondal heading CB has inserted 'A Serenade'. First published in *1902*.

E G. to M. R: the speaker is probably Edmund Gleneden. For the Gleneden group see introduction, p. 13; Paden, pp. 64–5.

23 *Gleneden's*: 'for honour's', CB in B above line, repeated in left-hand margin.

98. 'E.' above text in B, immediately before date. CB pencilled in a title, 'The Warning', revised to 'Warning a [*sic*] reply'. First published in *1850* with the title 'Warning and Reply'. There is nothing to link this poem with Gondal except its inclusion in B. Miles (p. 84) notes 'impressive lines charged to capacity with thought, feeling, and stress'; Hardy (pp. 97–8) distinguishes more and less successful stanzas.

8 *twined*: 'entwined' *1850*.

12 *its gloom and thee*: 'it shudderingly' *1850*.

15 *they'll*: 'they will' *1850*.

23 *broke*: 'breaks', CB in B, *1850*.

there: '—here', CB in B.

24 That *heart*: 'But that heart', CB in B, *1850*.

99. Facsimile of MS in *1934*, p. 318. First published in *1846*. The title, inserted above the text by EB, may have been added with publication in mind; 2 and 12 were apparently revised at the same time.

2 *den*: 'A place hollowed out of the ground, a cavern' (*OED*); here, bars and grating indicate a prison. Cf. the first sentence of Bunyan, *The Pilgrim's Progress*, where the 'Denn' of the dream stands for 'The Gaol'; cf. also **103**. 10. The metaphor links the 'prison caves' (**72**, title) of Gondal and Gaaldine with EB's more obviously figurative poetry.

5 Cf. 'Terror made me cruel', *WH*, p. 31.

100. The Gondal heading and Gondal date appear above the text on the left in B. A centre heading 'Rodric' has been added in pencil, it is not clear by whom. First published in *1902*. The speaker presumably belongs to the same family as 'Lord Lesley', A.G.A.'s devoted follower, who is murdered by Douglas in **81**. The battle he describes cannot be clearly located in Gondal history (but see Paden, p. 53). The Gondal date of 1830 is shared with **96**.

1 Cf. 'Soldier, rest! Thy warfare o'er', Scott, *Lady of the Lake*, I. xxxi.

10 *hundreds*: 'many', CB's alternative in B.

20 *monarch's legions*: 'war-worn comrades', CB's alternative in B.

101. First published in *1902*. A title, 'North and South', appears in a transcript by A. B. Nicholls (see *1941*). For this group of characters and the contrasted climates of Gondal and Gaaldine, see introduction, pp. 7, 13.

M G—For the U.S: probably 'Mary Gleneden for the Unique Society'. The poem was written about a year before the Gondal game at Haworth left the U.S. stranded on a desert island; see AB's record paper of 31 July 1845, appendix V.

9 *Ula's bowers*: 'Ula, a kingdom in Gaaldine' (*GGG*).

31–8 Cf. AB's Thorp Green poem of 19 August 1841: 'Far sweeter is the winter bare | With long dark nights and landscape drear | To them that are at home!' (*Poems of AB*, **16**. 22–4).

39–42 These lines were written a few days before AB and BB arrived home from Thorp Green for Christmas. CB was in Brussels, and EB could not yet have heard of her decision to return in January.

102. Written on a strip torn horizontally from a sheet of black-edged writing-paper, obviously used after Miss Branwell's death on 29 October 1843. The text shows more revisions than usual and may be a first draft, apart from a beginning ('Febuary 2^{d} 1844 | My Task is done') on the other side of the strip. First published in *1910*, with the title 'At Castle Wood'.

A S castle wood: the 'S' is flattened at the top and may be meant for 'J', though no Gondal figure is known with the initials 'A.J.' 'A.S.' usually denotes Alfred ?Sidonia (**76**, **92**), and 'castle wood' may be near his home at Aspin Castle. But the speaker's gloomy account of his life conflicts with what we know of Alfred, and his expected death in winter with Alfred's in May (**25**). Paden (pp. 33, 49–50) identifies the speaker with Alfred's estranged daughter, 'Alexandria' in his reconstruction, 'Angelica' in others. Cf. also Hinkley, p. 276; *GQ*, p. 101. The mood of stoical pessimism recalls some poems in MS A, e.g. **95**, **115**.

3 *as been*: quite clear in E, and may give a clue to EB's pronunciation (see appendix I).

5–6 Cf. **116**. 17–18.

8 EB first wrote 'I had no love for joys devine'. For 'harp', written unclearly over 'joys', *1941* reads 'ways'.

18 Apparently EB first tried 'On dying hearts <that> with pleasure glad', then 'On hearts that <happiness can> drink of happiness', then 'On spirits born akin', leaving the line incomplete. 'Akin', written below the line, may be a suggestion for 19.

19–20 'It looks as if Emily has been reading Keats' (*Life*, p. 163): with 'brede' (in a different sense) and the metaphorical 'foster child', cf. 'Ode on a Grecian Urn', 2, 41. With 19, cf. also Byron, *Prisoner of Chillon*, 258: 'I was the mate of misery'. *Brede* is probably an archaizing form of 'bred'.

103. Facsimile of MS in *1934*, pp. 318–19. First published in *1846*. The 'Comforter' may be a faculty like the imagination (cf. **108**, **110**), an imagined visitant, or 'an earlier poet or writer, whose words have comforted' EB (*Selected Brontë Poems*, ed. Edward Chitham and Tom Winnifrith (Oxford, 1985), p. 249).

Title: perhaps inserted into A later than the poem itself, with *1846* in view. Offsetting on the facing page shows that the notebook was closed before the ink of the title was dry; there may also be offsetting from the date.

4–10 The main metaphorical contrast of the poem is between light and dark: light comes into the den from the sun and from the soul, despite the clouds outside and the shadows within. By unmasking the sunlight, the Comforter confirms the inner light.

9 i.e. 'that its gentle ray . . .'.

control: hold in check; overpower (*OED*).

10 *sullen den*: dark and dismal cavern, like a prison (cf. **99**. 2).

11–20 Strongly suggestive of Bedlam, as depicted by Hogarth in the last plate of *The Rake's Progress.*

13 *wretches uttering praise*: Hogarth's Bedlam includes at least two examples of religious mania.

16 Cf. 'Back to the fostering world beguiled | To waste in self-consuming strife | The loveless brotherhood of life, | Reviling and reviled!' (Thomas Campbell, 'Lines on Leaving a Scene in Bavaria', 114–17). This poem may have given EB the name *Eldern* (see commentary on **27**. 6).

22 *glare of Hell*: a false light, which complicates the contrast of light and darkness and may be related to the misguided religion of 13.

24 *seraph's song and demon's moan*: probably joy and misery, corresponding to 'Heavens glorious sun' and 'Hell'. But possibly both are expressions of 'orthodox Christian belief' (*Selected Brontë Poems*, ed. Chitham and Winnifrith, p. 249).

104. 'E.' above text on right, before date. First published in *1902*.

A.G.A. to A.S.: cf. **25** (which shows that, despite the parting described here, A.G.A. was present at Alfred S.'s death), **76**, **92**.

21 *frenzied strife*: cf. **103**. 15, written three weeks before.

24 Cancelled 24 does not fit cancelled 21–3, and may have been written after EB had abandoned the original stanza and begun to revise.

105. Facsimile of MS in *1934*, pp. 321–3. First published in *1846*. The poem has been seen as the record of a mystical experience (Gérin, p. 152), but the ballad-like opening, the traditional devices of supernatural story-telling in 37–8, 69–72, and the exact reporting of the spirits' speeches (unlike the tentative rendering of the 'Comforter' in **103**) argue against a literal reading. It is an attempt to cast ideas and feelings familiar to EB (including a mood of 'peevish woe' and an impulse to resist it—cf. **54**) into dramatic form. There are many fairy visions in CB's early stories: EB's spirits may be compared with the 'thousands and tens of thousands of fairies and genii' with 'silver harps', who seem close to nature but sing to a mortal of a brighter world, in 'The Search After Happiness', ch. 4 (*CBEW*, i. 49–50). In EB's poem, through these spirits the loved natural world and the redemptive otherworld are united, instead of being opposed as in **86**. But Lyn Pykett suggests that the affirmative vision is 'subtly undermined (although not dispelled)' by the qualifying 'Or seemed' in 52 and by the final stanza (*Emily Brontë* (1989), p. 65).

Date: this alone makes a literal reading unlikely: the poem would have had to be written at least nine months after the visionary experience (cf. 3–4).

Title: visible in photographs at BPM, where it looks like a pencilled insertion into MS A; invisible in *1934*.

1 *brae*: hillside.

3–4 i.e. when May approaches June: cf. 'Nature knows not night's delay, But springs to meet her bridegroom, Day' (Thomas Moore, *Loves of the Angels*, 'First Angel's Story', 3–4, in *Poetical Works* (1841), viii. 16).

28 *unreal mockery*: cf. *Macbeth*, III. iv. 107.

41–2 Cf. Coleridge, *Ancient Mariner*, 238: 'a thousand thousand slimy things'; ibid. 313–14: 'The upper air burst into life! And a hundred fire-flags sheen' (followed at 349 by 'a troop of spirits blest').

49, 51 *rung . . . sung*: it is not clear why these preterite forms were introduced for *1846*, but the rhyme at **123**. 21–2 shows that EB had no objection to them.

59–60 *endless rest And everlasting day*: traditional Christian descriptions of heaven. 'Everlasting day' may have passed into hymnography from Milton, *Nativity Ode*, 13. For *rest*, see commentary on **12**. 1.

106. 'E' above text in B, to left of title. First published in *1850*.

Title: 'On a life perverted' inserted into B below the Gondal heading, in print-style script but probably by CB; 'The Wanderer from the Fold' *1850*.

E.W. to A.G.A.: omitted in *1850*. 'E.W.' has been identified with 'Lord Eldred': his remarks after the death of A.G.A., in a poem completed two months later, have a similar tone (**81**. 323–44, esp. 339–40); cf. also **107**. The masculine pronouns in 24–31 are explained by the 'pilot' metaphor, and apparently helped CB to convert the poem into a lament for BB, who died on 24 September 1848.

14 *Love and Gladness*: 'sinless sunshine' *1850*.

15 *Memory*: 'presence' *1850*.

16 'Like gladsome summer-day' *1850*.

20 *That*: 'Which' *1850*.

31 *that*: 'which' *1850*.

34 *whitening wave*: with foam, as the wind rises: cf. 'the sea whitens with the rising gale' (Pope, *Odyssey*, IX. 160).

107. First published in *1846*.

E W: unusually, this Gondal signature appears at the foot of the text. The speaker is probably Lord Eldred and the dead person A.G.A., as in **106**; see commentary on that poem. Like Julius Brenzaida (**116**. 6–8), A.G.A. has been buried on the moors. Commenting on the sounds and movements of nature in 1–6, 25–6, Grove remarks (p. 58): 'mortality brings not an end but a replacing, of life by life'.

5 Cf. *Fingal*, III, last sentence but one: 'The wild roes feed upon the green tomb of the mighty king of Morven' (James Macpherson, *Poems of Ossian* (Edinburgh, 1792), p. 50). For the Brontës' intensive study of Ossian, see Christine Alexander, *The Early Writings of Charlotte Brontë* (Oxford, 1983), p. 19.

5, 6 *wilddeer*, *wildbirds*: cf. **31**. 67, **60**. 24; probably pronounced in each case as one word, stressed on the first syllable.

17 *Honour's breath*: cf. 'What is honour? a word. What is in that word honour? . . . air' (*1 Henry IV*, V. i. 133–5); 'mouth-honour, breath' (*Macbeth*, V. iii. 27).

23–8 Cf. the last sentence of *WH*.

108. Facsimile of MS in *1934*, p. 323. First published in *1846*. One cannot be sure just what aspect of imagination EB had in view in this deeply felt poem. A reference to the Gondal world has been suggested (*Selected Brontë Poems*, ed. Chitham and Winnifrith, p. 250), and 'bright' in 16, 30 does find an echo in 'The Gondals still florish bright as ever' (record paper of 30 July 1845; see appendix V). Yet Gondal is certainly not free from pain and darkness, 'guile and hate and doubt'. The power EB celebrates seems that of happy fantasizing—untrustworthy (31), condemned by reason and truth in favour of 'Nature's sad reality', but possibly linked with a genuine otherworld (29–30). The shaping and rhythmic drive of the poem create a more positive effect than its semantics. For a closely related poem, see **110**.

Title: inserted into A later than the poem.

7 At this period the sisters were giving up their plan for a school, CB was tormented by love for M. Heger, BB was taking opium and was often ill, and their father suffered from cataracts which threatened the family income. But the poem goes beyond these facts in its dark picture of 'the world without'.

14–16 In revising for *1846*, it may be that EB changed 'sullied sky' to 'untroubled sky' for easier sense, then restored the sense of pollution by changing 'greif' to 'guilt'. For these revisions see Roper, p. 164.

30 The revised reading implies that though the world of imagination is unreal, it can tell us about 'real worlds' which are as bright as itself; in this context, 'divine' in 29 becomes literal and 'real worlds' seems to mean heaven. The original version says nothing of reality, and may mean only that other fictional worlds are as bright as the speaker's.

31 *phantom bliss*: this phrase sums up the ambiguity of the poem.

109. 'E' above text, left of heading. Facsimile of MS with printed extracts in Moore, *The Life and Eager Death of Emily Brontë*. First full printing in *1938*. The poem foresees the civil war in Gondal between Republicans and Royalists, which at Haworth was going on late in July 1945 (see EB's and AB's record papers, appendix V). *GQ* (p. 164) notes a poem of September 1846 by AB dealing with a similar theme: the speaker has killed, for his 'country's gain', a boyhood friend, and the poem begins with a dream that brings back their early intimacy (*Poems of AB*, 53). EB's speaker accepts the likelihood of such an outcome with an almost gay fatalism. For fuller treatment of civil war, see **126**, **127**. Miles (p. 84) notes the 'extraordinarily daring and complex' metrical pattern, which does much to establish the mood of the poem.

D G C. to J.A.: the first set of initials does not occur elsewhere in poems by EB or AB. The second may belong to Julius Brenzaida, also known as Angora, but Gondal reconstructions put this war after his death.

6 To clarify the stanza pattern, I follow *1941* in closing the line-break after 'heart'.

110. Facsimile of MS in *1934*, p. 324. First published in *1846*. The 'God of Visions' (39) seems to be an ambivalent faculty similar to 'Imagination' in **108**, though the paradox of 'Darling Pain' (31) is sharper than that of 'phantom bliss'. For comment see Hardy (pp. 113–14), who finds this poem

EB's 'most complex analysis of Imagination's struggle with Reason'; also Miles (pp. 90–1), who groups it with the 'visitant' poems.

Title: visible in photographs of A at BPM, where it appears to be a pencilled insertion into the MS; not to be seen in *1934* facsimile.

33 The *1846* revision from 'real' to 'earthly' aligns the visionary power with heaven; cf. the parallel revision in **108**. 30.

111. First published in *1846*.

I.M. to I G.: it is not clear why father and daughter have different surnames, nor which initials belong to which. Neither can be 'Isidora Montara' (see appendix VI), and no other known Gondal names fit these initials.

3 *matless*: mateless, without a child companion.

6 *Iernë*: an 'Iernë' appears in **182**, and 'Princess Iernë' has a role in CB's 1834 story 'A Leaf from an Unopened Volume' (*CBEW*, ii/I. 335, 345 ff.). In late Latin the name stands for Ireland (Claudian, *De laudibus Stilichonis*, 2, 251), but the Brontës probably found it in contemporary poetry or fiction.

7 *November's gusts*: on 6 November 1844 the wind near Haworth was weak (Dingle).

34 *fearful*: more probable, but B could as well read 'tearful'; cf. CB's misreading of **112**. 28 when copying for *1850*.

112. 'E J B' precedes composition date in B, followed by a closing parenthesis mark, then Gondal heading and date. First published in *1850*.

Title: CB adds '<T> Old Man's lecture' in B. For the Gondal heading, *1850* substitutes 'The Elder's Rebuke'.

From a Dungeon Wall in the Southern College: the idea of a school or college for young noblemen, with a 'subterranean dungeon' for offenders, goes back at least to June 1828 and the 'Islanders' Play', a game shared by all four Brontë children: see CB's 'Tales of the Islanders', *CBEW*, i. 24. Poems from the dungeons of the Northern College are **114**, **122**; for one from 'a Dungeon in the Southern P[alace] of I[nstruction]', with a Gondal date of April 1826, see *Poems of AB*, 35.

J B: Julius Brenzaida; see introduction, pp. 12–13.

Sept. 1825: the earliest of the six surviving Gondal dates (see appendix VI).

8 *these*: 'those' *1850*.

10 *ears*: 'ear' *1850*.

14 *a serious power*: in quotation marks in *1850*. The quotation has not been traced; CB may have been thinking of 'awful Power' in Wordsworth, 'Ode to Duty', 57.

18 *golden gifted*: 'golden-gifted' *1850*.

28 *tears*: 'fears' *1850*.

29–60 'Thus spake the ice-blooded elder gray; | The young man scoffed as he turned away, | Turned to the call of a sweet lute's measure, | Waked by the lightsome touch of pleasure: | Had he ne'er met a gentler teacher, | Woe had been wrought by that pitiless preacher' *1850*.

39 *Rosina*: Rosina Alcona, with whom Julius was later allied and who mourned him fifteen years after his death (88, **116**).

46 *those wonderous southern isles*: probably in Gaaldine, whose climate is contrasted with Gondal's in **101** and elsewhere. Brenzaida was at one time King of Almedore in Gaaldine.

51 *falcon eyes*: cf. Scott, *Lady of the Lake*, IV. xxvi. 28, 'Bent o'er the fall'n, with falcon eye.'

58 For Rosina's ambitiousness cf. **88**. 43.

113. First published in *1846*. One of the few poems by EB that owe something to Cavalier lyrics: 49–52, 63–4 recall 'I could not love thee (Deare) so much, | Lov'd I not Honour more' (Richard Lovelace, 'To Lucasta, Going to the Warres', 11–12).

M Douglas to E. R. Gleneden: 'M Douglas' must at least be related to the 'Douglas' of **31** and **81**, and is possibly the same man at a different stage of his life. What deed is to earn him the name of traitor is unknown, but it cannot be the murder of A.G.A. in **81**: that crime was performed the day it was planned, by a 'Douglas' devoted to Angelica. For conjectures, see *GQ*, p. 102; Hinkley, p. 281. 'E. R. Gleneden' does not appear elsewhere, but for the group see introduction, p. 13.

1 On 21 November 1844 the moon was four days from full (Dingle).

37 *my out-lawed race*: cf. **31**. 66, **81**. 35–40.

114. First published in *1846*; reprinted in the *Halifax Guardian*, 10 October 1846, probably from a review copy. Here EB returns to a subject she had treated more than seven years earlier in **4**: the death of Alexander Elbë, as witnessed and narrated by A.G.A. The MS is more heavily revised than any B text except **126**. The new readings of *1846* are fewer, and have been adopted except where their only purpose is to de-Gondalize: thus the Gondal heading and the names 'Elbë' and 'Elnor' (9, 11, 27) have been retained. For the stanza-form, see commentary on **5**.

From a D.W. in the N C: from a dungeon wall in the Northern College (see commentary on heading of **112**). Two weeks after EB wrote this poem, AB wrote a lament inscribed on a dungeon wall 'in the Southern P[alace] of I[nstruction]', with the Gondal date 'April 1826'; in this poem 'Alexander' complains of his unfeeling mistress (*Poems of AB*, **35**). This may be Alexander Elbë, doomed to die in battle six months later; but EB and AB usually wrote about different Gondal characters, and elsewhere AB's Alexander is surnamed 'Hybernia'.

11 *Elnor's lake*: probably the traditionally poetic 'Arden's' has been written over 'Elnor's' in B in preparation for *1846*; but possibly 'Elnor's' is the later reading and the earlier was 'Areon's' (cf. **17**. 45, **63**. 9). That Elbë died by Lake Elnor, in Gondal, is clear from **4**. 68.

13 In A, EB began with 'Beside thee, on my knee'; changed this to 'upon my bended knee'; then cancelled 'Upon' and 'bended', but neither restored the earlier readings nor substituted new ones.

15 ff. For the sea as a metaphor for death, cf. **5**. 38–40, **8**. 16–20, **58**. 17–20; also *WH*, p. 408.

22 *Eden isles*: in classical mythology the Isles of the Blest lay beyond the Pillars of Hercules; cf. Tennyson, 'Ulysses' (1842), 63–4.

43 *orbs*: CB was ridiculing this word as early as 1833: 'I beg you will call the resplendent mediums through which I see by the name of orbs not eyes' ('Arthuriana', *CBEW*, ii/II. 208).

115. Facsimile of MS in *1934*, pp. 324–6. First published in *1846*. The poem is a dialogue between a 'seer' (41) and a philosopher: from his chamber the philosopher has explored space, heaven and hell, but desires death because he has never glimpsed the transforming and reconciling vision granted to the seer—in the same place, an hour ago. The quotation-marks are confusing in A and in *1846*, and are here emended. The first speech should be closed after 6, when the seer's question ends. The philosopher then answers by quoting his 'sad refrain' (underlined in A, indented in *1846*), but evidently goes on speaking till 27, when a new speech opens. From then on A uses quotation-marks for the seer only: he relates his vision in 27–40, the philosopher replies in 41–56. The philosopher who desires oblivion may have been suggested by a story in *The Keepsake* for 1828 (see below, comment on 49–50).

Date: A. Mary F. Robinson gives the date of this poem as October 1845 (*Emily Brontë* (1883), p. 130). She states (p. 128) that she obtained this and other composition dates from EB's own marked copy of *1846*, and is right about the dates of **105** and **116**. Possibly EB wrote in the date of the final revision affecting 53–6. The whereabouts of this copy of *1846* is unknown.

Title: 'The Philosopher's Conclusion' is visible in BPM photographs of A as a pencilled addition, apparently by EB.

1 The forms of address here and at 27 recall the dialogues in the *Discourses* of Epictetus: cf. 'But what say you, philosopher?' (IV. i. 212); 'What would you have, man?' (I. xxi).

17–18 The three conflicting gods are interpreted by Barker as 'heart, soul and mind' (*The Brontës: Selected Poems*, p. 139). With a similar reading, Philippa Tristram sees the internal conflict as one externalized in *WH* (' "Divided Sources" ', *The Art of Emily Brontë*, ed. Anne Smith (1976), pp. 200–2; cf. Hewish, pp. 79–81). Tom Winnifrith is tempted to invoke 'the tripartite division of the soul in Plato's *Republic* or the threefold division of the personality by Freud' (*The Brontës* (New York, 1977), p. 43). EB's revised last stanza names two conflicting elements as power and will.

29 ff. The three rivers, combined and beautified in the seer's vision, correspond to the philosopher's three irreconcilable gods. The imagery may owe something to Revelation 8: 8 and 15: 2 (Hewish), but is closer to the vision in ch. 4 of CB's 'The Search After Happiness': 'The ruby sent forth a stream of crimson light, the topaz gold, the sapphire intensest purple and the dome poured a flood of deep, clear splendour, which overcame all the other gaudy lights by its mild, triumphant glory' (*CBEW*, i. 49). CB is remembering the description of a palace in 'The History of the Merchant Abudah', *Tales of the Genii*, i. 35–6.

49–50 A figure stretches out his hands towards a pool amid a volcano-lit landscape in John Martin's painting of 1812, 'Sadak in Search of the Waters of Oblivion'. To the right of the figure a waterfall plunges into darkness (cf. 115. 34). The painting was based on a story from *Tales of the Genii*, 'Sadak and Kalasrade'. *The Keepsake* for 1828 included an engraving of this painting, together with a quite different story, anonymously written, 'The Deev Alfakir' (pp. 160–9). This story presents Sadak as a world-weary philosopher, who is finally freed from the pains of consciousness by being thrown into the pool. An early poem by P. B. Shelley, 'Sadak the Wanderer', was also included. For Sadak, Martin, and the Brontës, see Christine Alexander, ' "The Burning Clime": Charlotte Brontë and John Martin', *Nineteenth-Century Literature*, 50 (1995); Alexander, 'Art and Artists in Charlotte Brontë's Juvenilia', BST 20/4 (1991), 191–5; Alexander and Jane Sellars, *The Art of the Brontës* (Cambridge, 1995), pp. 20–1. See also William Feaver, *The Art of John Martin* (Oxford, 1975), pp. 16–17 (with a reproduction of the 'Sadak' painting); P. B. Shelley, *Complete Poetical Works*, ed. Neville Rogers (Oxford, 1972), i. 20–2, 354.

53–6. EB rewrote the final stanza after this poem and the beginning, at least, of the next had been copied into A: the new stanza is inserted below the cancelled one, and overruns the dividing lines and the date of 118.

116. Facsimile of MS in Virginia Moore, *The Life and Eager Death of Emily Brontë* (1936). First published in *1846*. The verbal revisions of *1846* have been adopted into the text except where their only purpose is to de-Gondalize: thus the Gondal heading and 'Angora's shore' have been retained. EB's most anthologized poem has attracted much critical comment: see especially F. R. Leavis, 'Reality and Sincerity', *Scrutiny*, 19 (1952–3), 90–8 (repr. in *The Living Principle* (1975)); Hardy, pp. 116–18; D. W. Harding, 'The Process of Mourning', *TLS*, 4 July 1980, p. 747. Metrically the poem hesitates between a norm of five and one of six stresses, not always easy to distribute.

R Alcona to J Brenzaida: see introduction, pp. 12–13.

1 *Cold in the earth*: Thomas Moore uses the phrase twice in *Irish Melodies* (1801–34): see 'The Irish Peasant to his Mistress', 11, and the song beginning 'When cold in the earth lies the friend thou hast lov'd'. The latter is followed in Moore's sequence by the song 'Remember Thee!' For the Brontës' knowledge of *Irish Melodies*, see *Life*, p. 79. Cf. also AB's 'Night', written early in 1845: 'Cold in the grave for years has lain | The form it was my bliss to see' (*Poems of AB*, 37. 9–10). The phrase suggests both 'cold to the touch' and 'still feeling the weight and chill of the deep snow' (Grove, p. 58).

9 *fifteen wild Decembers*: this 'has struck many readers as prefiguring the eighteen years of Heathcliff's mourning for Catherine' (Visick, p. 15; *WH*, p. 351). The only related poem that bears a Gondal date is 112, recording Brenzaida's imprisonment (while a 'young man', seemingly a minor, and already under Rosina's influence) in September 1825. The Gondal date for the present poem, if one was worked out, cannot have been much earlier than the composition date.

15–18 EB revised 15, then changed 17–18 to avoid using 'other' four times.

117. Facsimile of MS in *1934*, p. 327. First published in *1846*. As Dingle remarks (p. 40), this is the only poem in which EB sustains a single

metaphor throughout. For a similar near-allegory, cf. the lament for a chief in Scott, *Lady of the Lake*, III. xv. 22 n., where the tree is the clan: 'Wide, wide around were spread its lofty branches— | But the topmost bough is lowly laid!' In EB's poem the tree is time; its root is eternity; the branch, which recovers from a defoliation by sorrow and guilt but is finally withered by a death, seems to be the speaker. It is not easy to find events in EB's own life to match these. Although the poem was not copied into the Gondal notebook, *GQ* (p. 111) regards it as a lament by Rosina for Brenzaida and a 'companion-piece' to **116**, written three weeks before; cf. Barker, ed. *Selected Poems*, p. 140. For comment, see Hardy, pp. 103–4.

30 *that perished sapling*: apparently the dead bough, though this sense is not recorded in *OED*.

118. Facsimile in *1934*, pp. 326–7. First published in *1846*. Modern criticism dwells on the symbolism of the poem. For Visick (pp. 36–8) it focuses a contrast found in some Gondal poems 'between the cool and gentle and the hot and vital', so as to liberate EB from Gondal and prepare her for *WH*. Grove (pp. 60–4) thinks it her finest poem, expressing divided feelings towards both the 'sheltering trance' of the night world and 'the world of adult passions'. A thematically related poem is Tennyson's 'Lady of Shalott' (1842), where Lancelot's disruption of the Lady's cool world is conveyed by images of archery, dazzling sunlight, and flame (73–7); though EB's domestic and realistic setting differs totally from Tennyson's. (For Tennyson, see also commentary to **17**.)

Title: the space above the text in A is overrun by the revised last stanza of **115**; what looks at first like 'stars' is probably the 'strife' (written over '?war') of **115**. 54.

12 *petrel*: a sea-bird supposed by tradition to enjoy storms. The night of 'changeful dreams' has its storms (perhaps imaginary conflicts, as of Gondal), but the dreamer masters them enjoyably without disturbing her 'peace'.

15 *sweet influence*: cf. 'the sweet influences of Pleiades', Job 38: 31; *influence*: a power (earlier, an etherial fluid) streaming down from the stars and affecting the destinies of human beings (*OED*).

119. First published in *1902*. None of the dramatis personae can be identified: the speaker (20–3), the mourner (8 ff.), or the corpse (21). For conjecture, see Paden, p. 69 n. 65.

27 *To sufferers*: 'For sufferers', CB's alternative in B.

32–3 Cf. **117**. 1–4, written twelve days before: a clear example of thematic continuity between Gondal and apparently non-Gondal poetry.

34 '*Life's conscious Death*: cf. 'Life-in-Death' in Coleridge, *Ancient Mariner*, 193.

120a. First published in *1850*. **120b** follows this poem without a break in B, and the two have always been seen as a pair. The theme of two contrasted children, or young people, occurs three years earlier in **90**; possibly relevant are 'two children' in cancelled **80**. 48 and 'two little children' in **191**. 22.

The contrasted pair prefigures *WH*: in **90** by the repetition over two generations, in **120** by the forsaken state of the boy (a parallel to both Heathcliff and Hareton) and the redemptive role of the fair girl (performed by the younger Catherine). On the boy's colouring, **120** is silent. For comment, see Dorothy Van Ghent, *The English Novel: Form and Function* (New York, 1953 repr. 1961), p. 165 ff., where the ' "two children" figure' is seen as 'a metamorphic figure of breakthrough and transformation'; Visick, pp. 16–20; Inga-Stina Ewbank in *WH*, p. 485.

A.E. and R.C.: these initials are not those of the heading in **90**, nor apparently those of the earlier pair remembered in that poem. It has been assumed that 'A.E.' stands for the boy and 'R.C.' for the fair girl, though the reverse may be be true. 'A.E.' may stand for Arthur Exina (Hinkley, p. 275), Alexander Elbë (Paden, pp. 37–8), or 'Amedeus' of **81**. 110 (*GQ*, pp. 71–7). A male 'A.E.' appears in three poems by AB written between October 1945 and August 1846 (*Poems of AB*, **47**, **51**, **52**). 'R.C.' does not appear elsewhere. The initials were replaced in *1850* by the title that CB inserted into B, 'The Two Children'.

7 *beats*: 'throbs' *1850*.

19 'Boyhood sad is merging' *1850*.

20 *Sterner*: 'In sadder' *1850*.

23 *unknowing*: 'unconscious' *1850*.

25 *Blossems*: 'Blossom' *1850*.

27–8 *your. . . Your*: 'thy . . . Thy' *1850*.

dew as: 'dew is' *1850*.

30, 32 *woke . . . roak*: in EB's pronunciation the two vowels may have been closer than in southern speech, which would help to explain her unusual spelling of 'rock' (see appendix I).

31 *your*: 'thy' *1850*.

32 *the*: 'a' *1850*.

33 'Wither, Orphan, wither', CB's alternative in B; 'Wither, soul and blossom!' *1850*.

Brothers: the boy and the kindred blossoms.

34 *You*: 'You both' *1850*.

120b. See general note to **120a**. The two poems may have a common speaker, or possibly **120a** voices the pitying thoughts of the fair child who arrives in **120b**. The change of metre is expressive, but it takes time for the new pattern to establish itself, and the four stresses in 6 and 8 are unexpected.

1 Cf. Thomas Moore, 'Maids from the West, with sun-bright hair', *Lalla Rookh* ('The Light of the Haram'), *Poetical Works* (1841), vii. 42.

5 *shouldest*: 'shouldst' *1850*.

7 *thy*: 'thine' *1850*.

8 *Borne*: 'Wafted' *1850*.

10 *And I do not*: 'Nor do I' *1850*.

15 ' "And I vowed—if need were—to share his sadness' *1850*.

16 *beamy*: 'sunny' *1850*.

20+ *1850* inserts:

"Watch in love by a fevered pillow,
"Cooling the fever with pity's balm;
"Safe as the petrel on tossing billow,
"Safe in mine own soul's golden calm!"

24 ' "And *my* love is truer than angel-care" ' *1850*.

121. Facsimile in *1934*, p. 328. First published in *1846*. In its theme and question-and-answer form the poem recalls Robert Southey, 'The Old Man's Comforts and How He Gained Them' (1799)—still a popular piece when Lewis Carroll parodied it in 1865 (*Alice's Adventures in Wonderland*, ch. v). When he wrote the poem Southey, like EB, admired the Stoical morality of Epictetus: see *New Letters of Robert Southey*, ed. Kenneth Curry (1965), i. 135, 266. For another Southey echo and similar moral cf. **128**. At the foot of the MS text CB has written 'Never was better stuff penned'. Stevie Davies asks whether CB understood the poem, which in Davies' view elevates EB's principles of non-commitment and 'voluntary self-retardation' to the level of a heroic philosophy (*Emily Brontë: Heretic* (1994), pp. 41–3).

16 For the effect of the *1846* revision see Roper, p. 164.

35–6 *tire With looking*: tire of looking.

40 Perhaps, as Gezari suggests, EB has in mind the distinction between the sublime and the beautiful—first theorized by Edmund Burke in his *Philosophical Enquiry* (1757), which emphasised 'terror' as a source of sublimity in nature and art.

45 *Glad comforter*: Hope.

122. First published in *1902*. A. B. Nicholls gave the poem the title 'The Captive's Lament', which was adopted in *1923* and *1934*. *GQ* (p. 167) locates it in the Royalist–Republican wars.

M.A.: the initials do not occur elsewhere; *N C*: Northern College (cf. **114**).

28 *guardian moon*: cf. **95**. 2.

123. Complete text first published in *1938*. From this poem EB extracted a much shorter one, consisting of 13–44 and 65–92 together with a new final stanza, which was published in *1846* as 'The Prisoner'. This became one of her best-known poems, and is printed separately here as **124**. Lines 1–12 were published in *1850* under the title 'The Visionary', with two additional stanzas probably by CB. Lines 113–20 were included in *Brontë Poems: Selections from the Poetry of Charlotte, Emily, Anne and Branwell Brontë*, ed. Arthur C. Benson (Smith, Elder & Co., 1915). Facsimiles of the first MS page, containing 1–44, are given in *1938* (p. 11) and *1941* (p. 238). For the main theme (which stands out more clearly in **124**), cf. Epictetus: 'We will allow those only to be free who do not endure captivity; but, as soon as they are taken, die, and escape' (*Discourses*, IV. i).

Julian M——and A. G. Rochelle: these names do not appear elsewhere and the characters have not been identified. *GQ* (168–73) locates the poem in the Royalist–Republican wars. Julian's family are fighting for 'Freedom'

(146), and reproach him for not taking the field as a 'patriot' (140; cf. **26**. 28 and comment).

Above 1 CB has pencilled 'The Signal Light', presumably a first attempt at a title for the twelve lines published in *1850*.

1–12 There are difficulties in relating the time, the setting (a parental house, as opposed to a castle with dungeons where Julian is master), and even the dramatis personae of these stanzas to the story that follows. But there is no sign of an intended break in B.

12 *winter*: 'frozen' in *1850*, where the line is followed by these two stanzas:

> What I love shall come like visitant of air,
> Safe in secret power from lurking human snare;
> What love's me, no word of mine shall e'er betray,
> Though for faith unstained my life must forfeit pay.
>
> Burn, then, little lamp; glimmer straight and clear—
> Hush! a rustling wing stirs, methinks, the air:
> He for whom I wait, thus ever comes to me;
> Strange Power! I trust thy might; trust thou my constancy.

No MS of these stanzas has been found, and recent critics assume that they are the work of CB.

26 *slumbering, unweaned child*: Helen Brown ('The Influence of Byron on Emily Brontë', *MLR*, 34 (1939), 376) compares Byron, *Don Juan*, II. lxx. 2, 'Ocean slumber'd like an unwean'd child'. In 1834 CB advised Ellen Nussey not to read *Don Juan* (*LL*, i. 122), but see Barker, p. 220.

65–92 The power of these lines, where the captivity of the prisoner becomes a metaphor for the confinement of soul in body, has often been pointed out: see Caroline F. E. Spurgeon, *Mysticism in English Literature* (Cambridge, 1913), pp. 80–4; Derek Stanford, *Emily Brontë: Her Life and Work* (with Muriel Spark, London, 1953), pp. 128–35; Hewish, pp. 83–6; Hardy, pp. 98–100. Their closeness to sexual experience is fully brought out by Davies in *Emily Brontë: Heretic*, pp. 126–30.

82 *inward essence*: for the soul as 'a distinct portion of the essence of God' see Epictetus, *Discourses*, I. xiv, xvii; II. viii.

103 *Two hours good*: a good two hours. Cf. the dungeon scene in Scott, *Legend of Montrose*, ch. 13, in which Dalgetty, being told that the gaoler never reappears till sunset, says 'Then, my friend, we shall have three hours good.'

124. See commentary on **123**.

33 *Still . . . know*: altered in B by EB from 'Yet, tell them, Julian, all', to prepare the passage for fair-copying for *1846* by removing the one Gondal name.

61–4 No MS has been discovered for this stanza, obviously a conclusion written for *1846*. It seems that 62–4 predict or relate the captive's death, which would be more in keeping with her speech than the ending in B.

125. Facsimile in *1934*, p. 329. First published in *1850*, with a sentence by CB: 'The following are the last lines my sister Emily ever wrote.'

Date: Barker reads ' "Jan 25" or possibly "Jan 23" ', following the *1934* facsimile, (p. 928 n. 18). But '2[d]' is clear in the BPM photographs and in Davidson Cook's 1926 transcript.

1 *No coward soul*: cf. 'No more repine, my coward Soul!' in a poem by Hester Chapone, prefixed to Elizabeth Carter's translation of *All the Works of Epictetus* (1758). Epictetus insists on the importance of overcoming the fear of death; for EB, Chapone, and Epictetus, see Maison, 'Emily Brontë and Epictetus', cited in commentary to 83.

5 'God himself is within you, and hears and sees all' (Epictetus, *Discourses*, II. viii; cf. I. xiv).

7 *hast*: 'has' *1850*.

14 *thy*: 'thine' *1850*.

17–20 Cf. Shelley, *Adonais*, 375–8.

21–4 Cf. *WH*, p. 101: 'If all else perished, and *he* remained, I should still continue to be; and, if all else remained, and he were annihilated, the Universe would turn to a mighty stranger.'

21 *moon*: 'man' *1850*.

23 *wert*: 'were' *1850*.

27 *Since Thou*: 'Thou—THOU' *1850*, a misreading.

126. This incomplete poem and 127, a renewed attempt at the beginning, are the last to appear in B. The first part may have been fair-copied, but from 149 onwards it is clear from the number and extent of alterations that EB is composing into the notebook. Lines 9–26 and 55–75 were included in *Brontë Poems*, ed. Benson. The first substantially complete text was published in *1938*, with a facsimile (p. 32) of the last MS page, containing lines from 212 to the end. In the present text, cancelled passages where EB supplies no alternative have been restored, but not words or phrases that she seems decisively to have rejected. For comment, see Jonathan Wordsworth, 'Wordsworth and the Poetry of Emily Brontë', *BST*, 16/82 (1972), 85–91; Mary Visick, 'The Last of Gondal', *BST*, 18/92 (1982), 75–85; *Life*, pp. 219–22; Davies, *Emily Brontë: Heretic*, pp. 240–7.

1 As the opening emphasizes, time and place are unimportant; but *GQ* (pp. 164, 174 ff.) places the poem 'very probably' in Gondal during the Royalist–Republican wars. The narrator is then an outsider (27–34) enlisted with the Republicans (96).

34 Cf. Scott, *Legend of Montrose*, ch. 3: 'Loyalty is your pass-word, my lord—Liberty, roars another chield from the other side of the strath. . . . Good watchwords all—excellent watchwords.'

35 ff. Cf. the 'ferocious cruelty' of the civil wars in Scotland 1570–3, as described by Scott in *Tales of a Grandfather*, vol. ii, ch. 32: 'Each party continued to execute their prisoners; and as skirmishes were daily fought, the number Of persons who fell by the sword, or died upon the gibbet, was fearfully great' (*Miscellaneous Prose Works*, xxiii. 148).

74–5 Cf. Scott, *Lady of the Lake*, II. xiv. 15–16: 'Where some once pleasant hamlet stood, | A mass of ashes slaked with blood'.

158 *dying bed*: cf. 81. 141 and comment.

196–201 With these lines and cancelled readings, cf. Scott, *Marmion*, VI. XXX. 16–21: Clare seeks water for the dying Marmion, but

Where raged the war, a dark red tide
  Was curdling in the streamlet blue.
Where shall she turn!—behold her mark
  A little fountain-cell,
Where water, clear as diamond-spark,
  In a stone basin fell.

198 *1941*, Gezari, Lloyd-Evans restore 'water', which EB has deleted without finding a satisfactory substitute.

220 *sin gender sin*: cf. 'sin plucks on sin', and similar proverbs (*Oxford Dictionary of English Proverbs*, ed. W. G. Smith, rev. F. P. Wilson (Oxford, 1970), p. 735).

222 After 'five', *1941* and Lloyd-Evans read 'tomorrow morn'; Gezari 'come morn', noting cancelled 'tomorrow'.

240–1 EB's first intention, shown by the two cancelled lines after 239, was that the wounded man agrees to save the narrator's son precisely because his own woe has been so bitter that he would not inflict it on any other human being. After deleting these lines, she wrote 240 above 242, and 241 in the left-hand margin.

244 *1941*, Gezari omit; Lloyd-Evans gives 'Write that they kill'.

245 *1941*, Gezari, Lloyd-Evans restore 'Write', which EB would probably not have used to begin three consecutive lines.

257 *1941* and Gezari omit; Lloyd-Evans reads 'And mercy's God [. . .]'.

258 *1941* omits; Gezari, 'The last [look] of that agony'; Lloyd-Evans, 'The last [. . .] of [. . .] House'.

127. The last lines in B, and the last lines EB (who died seven months later) is known to have written. Facsimile of MS in *GQ*, facing p. 176. First published in *Brontë Poems*, ed. Benson. Davies suggests that EB was moved to return to the poem by the civil strife that was widespread in Europe early in 1848 (*Emily Brontë: Heretic*, pp. 243–4).

128. Facsimile in *1934*, p. 313. C. W. Hatfield notes (*1941*, p. 24) that EB has pencilled the title 'Love and Friendship' into A; but photographs do not show that title, which was used on first publication in *1850*. The poem was attributed to CB when it was set to music in 1879 (*1941*, p. 131). For its subject and moral, cf. Robert Southey's much-anthologized poem 'The Holly Tree' (1798), which compares the bright summer trees with the holly's 'sober hue', but ends by wishing 'That in my age as cheerful I might be | As the green winter of the Holly Tree'. For another possible Southey echo and a similar moral, see **121**.

129. Facsimile in *1934*, p. 313. First published in *1846*, when the title was added.

15 *journey on, if*: EB probably began to write something like 'man press onward' in A, but changed her mind after 'man' and put 'journy onward', forgetting to delete 'man'. For 'man' as a form of address, cf. **115**. 27,

comment on **115**. 1; though possibly the redundant text reads 'mar', a beginning for 'march'.

130. The drafts of 1–27 (in ink, and including a stanza later dropped) and of 26–33 (in pencil) are on different scraps of paper in the D collection (D3, D8); they have similarities of theme and form but no lines in common, and do not come together until B. First published from the D texts in *1902*, 1–27 as a separate poem, 26–33 as a continuation of **91**. The B text was not printed until *1938*, though a facsimile is given in Virginia Moore, *The Life and Eager Death of Emily Brontë* (1936). In GQ (pp. 86–7) the lover whom A.G.A. compares to the moon is Alfred ?Sidonia, and to the sun Julius Brenzaida (though he is never clearly linked with A.G.A. in the poems). Cf. **118** for the contrast of night and day, *WH* for that of lovers.

131. First published in *1902*. With 4–6, cf. **34**. 14–20.

132. One of only two poems undated in C; EB may have omitted the date when transcribing from a draft, as happened with **20**. First published in *1910* with 19–22 omitted and the date 'July 26, 1837', which would make it one of EB's earliest dated poems. Most likely the editor misread the date of the previous C poem, **58** (26th July 1839), and supposed it would apply to both.

A A A: these initials do not occur elsewhere. GQ (p. 78) suggests they refer to Amedeus (cf. **81**. 110), and identifies the speaker as A.G.A. 'by the poetic language of her self-excuse'.

133. First published in *1941* (p. 117 n.). The line after the end of 3 may indicate a new beginning.

4 Cf. Scott, *Lay of the Last Minstrel*, epilogue, 1, 'Hush'd is the harp—the Minstrel gone'; Byron, 'Elegy on Newstead Abbey', xxiii, 'Hush'd is the harp, unstrung the warlike lyre'.

his: The only redundant initial *h* in EB's manuscripts, probably influenced by the surrounding words. In other places *h* is omitted.

134. First published in *1902*. This and the next eight poems and fragments were all written on D5, together with **23**, the only dated item. *1902* combines **134–140** into a single sequence, in that order.

135–140. See commentary on **134**.

135. In 2, D's 'fellings' seems much more likely to be a slip of the pen, anticipating the taller loop and then doubling the wrong letter, than a spelling variant.

141. First published in *1902*, where two other poems (**23** and **142**, which follow **141** in D5) are added under the same poem number. This composite poem is dated 'Mar 22 1838': **23** has only 'march 1838' in D, and **141**, **142** are undated.

142. See commentary on **141**.

143. First published in *1902*, where this poem and **144** are each dated 'November, 1837'. This date may have been derived from **16**, the preceding poem in D6. Apparently the speaker is a spectre: cf. **6** (written in July 1837).

2 *Hid*: 'H' is unclear but resembles the first letter of 'Had' in **9**. 2, on the same side of D6.

144. First published in *1902*, dated as described above. This fragment is thematically related to **57**.

145. First published in *1902*. In D8 the figure *2* has been written above the fragment—probably to indicate its place in a sequence, though no other figures have been found.

146. First published in *1902*. Thematically and stylistically similar to **65**, **104** (**146**. 21–4 closely follow **104**. 1–4), and **130**. *GQ* (pp. 84–7) relates **104**, **130**, and **146** to A.G.A.'s parting from Lord Alfred.

147. First published in *1902*, where **30**, **147**, **148**, and **150–156** are printed as a sequence with a single poem number, though as in D the items are separated by short rules. The date 'June 1838', which belongs to **30**, is placed at the head of the *1902* sequence.

148–156. See commentary on **147**. The cancelled **149** was omitted from *1902*, and has not been previously published.

154. For the phrase 'None but one', cf. **24**. 7.

157. First published in *1902*, followed after a short rule but under the same poem number by **1**, which follows **157** in D10^{v}. The composite poem is dated 'July 12 1836', the date given in D to **1**.

3 *Lake Wernas water*: the name *Werna* does not occur elsewhere.

158. First published in *1902* as one poem with **159**, which follows it in D10^{v}. After composing or (more likely) copying the first stanza into D, EB at first began to write what is now the third.

159. First published in *1902* as a continuation of **158**. Thematically similar to **191** and **192**.

160. First published in *1902*, with the date 'November 1887' above in brackets. The year is a misprint for 1837 and the date probably derives from **14** or **15**, which precede **160** in D11 and in *1902*.

9–16 The arrogance and misanthropy of the first speaker (and many of EB's speakers) is rebuked by the 'shade' who answers him.

161–162. First published in *1902*, as parts of one three-part sequence which begins with **36** and takes its date; the order is that of D11^{v}.

163. First published in *1902* as a final stanza to **2**, which precedes it in D11^{v}.

164–168. First published in *1902*, as parts of one sequence which begins with **10** and takes its date; the order, as in the present text, is that of D12.

165. See preceding note.

8 *Lake Elnors tide*: this lake in Gondal was the scene of the death of Alexander Elbë; cf. **4**, **114**.

166. For comment on 'this perfect imagist fragment', see Davies, *Emily Brontë: Heretic*, pp. 174–5.

168. See general note to **165–168**. This fragment may be related to **57**, perhaps as a draft for 5–8.

169–173. First published in *1902* as a sequence under one poem number following the order of D12^{v}, which is followed here. The metre and narrative of **173** suggest a direct continuation of **172**, but between them EB has placed a line of crosses—one of her methods for separating out poems and fragments.

171. See general note to **169–173**.

5–6 The picture is in a locket that also contains a woven cutting from the lady's hair (cf. **126**. 145–6). The pathos of decay is tacitly transferred from the picture to the lady herself.

174. Written in very pale ink, and upside-down to the other fragments on D12^{v}; previously unpublished. 'Harold' does not occur elsewhere in EB's or AB's poems.

175. Written in pencil on E2, a scrap of paper about 2″ x 1″ which contains no other writing. First published in *1910* as a continuation of **11**; first printed separately in *1941*.

176–177. These fragments, together with **69**, are pencilled on another scrap of paper (E3); they were first published in *1910* as a continuation of **69**. Below the poems in E is a calculation involving six dates.

178. Written on the upper half of a page torn from a small notebook. First published in *1910*. Neither the speaker nor the addressee has been identified. For comment see *Life*, pp. 150–2.

1 *thy bleeding branch*: the *locus classicus* for the story of the bleeding branch, broken from a tree which is really a man transformed as a punishment, is Virgil's *Aeneid*, III. 19–68 (III. 34–44 in Dryden's translation, of which BB owned a copy). The story passed into Ariosto, *Orlando Furioso*, vi. 26–53, and Spenser, *Faerie Queene*, I. ii, stanzas 30–44. The branch cut off and cast out or burned is a common biblical metaphor for divine punishment, e.g. John 15: 6. Chitham in *Life* refers to the broken branch of a pine drawn by EB; Gezari compares *WH*, pp. 30–1, where the branch of a fir is transformed into a bleeding limb.

179. This fragment and **180** are consecutive in E6 and were first printed in *1910* as one poem, in a sequence beginning with **71** (from E10, once part of the same leaf as E6).

180. See previous comment.

3 The first two words have been made exceptionally difficult by overwriting (*1941* reads 'I saw'), and the sixth is much distorted (*1910* reads 'torn'). The line could be read as 'Ah soul my young breast filled with sighs'.

5 No reading has been found for the fifth word that corresponds to what is visible, though 'bare' (*1910*) comes closer than 'first' (*1941*); *woe* is unclear and may be a continuation of the missing word.

181. First published in *1910*, with 1–8 of **193** following it as a continuation.

182. First published in *1941*. For 'Iernë', see **111**. 6 and comment.

2 With the chiming castle clock, cf. Coleridge, 'Christabel', 1.

183. First published in *1910*.

184. Below this poem on E12 is a tiny sketch of the sun or moon rising or setting between low hills, with a figure in the foreground. First published in *1910*. A place is found for **184** in the Gondal reconstructions by Hinkley (p. 278) and Paden (p. 39).

185. First published in *1910* with the date 'November 1838', probably derived from the draft of **61** which bears that date and precedes it in E12. Hinkley (p. 278), GQ (p. 55), and Paden (pp. 29, 39) read this as a poem about the death of Elbë, though **4** and **114** tell that he dies in bright evening sunshine.

1 *swept*: with MS *spwept*, cf. 'spweeping' at **58**. 6.

186. The Gondal heading was added to the right of 1–3; 'marcius' is in pencil. First published in *1910*. The poem is placed in Gondal history by Hinkley (p. 275), *GQ* (p. 108), and Paden (p. 22).

Arthr Ex: probably Arthur Exina, son or brother of Gerald, the monarch betrayed and overthrown by Julius Brenzaida (see introduction, p. 12). His name occurs in a list of Gondal names by AB and is one of the few to appear in both sisters' writings (see appendix VI).

marcius: not found elsewhere.

3 This line has been inserted after 2 and 4 were written.

187. First published in *1910*. For the theme, cf. and contrast **118**; here even the 'cloudless sky' is left behind.

188. E15 has a ragged top edge where the upper part of the leaf, apparently bearing some verse ending in a rule, has been torn off. 'Almeda' and '— October 30th | 2 October 30th' are written upside-down in the right-hand margin. First published in *1910* as a continuation of **82**.

M A A: not found elsewhere, though 'M.A.' is the speaker of **122**.

189. First published in *1910*.

190. E17, which bears this poem only, has been cut in two by an uneven cut passing below 16 without damage to letters. First published in *1910*. The poem laments the imprisonment of Gondal's king, Gerald Exina, after his overthrow by Julius Brenzaida (*GQ*, p. 99).

191. First published in *1910* as a continuation of **61**. For attempts to fit this poem into Gondal reconstructions, see Hinkley, p. 275; *GQ*, pp. 79–80; Paden, pp. 47–8.

1–2 Cf. Byron, 'To Inez', *Childe Harold*, I. lxxxiv: 'It is not love, it is not hate | . . . That bids me loathe my present state.'

22 *two little children*: see commentary on **120a**.

192. The single poem or fragment written on E19, a small piece of pale brown cardboard. First published in *1910*. Cf. the close of 'Alone She paced her ancient Hall' (1837), *Poems of BB*, p. 143.

193. First published in *1910* (1–8 only) as a continuation of **181**. Those two fragments may once have been on the same sheet, though not in the *1910* sequence.

194. First published in *1910*. The scene for this speech may be an imaginative version of Haworth churchyard. For the theme, cf. **98**.

1 *Start not*: Helen Brown ('The Influence of Byron on Emily Brontë', *MLR*, 34 (1939), 376) notes the opening of Byron's 'Lines Inscribed upon a Cup Formed from a Skull': 'Start not—nor deem my spirit fled'.

minster: Haworth Church seems thus transformed in **60**. 2.

7 *These stairs are steep*: perhaps a meiosis, predicting the descent into the grave; or EB may be imagining a crypt.

landed: having reached a stage in, or end of, a journey (*OED*).

195–197. First published in *1910*, and now printed for the first time as a separate poem and fragments: see commentary on **3**.

198. First published in *1902*.

199. First published in *1910*. The 'wild harp', an adjunct of the bard myth, had been made a cliché by frequent use in Thomas Moore's *Irish Melodies* (1808–34). This poem redeems it, especially by the transformation of sound into visual effects in the last stanza.

200. First published in *1902*.

17 Cf. *Hamlet*, I. iii. 78–80: 'to thine own self be true, | And it must follow, as the night the day, | Thou canst not then be false to any man.'

201. First published in *1850*. No manuscript of this poem has ever been reported, and its authenticity has been questioned. To C. W. Hatfield it 'savors more strongly of Charlotte than of Emily, seeming to express Charlotte's thoughts about her sister, rather than Emily's own thoughts' (*1941*, p. 255). In view of CB's revisions and expansions of EB's poems in *1850*, there is nothing improbable about her producing a complete poem on her sister's behalf to set her in a desired light. This **201** would have done by bringing EB out on the side of truth and nature as against the 'shadowy region' of romance, in a conflict which seems to have disturbed CB more than her sister. Stylistically, as Gezari points out, the iambic pentameter is uncharacteristic of EB; so is the wealth of feminine rhymes (matched only in **2**, **53**, and the first four stanzas of **7**) and the jingle of 'more glory and more grief'. But there is no firm evidence either way, and some reasons for accepting the poem as authentic are set out by Chitham in '"Often Rebuked": Emily's After All', *BST*, 18/93 (1983), 222–6.

APPENDIX I

Emily Brontë's Spelling

EB's spelling is neither consistent nor orthodox, though MSS A and B show fewer unusual spellings than the earlier manuscripts. Most of these are of kinds common among people more sensitive to the sound than to the look of words, and cause no real difficulty. She often writes *ei* for *ie* (*veiw*), and goes wrong over *ua*, *au* (*gardian*, *guant*), and double letters (*accross*, *disapear*, *tyrrany*). The use of *e* gave her problems: the reader is not likely to be held up by *rosey*, *tiney*, *truely*, *waveing*, *quenche*, but may be checked by *breath* (for 'breathe'). In some cases the absence of *e* probably results from a habit of writing rather than of spelling. Some words take a moment to recognize because the form used would normally produce a different sound from the one intended, as in *carless* ('careless'), *hopless* ('hopeless'), *matless* ('mateless'), *mared* ('marred'). Two strange forms used more often than not are *roak* for 'rock' (e.g. in **31**. 13, 17, 38, 56, a spelling previous editors have missed, or disbelieved) and *whach*, *whacher* for 'watch' and 'watcher' (e.g. **107**. 21, **48**. 1). A list follows of the spellings most likely to confuse, together with a few that are of interest because archaic ('desarts', 'holyday').

Some spellings may give a clue to pronunciation.[1] Since EB not only spells 'rock' *roak*, but rhymes it with 'woke' (**120a**. 30, 32), and also writes *chocked* for 'choaked' (**7**. 28), it seems that for her these two vowels were not far apart. In two places she begins a line with *A*, then deletes it for the required pronoun 'I' (**126**. 207, **191**. 21). Three times she omits the *h* from 'has' (**49**. 6, corrected; **29**. 9, **102**. 3). Another possibly phonetic spelling is *been* for 'being', in 'One been absent saddens all' (**45**. 44, written twice thus before being corrected). These spellings probably correspond to speech around Haworth then as now. Her occasional rhyming of *prayers* with *tears* and *care* with *dear* may suggest the local use of the diphthong 'Iə'; so too the spellings *scearce*, *scearcely*, which occur thirteen times (e.g. at **7**. 44). But EB also wrote *sceattered* (**26**. 39), which looks more like a trick of the pen. When she wrote *Wuthering Heights* she was certainly conscious of pronunciations like 'whear' and 'thear' as non-standard, and indicated them in Joseph's speech. Some of the archaic spellings, too, may reflect EB's pronunciation (*dongeon*).

[1] EB's use of local speech for Joseph in *WH* has been examined by K. M. Petyt in *Emily Brontë and the Haworth Dialect* (Yorkshire Dialect Society, 1970), and in *WH*, appendix VII. Her own speech may have been influenced by her Irish father's habits, and those of her Cornish mother and aunt, as well as Yorkshire ones. Mary Taylor remembered many years later that when CB arrived at Roe Head she had 'a strong Irish accent' (*LL*, i. 89).

Some Unusual Spellings

alter (altar)
beuty (beauty)
blithly (blithely)
bosem (bosom)
breath (breathe)
broard (broad)
brouze (browse)
buissy (busy)
cerfew (curfew)
chocked (choked)
controul (control)
corps (corpse)
dazzel (dazzle)
dazzlling (dazzling)
deifyed (deified)
desarts (deserts)
devided (divided)
devine (divine)
dispair (despair)
dispondancy (despondency)
dollful (doleful)
dongoen, dongeon (dungeon)
exsist (exist)
faultering (faltering)
firn (fern)
forebear (forbear)
forunners (forerunners)
grive (greive)
guant (gaunt)
hazle (hazel)
hid (hide)
holyday (holiday)
hopless (hopeless)
I'de (I'd)
knook (nook)
lenghened (lengthened)
levert (leveret)
lightening (lightning)
lonley (lonely)
majian (Magian)
majic (magic)
mared (marred)
matless (mateless)
ment (meant)
mistery (mystery)
oacen, ocaen (ocean)
ore, oe'r (o'er)
purefyed (purified)
rearl (real)
recives (receives)
roak (rock)
scearce (scarce)
sceattered (scattered)
seigh (siege)
shallt (shalt)
sooth (soothe)
souless (soulless)
specteral (spectral)
stranglers (stragglers)
streching (stretching)
symathy, symphathy (sympathy)
taan (taken)
their (there)
thrawl (thrall)
tyrrany (tyranny)
usless (useless)
virture (virtue)
voicless (voiceless)
were (where)
whach (watch)
whacher (watcher)
whithered (withered)
wholey (wholly)
whreched (wretched)
wistle (whistle)

APPENDIX II

Sequence of Poems in the Manuscripts

In each case, the first line of a poem, fragment, or draft is given as it appears in the manuscript under which it is listed.

Sequence in MS A	*Poem no.*	*Page*
Loud without the wind was roaring	39	66
A little while, a little while	40	69
How still, how happy! those are words	41	70
The bluebell is the sweetest flower	42	71
Fair sinks the summer evening now	62	92
Shall Earth no more inspire thee	84	121
In summer's mellow midnight	79	107
Riches I hold in light esteem	83	120
Aye there it is! It wakes to night	85	122
I'll not weep that thou art going to leave me	75	104
If greif for greif can touch thee	77	106
O Dream, where art thou now?	38	66
It is too late to call thee now	74	103
The wind I hear it sighing	66	96
Love is like the wild rose briar	128	195
There should be no dispair for you	129	195
"Well, some may hate and some may scorn"	68	98
Far, far away is mirth withdrawn	73	102
I see around me tombstones grey	86	123
The evening passes fast away	93	134
Hope was but a timid Friend	99	142
Well hast thou spoken—and yet not taught	103	146
How clear she shines! How quietly	95	138
On a sunny brae alone I lay	105	148
When weary with the long day's care	108	153
O, thy bright eyes must answer now	110	155
"Enough of Thought, Philosopher"	115	164
Ah! why, because the dazzeling sun	118	169
Death, that struck when I was most confiding	117	167
How beautiful the Earth is still	121	173
No coward soul is mine	125	183

Sequence in MS B		
There shines the moon, at noon of night	4	32
Lord of Elbë, on Elbë hill	8	40

Sequence in MS C

Leaves have been removed from this notebook, and some texts are incomplete (see introduction, pp. 17–18). The notebook now begins in mid-poem, with the line shown below.

	Poem no.	*Page*
If I might hear thy voice in the hall	8	40
O transient voyager of heaven!	18	49
Awake! awake! how loud the stormy morning	20	51
King Julius left the south country	46	76
O wander not so far away	25	54
This shall be thy lullaby	27	57
Sacred watcher wave thy bells	48	79
I die but when the grave shall press	19	50
O between distress and pleasure	65	95
O Dream where art thou now?	38	66
Shed no tears o'er that tomb	58	89
Sleep not dream not this bright day	132	198
From our evening fireside now	45	75
I did not sleep 'twas noon of day	51	82
Far away is the land of rest	12	44
The soft unclouded blue of air	47	77

Sequences in the Single-Leaf Manuscripts

The sequence of poems on each leaf is shown, but not the distinction between recto and verso sides, since it does not seem to be significant and the choice of designation is almost always arbitrary. Fragmentary drafts are entered by the first line of the fragment and, if other texts exist, identified by the number of the poem under which they are collated.

D1		
And now the housedog streched once more	56	86
D2		
The night of storms has past	5	34
I saw thee child one summers day	6	36
D3		
Come hither child—who gifted thee	57	88
Alas that she	133	199
I'm standing in the forest now	130	196
D4		
O God of heaven! the dream of horror	7	38
D5		
Deep deep down in the silent grave	134	199
Here with my knee upon thy stone	135	200
O come again what chains withhold	136	200
Was it with the feilds of green	137	200

	Poem no.	*Page*
D11		
Now trust a breast that trusts in you	14	45
Sleep brings no joy to me	15	46
Strong I stand though I have borne	160	207
Where were ye all? and where wert thou	36	64
I paused on the threshold I turned to the sky	161	208
O come with me thus ran the song	162	208
High waveing heather 'neath stormy blasts bending	2	31
Woods you need not frown on me	163	208
D12		
The battle had passed from the height	10	41
How golden bright from earth and heaven	164	209
Not a vapour had stained the breezless blue	165	209
Only some spires of bright green grass	166	209
The sun has set and the long grass now	167	209
Lady in your palace Hall	168	210
And first an hour of mournful museing	169	210
Wind sink to rest in the heather	170	210
Long neglect has worn away	171	211
Awaking morning laughs from heaven	172	211
Her sisters and her brothers feet	173	212
O Harold while the darkness falls	174	212
D13		
That wind I used to hear it swelling	70	99
D14		
How long will you remain the midnight hour	60	91
D15		
Companions all day long we've stood	80	108
D16		
Alcona in its changing mood	63	93
E1		
May Flowers are opening	50	81
E2		
Tis evening now the sun descends	175	212
E3		
The wind was rough which tore	69	99
We wander on we have no rest	176	212
What Shadow is it	177	212
E4		
There let thy bleeding branch atone	178	213
E5		
What winter floods what showers of Spring	44	75

E6	*Poem no.*	*Page*
Upon her aching breast	179	213
I gazed within thine ernest eyes	180	213
E7		
There was a time when my cheek burned	67	97
E8		
All hushed and still within the house	181	213
Iernës eyes were glazed and dim	182	214
E9		
And like myself lone wholey lone	82	120
E10		
Heavens glory shone where he was laid	71	99
E11		
Tis moon light summer moonlight	78	106
E12		
When days of Beauty deck the earth	183	214
Still beside that dreary water	184	214
The starry night shall comfort bring	61	92
There swept adown that dreary glen	185	215
In dungeons dark I cannot sing	186	215
The evening sun was sinking down	33	62
Fall leaves fall die flowers away	21	51
Loud without the wind was roaring	39	66
E13		
Weaned from life and torn away	22	52
O transient v[oyager of heaven!]	18	49
I'm happiest when most away	187	216
E14		
I know not how it falls on me	52	83
The hours of day have glided by	53	83
The buissy day has glided by	53	83
E15		
Methinks this heart should rest a while	188	216
E16		
That dreary lake that midnight sky	189	217
E17		
His land may burst the galling chain	190	217
E18		
it is not pride it is not shame	191	218
E19		
She dried her tears and they did smile	192	219

E20	*Poem no.*	*Page*
The day is done—the winter sun	102	145
F1		
The organ swells the trumpets sound	64	95
F2		
But the hearts that once adored me	193	219
T1		
I am the only being whose doom	49	80
T2		
A sudden chasm of ghastly light	11	42
T3		
Start not upon the minster wall	194	219
Red breast early in the morning	3	32
My heart is not enrapturd now	195	220
What woke it then? a little child	196	220
I heard it then you heard it too	197	220
Through the hours of yester night	198	220
Darkness was over Gondall every face	28	57
Harp of wild and dream like Strain	199	221
The Old church tower and Garden wall	13	44
T4		
Mild the mist upon the hill	59	90
T5		
All day I've toiled but not with pain	200	221
T6		
"The starry night shall tidings bring"	61	92
T7		
None of my kindred now can tell	29	58
T8		
Month after month year after year	54	85

APPENDIX III

Sequence of Poems in *1846* and *1850*

Poems by Currer, Ellis, and Acton Bell (1846)

These poems by 'Ellis' are interspersed with others by 'Currer' and 'Acton', in rough rotation. Most were given titles, by which they are listed below.

	Poem no.	*Page*
Faith and Despondency	111	156
Stars	118	169
The Philosopher	115	164
Remembrance	116	166
A Death-Scene	114	162
Song	107	152
Anticipation	121	173
The Prisoner	124	181
Hope	99	142
A Day Dream	105	148
To Imagination	108	153
How Clear She Shines	95	138
Sympathy	129	195
Plead for Me	110	155
Self-Interrogation	93	134
Death	117	167
Stanzas to—	68	98
Honour's Martyr	113	160
Stanzas	75	104
My Comforter	103	146
The Old Stoic	83	120

Wuthering Heights and Agnes Grey (1850)

In this selection, poems by 'Ellis' were placed together, some with titles supplied by CB (see commentary for these and for CB's alterations). First lines are given below as they appeared in *1850*.

A little while, a little while	40	69
The Bluebell is the sweetest flower	42	71
Loud without the wind was roaring	39	66
Shall earth no more inspire thee	84	121
In summer's mellow midnight	79	107
Ay—there it is! it wakes to-night	85	122
Love is like the wild rose-briar	128	195
"Listen! When your hair, like mine"	112	158
How few, of all the hearts that loved	106	150

	Poem no.	Page
In the earth—the earth—thou shalt be laid	98	141
I knew not 'twas so dire a crime	35	63
For him who struck thy foreign string	32	61
Heavy hangs the rain-drop	120a	171
Child of delight, with sun-bright hair	120b	173
Silent is the house; all are laid asleep	123	176
I do not weep; I would not weep	89	128
Often rebuked, yet always back returning	201	222
No coward soul is mine	125	183

APPENDIX IV

Editions after *1850*

1902

Poems by Charlotte, Emily, and Anne Brontë, Now for the First Time Printed (New York, 1902) was published by the rare-book dealers Dodd, Mead and Company in an edition of 110 copies. It includes ninety-nine poems and fragments by EB, all but three of them previously unpublished.[1] The table of contents lists only sixty-six of her pieces, eight of them ultimately derived from MS A, twenty-six from MS B (plus the 'Song' in 31, listed separately), and thirty-two from the D MSS. But the total from D is larger than it appears, since, as printed, these poems incorporate thirty-three other short poems and fragments found in sequences on the same leaves. The volume includes almost all the D pieces, together with most of the A and B poems that had been excluded from *1846* and *1850*. It also includes ten poems by CB and twelve by AB.

It is not known who edited the volume, or who then owned the manuscripts he used;[2] but it is clear what these sources must have been. The editor had no access to A, which in 1902 was at Honresfeld, nor to B, which Nicholls kept till his death in 1906. His prefatory note refers to two kinds of manuscript: some 'written in an ordinary, quite legible handwriting', and others 'written on little scraps of paper of various sizes, in minute angular characters, almost illegible, without punctuation, and the spelling often at fault'. These were, on the one hand, Nicholls' transcripts of poems from A and B, and on the other the D holographs.

That Nicholls' transcripts were used for the A and B poems is clear from the appearance in *1902* of misreadings from those transcripts, like 'Tell me, whether' for 'Tell me, whacher' in **26**. 1, and of headings that Nicholls supplied, such as 'Grave in the Ocean' for **96**. The volume also follows Nicholls in presenting unpublished parts of B poems as though they could stand complete, as with 39–60 of **112**. The transcripts used must have been those now in the Huntington Library, since they agree with that manuscript in reading 'piteous' in **86**. 1 as against the 'hideous' of the Huntington

[1] The three exceptions were **55**, which had appeared in the *Cornhill Magazine* (May 1860); **26**, which Clement Shorter had printed in *Charlotte Brontë and her Circle* (1896); and **72**, published in *The Woman at Home* (Aug. 1897).

[2] Clement Shorter states that *1902* was printed 'from a manuscript in the collection of a bookman in the United States' (introduction to *Wuthering Heights* (1911), pp. vii–viii). It is possible that Dodd, Mead (who had other dealings with Wise) were the purchasers of the source MSS, and that the bibliographer Luther S. Livingston was the editor. Livingston was working for the firm in 1902 and had become a partner by 1913: see John Carter and Graham Pollard, *The Firm of Charles Ottley, Landon & Co.* (1948), p. 21.

notebook.[3] The editor seems to have mistaken these copies for holographs, claiming in the preface that 'The poems have been deciphered . . . from the original manuscripts.'

The poems and fragments from the D MSS would have had to be transcribed for the press. The editor states that 'The effort has been made to print them here exactly as they were written, without attempt at correction.' They were indeed carefully and fairly accurately transcribed, preserving spellings like 'breezless', 'chocked' (for *choked*), 'dispair', 'thrawl', and 'whached'. Some passages which defeated the editor have become no clearer since. Composition dates, Gondal headings, and signatures were all retained whenever found, though in the case of transcripts from A and B the headings and signatures had been removed by Nicholls. The poems were also arranged as far as possible in order of composition, though one dated poem (91) was left out of sequence and had to be added near the end.

This was a valuable edition in its time, and a more scholarly one than *1910*. It is remarkable that in *1902* no pieces were misattributed to EB. Its major errors were reliance on Nicholls' transcripts from A and B, and the incorporation into some D poems of unrelated fragments from the same leaves, even when these differed in subject and metre (e.g. 163 is printed as a continuation of 2).

1910

The Complete Poems of Emily Brontë, edited by Clement Shorter (London: Hodder & Stoughton, 1910), was the first volume of an edition of her works. The second appeared in 1911 and included *Wuthering Heights*, an introduction serving for both volumes, and facsimiles of some verse manuscripts. The *Complete Poems* added fifty-eight poems and fragments to the 135 already published,[4] drawing on two main sources. One of these was MS C, which was in Wise's possession and is reproduced among the facsimiles in the 1911 volume. The other, comprising what are now designated the E, F, and T MSS, was the second of the two batches into which the single-leaf manuscripts had been divided by Wise, a batch which was now in the possession of his associate H. Buxton Forman.[5] In addition, part of a new D poem was included. Spelling and punctuation were normalized.

[3] Nicholls' transcripts are listed in Barbara Rosenbaum and Pamela White, *Index of English Literary Manuscripts*, IV/I. (1982) 82–103.

[4] Besides including some manifest errors, the totals for old and new poems given by Shorter in his introduction, pp. vii–viii, are misleading because of the large number of pieces either misassigned or lost by amalgamation.

[5] See introduction, above, pp. 18–19. The facsimiles in the 1911 volume are said to be 'reproduced from the Original Manuscripts in the possession of Mr Thomas J. Wise and Mr Walter Slater'. Walter Brindley Slater was 'one of Wise's earliest and closest friends, whose collection contained an almost complete run of forgeries and many other of Wise's productions' (Carter and Pollard, *Firm of Charles Ottley*, p. 30). Apart from MS C and D15, none of the MSS reproduced is by EB.

The first of the four parts of *1910* simply reprints the twenty-one poems of *1846* in the order in which they stood in that volume. The second part does the same for the selection of *1850*. The third, headed 'Privately Printed Poems', is substantially a reprint of *1902* with normalized accidentals (except for a few instances that are probably mistakes, as where 'Isles' for 'aisles' is retained from *1902*). In his introduction Shorter disclaims responsibility for the accuracy of the *1902* texts, claiming only to have reproduced them from the earlier volume. In fact, he occasionally consults C for alternative texts (he reports C's title for **20**), and sometimes adopts C readings into B and D poems from *1902*. Thus he follows C in some lines of **8** and **45** (though this means substituting EB's cancelled draft readings for her final ones) and of **27**. Otherwise the A and B poems are corrected only by guesswork: thus in **37**. 21, where *1902* offers the bracketed alternatives 'hand' (B's reading) and 'head', *1910* replaces both by the unlikely 'hair'.

The copies of EB's manuscripts that were made for Wise before he sold them were available to Shorter, who later passed them to Hatfield. It also looks as though he had some co-operation from the unknown owner of the original D MSS. One of the few D poems to be omitted from *1902* was **80**, 'Companions all day long we've stood': the first thirty-six lines of this piece are printed among the new poems in *1910*, and in the 1911 volume a facsimile of the complete poem is reproduced from D15. Four texts from the two sides of D5 are now rearranged so as partly to undo one of the *1902* amalgamations, the sequence **141–23–142**, by removing **142**. (**142** is still not seen to be a complete piece, and now reappears at the head of a sequence continuing with **135**; in the process, the two-line fragment **134** disappears entirely.) Other D poems are accurately corrected, sometimes where the *1902* misreading was obvious (e.g. 'bursts' in **14**. 1, corrected to 'trusts'), occasionally where it was not ('lifeless' in **156**. 3, corrected to 'roofless'). But in many more D poems the misreadings of *1902* are either corrected by guesswork or allowed to stand.

The last part of *1910* comprises 'Unpublished Poems', which Shorter declares 'have been carefully collated by me, and . . . are unquestionably Emily's work' (p. viii in the 1911 volume). Twenty-two of these poems are now agreed to be by AB, BB, or CB, and another, 'To the horse black Eagle', was rightly excluded from most later editions (see introduction, p. 25, n. 2). The first in sequence of the authentic poems is the incomplete text of **80**, from D, which ends with the misreading 'And flout against her sky' for 'And Ula's Eden sky'. Then come forty-eight poems and fragments from MSS E, F, and T, interspersed with poems by the other Brontës. Eleven new pieces of EB's verse in this batch do not appear in the table of contents because they are combined with other pieces, as happened with the D pieces in *1902*. The first five lines of **53** are duplicated: they are given from E14 as a separate fragment (p. 303), although the complete text from B had already been printed in *1902* and reprinted in the previous section of *1910* (pp. 142–3). The standard of transcription is variable but less satisfactory than in the D poems of *1902*, and again the editor sometimes falls back on invention.

Last come nine previously unpublished poems from C. This holograph, in an ordinary cursive hand, is more accurately copied, though one odd error is 'morning's brow' for 'mourning brow' (18. 6), and a date is wrongly assigned. More editorial activity has gone into this volume, for better or worse, than Shorter's introduction suggests, but the standard of care leaves much to be desired. As Tom Winnifrith remarks in another context, 'Shorter was not interested in accuracy.'[6]

1923

By 1910 nearly all EB's poems had been published, and the problems now were to improve the texts and to eliminate poems wrongly attributed to her. Over the next thirty years both problems were largely solved by the devoted work of C. W. Hatfield,[7] who a few years after *1910* appeared was invited by Shorter to prepare an improved version of it. Hatfield was not a professional man of letters but a civil servant, and his access to sources was limited.[8] At this time he was unaware of the existence of MS A, and he was not allowed fully to examine either MS B[9] or the E MSS. MS C had appeared in facsimile in the companion volume to *1910*, but Hatfield (who had no copy of that volume) had not learned of the fact.[10] He knew enough of the juvenile literature to distinguish Gondal from Angrian names, and he seems to have formed his first conclusions about the Brontës' differing print styles by studying parts of B (possibly in photographs) and by correspondence with H. H. Bonnell of Philadelphia, who owned the D MSS. Shorter also gave him transcripts that had been made for Wise before the manuscripts were dispersed, which were often more plausible than the texts printed so far. By these means, Hatfield eliminated twenty-three poems by AB, BB, and CB from among the poems Shorter had added in *1910*, and improved the texts of many others. For this work he received no reward, and *The Complete Poems of Emily Jane Brontë* (1923) was published as 'edited by Clement Shorter' and 'arranged and collated, with bibliography and notes, by C. W. Hatfield'.

1934

In 1926 MS A was brought into the view of scholars and photographed by Davidson Cook during researches in the Law family library. In the same year H. H. Bonnell had good photographs made of the D MSS and sent them to Hatfield. At about the same time, the E MSS were bought by another

[6] *The Brontës and their Background* (1973; repr. 1988), p. 12.

[7] For Hatfield see Edward Chitham and Tom Winnifrith, *Brontë Facts and Brontë Problems* (1983), ch. 2.

[8] For Hatfield's sources for his two editions, see *1941*, pp. 7–10.

[9] MS B was still owned by the family of George Smith, CB's publisher, and in 1915 **127** and part of **126** had been printed from it in A. C. Benson's selection *Brontë Poems*, published by Smith, Elder. Although Hatfield was not given access to B (*1941*, p. 9), *1923* includes a facsimile reproduction of part of **116** from that MS.

[10] Winnifrith, in *Brontë Facts and Brontë Problems*, p. 18.

co-operative collector, W. T. H. Howe of New York, who also sent photographs to Hatfield. In 1933 MS B was bequeathed to the British Museum. The sources available to Thomas Wise and A. J. Symington, editors of 'what should have been the great edition of the works of the Brontës, the Shakespeare Head',[11] were better than at any time since the manuscripts were dispersed.

Little use was made of these materials in *The Poems of Emily Jane Brontë and Anne Brontë* (1934). Some unauthentic readings were corrected, particularly in the *1850* poems (EB's deer were reinstated in **40**. 40 in place of CB's sheep); but many misreadings and misattributions remained, and the level of competence was low. Hatfield took part in the proof-reading, but wrote afterwards that he alone seemed to have made any corrections, and disgust caused him to limit his own participation.[12] This disappointing volume is useful chiefly for including complete facsimiles of MS A and a poetry manuscript by AB.

1938

MS B was not consulted in the preparation of *1934*, possibly because time did not allow it. Later, Helen Brown and Joan Mott edited a supplementary volume to *1934* with the title *Gondal Poems, by Emily Jane Brontë: Now first Published from the MS. in the British Museum* (1938). It contained six B poems not previously printed in full (**4**, **130**, **112**, **109**, **123**, **126**), together with a list of the B poems with their headings and composition dates, notes on some variants, and two facsimiles.

1941

The Complete Poems of Emily Jane Brontë (1941) was the culmination of thirty years' efforts by Hatfield. The difference that these efforts had made to the corpus as a whole and to the text of almost every poem can be seen simply by comparing *1941* with *1910*. Hatfield now had access to the originals or to photographs of all EB's poem manuscripts except for the T MSS, for which he followed the transcripts that had been prepared for *1910*. In his concern for accuracy Hatfield stood alone among Brontë scholars of his day, and it was forty years before his texts could be significantly improved. His decision to relegate the readings of *1846* to the status of variants was defensible, and his method of presenting variants, though unusual, was perfectly clear. Other aspects of *1941* were more open to question, especially its placing of every poem in one quasi-chronological sequence, whether evidence of its date existed or not. These defects are small compared with Hatfield's achievement, for which any later editor must feel admiration and gratitude.

[11] *The Poems of Charlotte Brontë*, ed. Victor Neufeldt (New York, 1985), p. xxx, q.v. for a discussion of the Shakespeare Head edition; see also Winnifrith, *Brontës and their Background*, ch. 2.

[12] Letters quoted by Neufeldt, *Poems of Charlotte Brontë*, pp. xxxi, xlvii.

Later Editions

The Complete Poems of Emily Brontë (1951), edited by Philip Henderson for the Folio Society, prints the fragments at the end, but otherwise does not differ significantly in text or arrangement from *1941*.

Emily Jane Brontë: The Complete Poems, edited by Janet Gezari (Penguin Classics, 1992), is the first edition to profit by the accessibility of the T MSS, purchased by Mr Robert H. Taylor in 1982 and now part of the Taylor Collection at Princeton University Library. In this respect it represents a significant advance on *1941*.

The Poems of Emily Brontë, edited by Barbara Lloyd-Evans (Batsford, 1992), is a pleasantly produced volume which prints only the poems in MSS A, B, and C, but usefully gives those poems in the order in which they appear in the manuscripts.

APPENDIX V
Gondal Records

Outside the poems, most of what we know about Gondal comes from a series of notes made for record purposes by EB and AB, sometimes called 'birthday notes' or 'diary papers'. They have often been reprinted: this appendix gives only extracts.

EB's Record Paper, November 1834

From a note written when EB was sixteen, AB fourteen, headed 'November the 24 1834':

papa opened the parlour door and gave Branwell a Letter saying here Branwell read this and show it to your Aunt and Charlotte—The Gondals are discovering the interior of Gaaldine   Sally mosley is washing in the back-kitchin

It is past Twelve o'clock   Anne and I have not tided ourselves, done our bed work or done our lessons and we want to go out to play . . .

Emily and Anne

MS at BPM. Facsimiles of recto in *GQ*, facing p. 16; Wilks, p. 73; Lloyd-Evans, p. 60. The paper ends by wondering about their doings in 'the year 1874'.

EB's Record Paper, June 1837

From a note written on BB's twentieth birthday, headed 'Monday evening June 26 1837':

A bit past 4 o'Clock . . . Anne and I writing in the drawing room—Anne a poem beginning 'fair was the Evening and brightly the Sun[']—I Agustus-Almedas life 1st vol—4th page from the last   a fine rather coolish thin grey cloudy but Sunny day Aunt working in the little Room papa—gone out. Tabby in the Kitchin—the Emperors and Empresses of Gondal and Gaaldine preparing to depart from Gaaldine to Gondal to prepare for the coronation which will be on the 12th of July   Queen Vittiora ascended the throne this month Northangerland in Monceys Isle—Zamorna at Eversham.

MS at BPM. Facsimiles in *GQ*, facing p. 177; Winifred Gérin, *Anne Brontë* (1959), facing p. 112; Wilks, p. 55; Lloyd-Evans, p. 61; Juliet Barker, *The Brontës* (1994), after p. 332. AB's poem was a Gondal piece concerning Alexander Hybernia and Zenobia (*Poems of AB*, 2). 'Agustus' seems to be a slip for 'Augusta'. The coronation was happening in the Gondal game 'at present': EB's biography of A.G.A. need not have been synchronous. The historical Victoria inherited the throne on 20 June 1837 and was crowned a year later. As 'Princess Vittoria', she had been one of EB's chief characters in the 'Islanders' Play' (Christine Alexander, *The Early Writings of Charlotte Brontë* (Oxford, 1983), pp. 32, 48, 262–3). 'Northangerland' and 'Zamorna' are characters from the parallel game of Angria played by CB and BB; clearly EB was still kept informed about Angria at this date. The paper ends by glancing forward to 'this day 4 years', and EB seems now to have instituted the practice of opening old papers and writing new ones at four-year intervals, though the date shifts from BB's birthday to her own.

EB's Record Paper, July 1841

From a manuscript headed 'A Paper to be opened when Anne is 25 years old or my next birthday after—if all be well—Emily Jane Brontë July the 30th 1841':

The Gondalians are at present in a threatening state but there is no open rupture as yet—all the princes and princesses of the Royal royaltys are at the palace of Instruction—I have a good many books on hands but I am sorry to say that as usual I make small progress with any—however I have just made a new regularity paper! and I mean verb sap—to do great things.

The whereabouts of this record paper and the next is unknown; text from the facsimile in Shorter, facing p. 146. 'Gondalians' is followed by a long deletion which obscures part of the word, transcribed by Shorter as 'Gondaliand'. In the last sentence 'mean' is unclear.

AB's Record Paper, July 1841

From a paper written at Thorp Green, headed 'July the 30th, AD 1841': 'How will it be when we open this paper and the one Emily has written? I wonder whether the *Gondalian*[*s*] will still be flourishing, and what will be their condition. I am now engaged in writing the fourth volume of *Solala Vernon's Life*.' Text as transcribed by Shorter, p. 149, but amending his 'Gondaliand'.

EB's Record Paper, July 1845

From a paper headed 'Haworth, Thursday, July 30th 1845':

Anne and I went our first long Journey by ourselves together—leaving Home on the 30th of June, monday sleeping at York—returning to Keighly Tuesday evening sleeping there and walking home on wednesday morning—though the weather was broken, we enjoyed ourselves very much, except during a ?few ?hours at Bradford and during our Excursion we were Ronald Macalgin, Henry Angora, Juliet Angusteena, Rosabelle Esmaldan, Ella and Julian Egremont, Catherine Navarre and Cordelia Fitzaphnold, escaping from the palaces of Instruction to join the Royalists who are hard driven at present by the victorious Republicans. The Gondals Still florish bright as ever I am at present writing a work on the First Wars Anne has been writing some articles on this and a book by Henry Sophona—We intend sticking firm by the rascals as long as they delight us which I am glad to say they do at present.

Text from manuscript owned by Mr William Self, by kind permission. Facsimile of part in Shorter, facing p. 154. Shorter's facsimile is reproduced by F. B. Pinion, *A Brontë Companion* (1975), pl. 22, and by Lloyd-Evans, p. 62. The paper was written and EB's birthday celebrated on 31 July, as AB's paper makes clear. None of the Gondal names listed appears elsewhere, though the civil war is a theme in poems both by EB and AB.

AB's Record Paper, July 1845

From a paper dated 'Thursday July the 31st 1845':

Yesterday was Emily's birthday and the time when we should have opened our 1845 [i.e. 1841] paper but by mistake we opened it to day instead. . . . Emily is engeaged in writing the Emperor Julius's life she has read some of it and I want very much to hear the rest—she is writing some poetry too. I wonder what it is about—I ~~am writing~~ have begun the third volume of passages in the life of an Individual, I wish I had finished it. . . . We have not yet finished our Gondal chronicles that we began three years and a half ago when will they be done?—The Gondals are at present in a sad state the Republicans are uppermost but the Royalists are not quite overcome—the Young Sovereigns with their brothers and sisters are still at the palace of Instruction—the Unique Society ~~are~~ above half a year ago were wrecked on a dezart Island as they were returning from Garldin—they are still there but we have not played at them much yet—The Gondals in general are not in first-rate playing condition—will they improve?

Text from manuscript owned by Mr William Self, by kind permission. For the Unique Society, see **101**.

Other Gondal Documents

Besides the above records, there are in existence four lists of what are apparently Gondal names, two by AB and two by EB. These have been incorporated into the complete list of names in appendix VI, with references to the manuscripts or printed texts used. Appendix VI also includes the Gondal place-names AB pencilled into J. Goldsmith's *Grammar of General Geography*.

APPENDIX VI

Gondal Names and Dates

Personal Names and Initials

The following list includes all personal names and sets of initials found in the poems of EB and AB, and in their record papers and lists of characters. Most of these characters must belong to Gondal, and perhaps all of them do, but the possibility remains that some belong to unknown non-Gondal fictions. On the surviving evidence, very few names were used by both sisters: only 'Alexandria', 'Arthur Exina', the ambiguous 'A.E.', and 'Flora'. A few of the Christian names (Adrian, Alexander, Julius) had already been used in the Angrian stories.

It is likely enough that some of these figures were never very substantial. 'Maria', for example, need be no more than a name quickly found for the recipient of AB's 'A Student's Serenade', and 'Amedeus' in E81[1] may have no story beyond what is told in that poem. The lists and record papers may include names invented for the pleasure of invention, or used in play but not otherwise written down. But it is also true that any of these figures may once have loomed large in the lost Gondal chronicles. 'Solala Vernon' is now only a name in one record paper, but we know from that paper that AB devoted at least four 'volumes' to her biography.

The poems and records may refer to the same Gondal character in several different ways: thus Julius Brenzaida may be called 'King Julius' or 'the Emperor Julius', or by his full name, his surname, his initials, or his titles of Angora and Almedore. The opposite difficulty occurs when the same initials may stand for more than one person: 'A.E.' may mean 'Alexander Elbë' or 'Arthur Exina'. Some Christian names, like 'Henry' and 'Isabella', are given to more than one character, so where an unattached Christian name recurs ('Blanche', 'Iernë'), we cannot be sure that it indicates the same figure. In AB's two lists several names have been changed or deleted, as shown. This may mean the correction of a mistake, the rechristening of a character, a marriage, or a change in the dramatis personae of the story or game to which the list refers.

In principle, the list that follows is a list of names and appearances, not an attempt to sort out characters. Although the figure referred to only as 'A.S.' in E25 may well be the same person as 'Alfred S.' in E76, the earlier appearance is entered under 'A.S.', with a cross-reference. But each appearance is listed under the fullest form that the text permits. Thus the appearance of 'A.E.' in E8 is listed under Alexander

[1] Poem numbers in this appendix are given a letter prefix to distinguish EB's from AB's; bold type has not been used.

Elbë, because though the heading refers to him as 'A.E.', the poem itself addresses him as 'Alexander' and 'Lord of Elbë'. Also, appearances under different names in different texts are listed together in a few cases where the evidence of the poems amounts to proof of a common identity. Thus a consolidated entry covers all unmistakable appearances of Julius Brenzaida; conceivably the 'Brenzaida' of E87 could be an unknown man of the same family, but in view of Julius's well-established connection with 'Geraldine', who speaks the poem (see E34, E35), it seemed more helpful to simplify the list by disregarding this possibility. But to multiply exceptions of this kind would have meant going too far down the path of reconstruction.

In principle, again, each appearance is listed only once: since the appearance of 'A.E.' in E8 is listed under 'Alexander Elbë', this poem is not counted again under 'A.E.' The few exceptions occur where different names in one poem may or may not refer to the same person, and where AB has revised a name in her lists. Appearances are listed as follows:

A in a poem by AB (poem number from *Poems of AB* follows);
E in a poem by EB (poem number from this edition follows);
a in EB's record paper of 26 June 1837;
b in AB's record paper of 30 July 1841;
c in EB's record paper of 30 July 1845;
d in AB's record paper of 31 July 1845;
e in an undated list of characters by AB in BPM (text from *Poems of AB*, p. 189);
f in an undated list of characters by AB at the University of Texas (text from *Poems of AB*, pp. 189–90);
g in a list of characters by EB on MS D8 in BPM, probably made between late 1838 and July 1842 (see David R. Isenberg, 'A Gondal Fragment', *BST*, 14/72 (1962), 24–6);
h in a list of names by EB on MS F2 at the University of Texas (text from a photograph).

A.A.	E27
A.A.A.	E132
A.E.	A47, A51, A52, E120 (see also Elbë; Exina)
A.G.A. (Augusta G. Almeda)	E4, E8, E15, E18, E24, E25, E32, E36, E37, E44, E48, E72, E76, E81, E104, E106, E114, E130, a
A.H.	A15 (*see also* Hybernia)
A.S.	E25, E89, E90, E96, E102, E104 (*see also* Alfred, [S.])
Abrantez, Isabella	e, f
Adrian	h
Alcona	E63 (*see also* Alcona, R[osina])
Alcona, R[osina]	E88, E112, E116 (*see also* Alcona)

Alexander	A2, A35, f, h[2] (*see also* Alexander, D.; Elbë; Hybernia)
Alexander, D.	f (*see also* Alexander)
Alexandria[3]	E55 (*see also* Hybernia)
Alexandrina, *see* Zenobia	
Alfred, Lord of Aspin	E92 (*see also* A.S.; Alfred, [S.])
Alfred, [S.]	E76 (*see also* A.S.; Alfred, Lord of Aspin)
Almeda, *see* A.G.A.	
Almedore, *see* Brenzaida	
Alzerno (man)	A7
Alzerno, Cornelia	f
Alzerno, Flora	e (*see also* Flora)
Amedeus	E81
Angelica	E81
Angora, Henry	c (*see also* H.A.)
Angora, Julius, *see* Brenzaida	
Angora, Lucia	e, f
Angusteena, Juliet	c
Augusta, *see* A.G.A.	
Augusteena,[4] Catherina T. G.	f
Blanche	E27, E29
Brenzaida, Julius	E20, E23, E34, E35, E46, E87, E88, E112, E116, d (*see also* J.A.)
Campbell, Una	e
Caverndel, Hespera	A25
Claudia	E51
Clifford, Halbert	f
D.G.C.	E109
Desmond[5]	E45
Douglas (man)	E31, E81
Douglas, Helen	f
Douglas, M. (man)	E113
E.J.[6]	E55
E.W.	E106, E107 (*see also* Eldred, Lord)
E.Z.	A53
Eagle, Harriet	f
Edmund	E80 (*see also* Gleneden)
Egremont, Ella	c

[2] This writing of the name is divided between F2 and E8, which originally formed one MS.

[3] Also refers to 'a kingdom in Gaaldine'; see (though misspelt) AB's entry in *GGG*, below.

[4] Ratchford reads 'Angusteena' in *GQ*, p. 195.

[5] It is not clear whether 'Desmond' is a person or a place; see commentary for E45. 21–4.

[6] 'E.J.' at the head of this poem may be an incomplete signature by EB.

Egremont, Julian	c
Elbë, Alexander	E4, E8, E114 (*see also* A.E.)
Eldred, Lord	E81 (*see also* E.W.)
Eliza	A7 (*see also* Hybernia)
Esmaldan, Rosabelle	c
Eustacce [*sic*]	e (*see also* Sophona)
Exina	E88
Exina, Arthur	E186, f (*see also* A.E.)
Exina, Gerald	e, f (*see also* Gerald)
Fernando	E6, E17 (*see also* Samara)
Fitzaphnold, Cordelia	c
Fizher, Rosalind[7]	f
Flora	A8, E80, g (*see also* Alzerno)
Florian	A8
Francesca	g
Fred	h
Gerald	E23, E190, f (*see also* Exina; ?~~Gerald F~~.; Gerald S.
?~~Gerald F~~[8]	f (*see also* Gerald)
Gerald, S.	E89 (*see also* Gerald)
Geralda, Lady	A1
Geraldine, S.	E34, E35, E87
Gleneden (probably man)	E26 (*see also other* Gleneden *entries*)
Gleneden, Arthur	E45 (*see also* Gleneden)
Gleneden, E. (man)	E97 (*see also* Gleneden)
Gleneden, E. R. (woman)	E113
?Gleneden, Mary, *see* M.G., Mary, Mary R.	
Gleneden, R.	E45, E80 (*see also* Gleneden)
H.A.	E90 (*see also* Angora, Henry)
H.G.	E22
Harold	E174
Hybernia, Alexander	A29, e (*see also* A.H.; Alexander)
Hybernia, Alexandria Zenobia	f (*see also* Zenobia)
Hybernia, Edward	e, f
Hybernia, Eliza	f
~~Hybernia~~ Exina, Gerald	e
I.G.	E111
I.M.	E111
Iernë	E111, E182

[7] End of surname almost illegible; transcribed 'Fizhorch' in *GQ*, p. 195. Perhaps an abbreviation for Fitzherbert.

[8] So read in *GQ*, p. 195; Chitham in *Poems of AB* is uncertain.

J.A.	E109 (*see also* Brenzaida, Julius, a.k.a. Angora)
J.B., *see* Brenzaida, Julius	
Julian, M.	E123
Lesley, Lord	E81 (*see also* Lesley, Rodric)
Lesley, Rodric	E100 (*see also* Lesley, Lord)
M.A.	E122
M.A.A.	E188
M.G.	E101 (*see also* Mary; Mary R.)
M.R.	E97
Macalgin, Ronald	c
~~MacElgin~~ Angora, Lucia	e
MacRay, Archibald	f
Marcius	E186
Maria	A29
Mary	E80 (*see also* M.G.; Mary, R.)
Mary, R.	E97 (*see also* M.G.; Mary)
Mertleheath, John	e
Montara, Isidora[9]	f
Navarre, Catharine	c
Orlando	A48
R.C.	E120
Regina[10]	g
Rochelle, A. G.	E123
Rosina, *see* Alcona, R.	
Sabia, Marina	A3
St Albert, Adolphus	f
Samara, F[ernando] De	E37, E72 (*see also* Fernando)
Senland, Isabella	e, f
Senland, Xirilla	f
Sidonia	E92 (*see also* A.S.; Alfred, [S.])
Sophona, Eustace	e, f
Sophona, Henry	c, f
St[e]wart, Marcellus	g
St[e]wart, Ronald	g
Surry	E81
Vernon, Albert	e (erased), f
~~Vernon, Emily~~	e
Vernon, Olivia	A9
Vernon, Solala	b
Zenobia	A2

[9] This character cannot be 'I.M.' in E111; the Christian name of the only woman speaker in that poem is Iernë, who may be 'I.M.' or 'I.G.'

[10] This is also the name of the capital of Gondal: see E5. 47–8 and comment.

Zenobia, Alexandrina	A4, A5, A7, A8 (*see also* Hybernia; Zenobia)
Zerona, [Z.]	A47, A50

Geographical Names

The following names were pencilled by AB into their alphabetical places in 'A Vocabulary of Proper Names' in the Parsonage, now BPM, copy of *A Grammar of General Geography, for the Use of Schools and Young Persons*, by J. Goldsmith (1823):

ALEXANDIA, a kingdom in Gaaldine.
ALMEDORE, A kingdom in Gaaldine.
ELSERADEN, a kingdom in Gaaldine.
GAALDINE, a large island newly discovered in the South Pacific.
GONDAL, a large island in the North Pacific.
REGINA, the capital of Gondal.
ULA, a kingdom in Gaaldine, Governed by 4 Sovereigns.
ZELONA, a kingdom in Gaaldine.
ZEDORA, a large Provence in Gaaldine, governed by a Viceroy.

The fact that Gaaldine is 'newly discovered' but already occupied and subdivided suggests a date for these insertions soon after the exploration mentioned in the record paper of November 1834. Some Gondal stories probably described rapid colonization, like the Glasstown saga over which all four children had presided. The four sovereigns of Ula may have been the Brontës or their representatives, as with the 'Little King and Queens' of the Islanders' Play: see Alexander, *Early Writings of Charlotte Brontë*, pp. 46, 51. But there is no real evidence that CB or BB took part in Gondal.

Gondal Dates

The presence of Gondal dates in five poems by EB and one by AB suggests that the chronology may have been worked out with some care in the prose, as EB later worked out that of *WH*. This was not done with a view to period characteristics: the poems suggest the fifteenth and sixteenth century rather than the early nineteenth (see introduction, pp. 8–9).

Gondal date	*Poem number*	*Event*
Sept. 1825	E112	Young Julius Brenzaida imprisoned in Southern College after connection with Rosina
April 1826	A35	Alexander ?Hybernia is imprisoned in a dungeon in the Southern Palace of Instruction
Sept. 1826	E114	A.G.A., writing on a dungeon wall in the Northern College, recalls Elbë's death
10 Jan. 1827	E53	Leaders who died resisting tyranny are commemorated by friends returning to the Palace of Instruction

1830	E96	A.S. is urged not to mourn a lady buried at sea
1830	E100	Rodric Lesley dies after a battle

APPENDIX VII

Gondal Reconstructions

The following outlines do no more than indicate the main sequence of events in each of the three main attempts to reconstruct Gondal history, with reference to the relevant poems.

1. Laura L. Hinkley in *The Brontës: Charlotte and Emily* (1947), Appendix A

Julius Brenzaida, Prince of Angora in northern Gondal, loves and is loved by Rosina, Princess of Alcona in southern Gondal. The affair begins while he is still a student, but disciplinary action by the college separates the lovers (112). Released from prison, Julius raises an expedition and sails to Gaaldine, where he conquers first Almedore (20), then Zalona (94). He courts (34) and secretly marries Geraldine Sidonia, a native of Zadora, but breaks with her when she refuses to follow him to Gondal (35). His child, to whom Geraldine then gives birth, is A.G.A. (87). On a voyage to Gondal Geraldine is drowned, but A.G.A. survives and Julius has her brought up in the mountains of Angora. He marries Rosina, who treats A.G.A. coldly when she is brought to their court (191). Julius swears an oath of alliance with his remaining rival, Gerald, King of Exina (23); but breaks this oath, throws Gerald (190) and his brother Arthur (186) into prison, and makes himself Emperor of Gondal and Gaaldine. He defeats a rebellion from Exina, but is assassinated (88) by Douglas, who escapes (31). Rosina then rules as regent on behalf of their son Henry Angora.

As A.G.A. grows up, she becomes a centre of intrigue, in which her first lover Amedeus is involved; Amedeus dies in exile, for which his former love Angelica blames A.G.A. (81). The first great love of A.G.A.'s life is Alexander of Elbë, who is already married. They become lovers and A.G.A. bears a child, Alexandria, whom she leaves to die in a snowstorm (55) to preserve her own royal rights. Elbë's wife dies, he and A.G.A. are married, and they make war on Rosina. Alexander is killed in battle, A.G.A. watches him die (4) and is imprisoned (114). After being released by her 'noble foe' Rosina, she has an affair with Fernando De Samara, who deserts his childhood sweetheart on her account (17). He is imprisoned for political offences and she soon forgets him (72); later he kills himself (37).

A.G.A.'s second great love is for her mother's brother Alfred Sidonia, of Aspin Castle in Gondal, a widower who neglects his young daughter in his devotion to A.G.A. (92). They marry, and A.G.A. becomes queen, perhaps at the death of Rosina. His health declines; A.G.A. comes to feel that their union is a sin, and sends him to England to die (104). A Republican revolution breaks out, causing divided loyalties among the Gleneden family (113), who were involved in the earlier rebellion against Julius (26). A.G.A.

flees into the mountains of Angora, where, at Angelica's instigation, she is murdered by Douglas (81). She is mourned by Lord Eldred (106) and buried on the moors (107).

2. Fannie E. Ratchford in *Gondal's Queen* (Austin, Tex., 1955)

In this reconstruction A.G.A., Rosina Alcona, and Geraldine S. are regarded as the same person.

A.G.A., a princess of Alcona, tempts Julius Brenzaida from the paths of duty while both are still at the Palace of Instruction, bringing about his imprisonment (112). She then elopes with Alexander of Elbë, who deserts his wife for her. Alexander and Julius lead their armies to battle near Lake Elnor, where Elbë is mortally wounded and A.G.A. watches him die (4). She is imprisoned (114, 18), and is eventually released and sails for Gaaldine (7). After a spell of mourning for Elbë (8), she falls in love with Lord Alfred of Aspin Castle (76), who neglects his daughter Angelica for her sake (92). Angelica nevertheless adores A.G.A., until she steals Angelica's lover Amedeus (81, 132), then tires of him and has him exiled. A.G.A.'s next affair, the one deep and lasting love of her life, is with Julius Brenzaida (35); he demands that she renounce Lord Alfred (36), to which she agrees (104, 146, 130). Alfred goes to England and commits suicide; his ghost returns and haunts Aspin (92).

Julius, who is King of Almedore, now sets out to make himself sole ruler of Gondal and Gaaldine. He begins by capturing Zalona (20, 94), then prepares to invade Gondal despite ill omens (5). Gerald Exina, King of Gondal, allows Julius to be crowned as joint sovereign with himself (23). Julius breaks his oath of loyalty, imprisons Gerald (190), and reigns as Emperor of Gondal, with A.G.A. as Empress. A plot against him is led by Angelica; M. Douglas joins the conspiracy despite misgivings about his traitor's role (113), and the fatal blow is struck (88) by Amedeus (81). A.G.A., appalled by the news (117), takes flight with her baby Alexandria (87), though she soon rids herself of this encumbrance (55). Meanwhile the young nobles of Gondal return to the Palace of Instruction, mourning comrades who had died resisting Julius's tyranny (53).

Later A.G.A. is restored to her throne, mourns Julius (64, 116), and is oppressed by memories (48, 44, 199, 15). Among them are memories of Fernando De Samara, who deserted his childhood sweetheart for A.G.A. and, after a brief affair, was banished and imprisoned and committed suicide (17, 72, 37, 32). Finally she falls victim to Angelica's vengeance and to Douglas (81), who escapes (31). She is mourned by Lord Eldred (106) and buried on the moors (107).

3. W. D. Paden in *An Investigation of Gondal* (New York, 1958)

Alexander of Elbë sails as one of the *conquistadores* from Gondal to Gaaldine *c.*1820. For several years there is no news of him (8); his young wife Augusta (A.G.A.) falls in love (130, 76) with her cousin Alfred (one of the three children of the old King of Gondal, the others being Gerald and Geraldine).

In 1824 she and Alfred are married after A.G.A. has fabricated news of Elbë's death. In 1825 Elbë returns. Alfred rejects A.G.A.'s attempt to send him away (**104**), and treacherously murders Elbë near Lake Elnor. A.G.A., who has found her husband dying (**4**), later finds Alfred (**184**), who flees to England. She then wanders among the mountains, gives birth to Alfred's daughter Alexandria, and abandons her in a snowstorm (**55**). The child is rescued and carried to Gaaldine by A.G.A.'s friend or servant Blanche (**27**). In 1826 A.G.A. is captured and imprisoned in the Northern College, where she writes her first lament for Elbë (**114**).

Meanwhile Julius Brenzaida, a member of Rosina Alcona's circle who has already been imprisoned on ethical grounds (**112**), captivates the princess Geraldine (**34**) and takes her to Gaaldine (**35**), where she bears his child (**87**). There he rises to military eminence and becomes ruler of Almedore (**20**), with Geraldine as his consort. In 1828 he invades Gondal; Rosina makes his cause her own. The old king now dead, his son Gerald and Julius are crowned joint monarchs of Gondal (**23**); soon afterwards Julius imprisons Gerald (**190**) and the young prince Arthur (**186**), and puts them to death. In 1829 Julius is assassinated (**88**). This precipitates a civil war between the factions of Angora and Exina, during which A.G.A. escapes to England. She finds Alfred in time to witness his death (**25**); his ashes remain in England, but his ghost haunts Aspin in Gondal (**92**).

After the war the victorious Exina party recalls A.G.A. and raises her to the throne as the sole adult descendant of Gondal's royal race, since Geraldine has died of grief and Angelica, Alfred's daughter by his first wife, is still a minor. Angelica grows up at A.G.A.'s court. A popular queen, but oppressed by inner woes, A.G.A. takes young men as lovers; but her pleasure in each of them turns into hatred, and she sends them into exile (Fernando, **72**, **37**; Amedeus, **81**). She uses the affair with Amedeus as an excuse to exile his former love Angelica, the heir-presumptive.

After eleven or more years of rule, A.G.A. is murdered by Douglas at Angelica's instigation (**81**). Douglas escapes (**31**), but Angelica is executed; the royal line being apparently extinct, a Republican party bids for power. The old nurse Blanche reveals the existence of Alexandria, who now marries Henry Angora (son of Julius and Geraldine); they are crowned as joint monarchs. But civil war breaks out, and in the last known writings the Republicans have the upper hand (EB's record paper of 1845, **126**, **127**).